Penguin Books
AUSTRALIA'S PEARL HARBOUR

Douglas Lockwood (1918–1980) was born in Natimuk in the central west of Victoria. He was sent to Darwin as a correspondent for the Melbourne *Herald* in 1941 and thus witnessed the Japanese air raids of February 1942 that are the subject of this book. He later served in the AIF and as a war correspondent in the southern Pacific region, returning to Darwin in 1946. He lived there until 1968, after which he held various positions as a newspaper executive, including managership of the Melbourne *Herald* 1971–73. He wrote a number of books, mostly on the people and places of the Northern Territory, including the award-winning biography *I, the Aboriginal* (1962). To research *Australia's Pearl Harbour* he travelled extensively to interview the survivors, including Japanese and US airmen as well as Darwin residents.

Sir Edward Dunlop, AC, CMG, OBE, KCSJ, MS, FRCS, FRACS, LLD(Hon.), DSc. Punjabi (Hon.), FACS, was born in 1907 near Shepparton in rural Victoria. 'Weary', as he is known, graduated in medicine and surgery just before the outbreak of the Second World War. He served with the AIF in the Middle East, Europe and the Pacific during the war. Captured in Java by the Japanese in 1942, he survived more than three and a half years in some of the most notorious Japanese prison camps; his devotion to his men and his inspirational leadership are legendary. Since his return to Melbourne in 1945 Sir Edward has continued to practise as a surgeon and has been actively involved in community service in Australia and abroad. He was knighted in 1969. *The War Diaries of Weary Dunlop*, his exceptional account of prison-camp life, was published in 1986.

OTHER TITLES IN THIS SERIES

The Coast Watchers by Eric Feldt
Behind Bamboo by Rohan Rivett
We Were the Rats by Lawson Glassop
No Moon Tonight by Don Charlwood

Publisher's Note: In this edition we have retained the spelling 'Pearl Harbour', as this was the form adopted when the book was originally published.

AUSTRALIAN WAR CLASSICS
PRESENTED BY E. E. (WEARY) DUNLOP

AUSTRALIA'S PEARL HARBOUR
DARWIN 1942
DOUGLAS LOCKWOOD

PENGUIN BOOKS

Penguin Books Australia Ltd
487 Maroondah Highway, PO Box 257
Ringwood, Victoria 3134, Australia
Penguin Books Ltd
Harmondsworth, Middlesex, England
Viking Penguin, A Division of Penguin Books USA Inc.
375 Hudson Street, New York, New York 10014, USA
Penguin Books Canada Limited
10 Alcorn Avenue, Toronto, Ontario, Canada M4V 1E4
Penguin Books (N.Z.) Ltd
182-190 Wairau Road, Auckland 10, New Zealand

First published by Cassell Australia Ltd 1966
Revised edition 1967
Paperback edition published by Seal Books 1972
Reprinted 1975, 1977, 1984
Revised paperback edition published by Ian Drakeford Publishing 1988
This edition published by Penguin Books Australia Ltd 1992

10 9 8 7 6 5 4 3 2 1

Copyright © Ruth Lockwood, 1966

All rights reserved. Without limiting the rights under copyright reserved above, no part of this publication may be reproduced, stored in or introduced into a retrieval system, or transmitted, in any form or by any means (electronic, mechanical, photocopying, recording or otherwise), without the prior written permission of both the copyright owner and the above publisher of this book.

Produced by Viking O'Neil
56 Claremont Street, South Yarra, Victoria 3141, Australia
A Division of Penguin Books Australia Ltd

Cover design by Jan Schmoeger
Printed in Australia by The Book Printer, Maryborough, Vic.

National Library of Australia
Cataloguing-in-Publication data

Lockwood, Douglas, 1918–1980.
  Australia's Pearl Harbour, Darwin 1942.

  Rev. ed.
  Includes index.
  ISBN 0 14 016820 6.

  1. World War, 1939-1945 – Northern Territory – Darwin –
  Aerial operations, Japanese. 2. Darwin (N.T.) – History –
  Bombardment, 1942. I. Title. (Series: Australian war classics).

940.5426

Foreword

This engrossing book records in detail the greatest military disaster on Australian soil.

Most Australians are well aware of the devastating Japanese attack on the Hawaiian military base of Pearl Harbour on 7 December 1941, which destroyed much of the American Pacific fleet. This offensive occurred without a declaration of hostilities and precipitated the entry of the USA into the Second World War. Less publicised was the bombing raid on Darwin some ten weeks later by the same powerful task force, composed of Japanese airmen and aircraft carriers protected by cruisers and destroyers. This force had the same commanding admiral, Chuicho Nagumo, and the same air leader and planner, Commander Mitsuo Fuchida, as the Pearl Harbour force. Fuchida proved to be a dynamic and courageous foe. As a result of the attack the township of Darwin and its port facilities were largely destroyed, and commercial life came to a halt. Eight major Australian ships were sunk and others severely damaged or beached and burnt.

February the nineteenth 1942 was a day of tragedy and loss. Douglas Lockwood has gone to great pains to uncover as many documents as possible – both Australian and Japanese – which throw light on the raid. The town, ill-prepared for such an attack, reacted for the most part with commendable courage, but there were also instances of both confusion and shame. Unhappily the planned orderly evacuation of civilians became something of a rout and even some members of the military forces retreated in disorder.

As Lockwood reveals, there were also many episodes of heroism that were often ignored and in some cases misrepresented in contemporary accounts. Darwin's 'much-maligned wharfies', of whom twenty-two were killed as the Japanese bombarded the port area, undertook courageous rescue and salvage work in the face of continual bombing and strafing. Most of the region's Aboriginal population were evacuated to 'control camps' or returned to their native territories and left virtually to fend for themselves. There are many stories attesting to their continuing loyalty.

Just prior to the bombing of Darwin Japan had launched its decisive advance south through the Pacific. The Japanese soon drove the Allied forces down the Malay peninsula to Singapore, which capitulated on 15 February. The Japanese domination of the region continued, and the Allies were faring little better in Europe. In the context of this tide of disaster the raid on Darwin received minimal attention, and in any case all reportage of the events was censored by the military authorities. On the day following the raids the Minister for Air, the Hon. A.S. Drakeford, stated that 'fifteen people were killed and twenty-four wounded'. The royal commission into the circumstances surrounding the raids later found that the figures were closer to 250 killed and 300-400 wounded.

In addition to recounting the events of 19 February Lockwood appraises the reports that emanated from the royal commission led by Mr Justice Lowe a month after the bombardment. Lowe was sternly critical of the Northern Territory Administrator, Mr C.L.A. Abbott, of RAAF serving officers and men, and even to some extent of the Chief of Air Staff, the Air Board and the Federal Government.

The civil inquest censured the Administrator for his lack of foresight and planning, and was also critical of the inadequate co-operation between the Air Raids Precaution group and the police, which resulted in rioting and some looting after the raid. Notable among the findings of the military hearing was its revelation that despite the predictability of a Japanese attack on northern Australia the RAAF did not have as single serviceable fighter plane with which to defend Darwin, and that there were serious defects in the RAAF's communications facilities. The report also found it 'inexplicable' that the RAAF and the Area Combined Headquarters failed to relay a general alarm in time for effective action to be taken. The criticisms of the Administrator were met with a dignified reply from Mr Abbott, who asserted that evidence from some of the witnesses was inaccurate and 'malicious'. Lockwood indicates that his own research suggested that some of the evidence was indeed biased and unreliable.

Today humankind has at its disposal a range of ever more devastating weapons. This calls for thoughtful analysis, particularly by Australians who cannot count for ever upon the support of 'great and powerful friends'. Fifty years after the bombing of Darwin, at a time when we are reducing our defence facilities and pruning military expenditure, this book repays careful reading.

E.E. Dunlop

Contents

Foreword by E.E. ('Weary') Dunlop	v
List of Illustrations	ix
Foreword to the 1966 Edition	xi
Author's Note	xiii
1. The Japanese Task Force	1
2. The Irresolute Evacuation	12
3. The Warnings Ignored	22
4. The Aerodromes: Raid 1	30
5. Pearl Harbour Parallel	44
6. The Much Maligned Wharfies	65
7. The Militia Tested	84
8. The Silent Lines	93
9. Death & Escape at Government House	106
10. "All Patients Under Beds!"	125
11. R.A.A.F. — Second Raid	138
12. "Kill Twenty Japs Each!"	148
13. The Adelaide River Stakes	155
14. The Forsaken Aborigines	177
15. Aftermath	192
1. The Military Inquest	
2. The Civil Inquest	
3. Reckoning for the Japanese	
Bibliography	213
Appendixes	
I Civilian Evacuation Order	214
II Fate of the Rev. Leonard Kentish	216
III Attack on *Florence D* and Catalina	218
IV Japanese Aircraft Used and Lost	220
V Japanese Activity near Darwin before February 19, 1942	222
VI Air Raids on Darwin after February 19, 1942	223
Index	225

List of Illustrations

The photographs used in this book include some taken with 'Box Brownie' and similar cameras. Frequently the films remained undeveloped in the tropics for months afterwards and in one case for several years. That explains, if explanation is necessary, why a few of the reproductions are not of professional quality. A number have not previously been published, particularly the several pictures of ships on fire and exploding which were taken by Leading Signalman Douglas Fraser, a member of the crew of H.M.A.S. *Deloraine*. He used his small camera to good effect while red-hot metal was falling around him, and fortunately preserved his film.

Following page 80

These land-based 'Betty' bombers were among 54 that took part in the raid on Darwin *(Japanese War History)*

A 'Betty' bomber releasing its load over Darwin
(Japanese War History)

Vice Admiral Chuichi Nagumo

The explosion from the first bombs ever to land on Australia
(Douglas Fraser)

m.v. *Neptuna* hit and on fire *(Douglas Fraser)*

U.S.S. *Peary*, a destroyer, exploded and sank *(Douglas Fraser)*

The tanker *British Motorist* with propeller clear of the water and still on fire

Lieut. Robert Oestreicher with U.S.A.F. air crew
(U.S. Air Force)

The remains of a U.S.A.F. P.40 fighter destroyed on the ground
(Dr. D. C. Howle)

Only the shell remains of this store at the R.A.A.F. base
(Dr. D. C. Howle)

Damage to hangar and remains of aircraft at R.A.A.F. station
(Aust. War Memorial)

Ruins of R.A.A.F. equipment store *(Dr. D. C. Howle)*

The R.A.A.F. nursing staff with the R.A.A.F. doctor (Sqdn. Leader D. C. Howle, centre) at Daly Waters, N.T.

Sir Frederick Scherger, in the uniform of Air Commodore
(Aust. War Memorial)

Following page 136

The Administrator of the Northern Territory, Mr. C. L. A. Abbott
(Aust. War Memorial)

A seaward view of bombs bursting near the police barracks and Government House *(Aust. War Memorial)*

The office occupied by the N.T. Administrator in the grounds of Government House

The remains of the Post Office, where 10 people died
(Aust. War Memorial)

Crater of bomb which destroyed postmaster's residence in background
(P.M.G.)

The remains of the wharf, showing twisted rails and bogies
(Comm. J. C. B. McManus)

The severed wharf; the railway trucks are on the seaward side

Barbed wire entanglements were erected in the town as invasion appeared imminent *(Comm. J. C. B. McManus)*

Surgeon Commander Clive James with staff at civil hospital after bombing *(P. A. Mackenzie)*

Oil storage tanks on fire during a subsequent raid
(Aust. War Memorial)

Mitsuo Fuchida – a photograph taken in 1961

Foreword to the 1966 Edition

The Japanese air raids at Darwin on February 19, 1942, were well planned, carefully co-ordinated and efficiently carried out. Apparently they were intended to eliminate any possibility of Allied naval and air interference with the Japanese occupation of the Netherlands East Indies.

At that time my appointment was as Senior Air Staff Officer of the recently formed North Western Area Command of the R.A.A.F. My Commanding Officer, the late Air Commodore D. E. L. Wilson, was absent in Java at a conference of the A.B.D.A. (American, British, Dutch, Australian) Command.

The air attack was unexpected for two reasons. The first was that we did not believe the meagre forces in Darwin could be assessed by the Japanese as being a danger to them. The second was that we had no reliable warning of the Japanese Carrier Task Force in the area. We had prepared our defences as well as we could, but with little anti-aircraft artillery and no fighters we were almost defenceless.

On the morning of February 19 a small force of American P.40 (Kittyhawk) fighters had taken off for the Netherlands East Indies to boost the defence there, but turned back because of bad weather. Also, a small number of R.A.A.F. Hudson bombers had arrived from Koepang. Air Marshal R. Williams, R.A.A.F., telephoned me from Darwin to say that he had arrived by air and would like to see the Air Force station before his departure later in the morning. I was on my way into Darwin to meet him when the first high-level raid hit the town and the low-level attacks on the aerodrome began.

It later transpired that observers on Bathurst Island, north of Darwin, had seen a large number of aircraft flying towards us, and had reported them. But our Operations Room was still undecided whether they were returning Kittyhawks, five of which had already landed, when the bombs started to fall.

The author has told the story of 'Australia's Pearl Harbour' in great detail. It is perhaps sufficient for me to add that the lessons we learned from this first enemy attack on Australian soil were well learned. I can only hope that new generations of Australians will read the story of Darwin and also be instructed.

F. R. W. Scherger

May, 1966

Chairman
Chiefs of Staff Committee
Department of Defence
Canberra

Author's Note

The Japanese attack against Pearl Harbour on December 7, 1941, has become synonymous with treachery. Diplomatic negotiations were proceeding in Washington and war had not been declared when the operation began.

No such treachery occurred when Darwin was bombed on February 19, 1942. Singapore had already fallen and Java was about to be invaded. The Pacific War had in fact reached the stage at which the aerial bombing of Darwin, if not invasion, appeared inevitable.

In these circumstances it may be said that the title *Australia's Pearl Harbour* is misleading. I should make it clear, therefore, that my analogy is not based upon any suggestion of deception but upon other similarities.

The Japanese task force at Darwin consisted of airmen, seamen and aircraft carriers that had been at Pearl Harbour. The commanding admiral, the air attack leader and the chief planner were identical officers in both operations. And the devastation, though on a smaller scale, was equally grim.

Eight ships were sunk and others beached and burnt. Two hundred and forty three people were killed in less than one hour and more than three hundred wounded. Much of the town was destroyed and commercial life ceased at once. The banks were closed by government decree and the centre of N.T. Administration shortly removed to Alice Springs. Thereafter, although martial law was never proclaimed, Darwin was a town under military control. There were more than fifty subsequent attacks upon it by the Japanese.

The death toll on that first day made it the worst disaster in history on Australian soil. In spite of that, comparatively little is known of what happened. Two or three writers have discussed it only briefly. The Official War History, in each of several volumes, gives the barest outline.

Few Australians know that part of their country was so heavily attacked. One reason is that much was happening elsewhere at the time. The fall of Singapore only four days earlier had shocked the nation because with it were lost 17,000 men of the 8th Division. Rommel had the upper hand in the Western Desert.

The Russian front was ablaze and the Battle of the Atlantic at its height.

The news of the bombing of Darwin had to compete for space in the newspapers with all these other events. While it was the main story of the day following an announcement by the Prime Minister, it was quickly forgotten. There then also developed a threat to the east coast of Australia with the Japanese invasion of New Britain and the Solomons, the landings on the north coast of New Guinea, and the thrust across the Owen Stanley Ranges towards Port Moresby.

This all took the spotlight away from Darwin. Japanese and Allied strategy was such that it was to become something of a military backwater in the last years of the war. Nevertheless, it was Australia's Pearl Harbour.

I have attempted here to tell the story of February 19, 1942, and the events that immediately preceded and followed the bombing. I have deliberately refrained from extending it beyond that period.

I was fortunate in having been present and thus am able to write from personal experience. However, I had realised for some years that to give a full account would require interviews with American, Japanese and other nationals who took part. It has been possible only in recent times for me to go abroad for that purpose, but I was able to trace many survivors, notably the leader of the Japanese air attack force, Commander Mitsuo Fuchida, the Japanese who planned the operation, and Japanese historians who had access to vital records. In America I found former airmen who had flown against the Japanese that day and been shot down.

Meanwhile, for several years, I had been interviewing Australians who were present. From all of this I have attempted to write a comprehensive story.

When planning the book I had to choose between a strictly chronological account of the battle as it developed, and one that would describe the events in particular sectors. It seemed to me that the latter was the better method. To have attempted it chronologically would have meant frequent transfer of the scene of action from one sector to another. That would have presented difficulties in maintaining continuity and must have impaired clarity.

In separate sections, therefore, I have described what happened in the air, at the aerodromes, in the harbour, on the wharf, at the anti-aircraft batteries, and in the town and the hospitals.

As far as possible, I have told the story through eyes other than mine. Direct quotation has been used only after careful questioning of the person concerned. Conversation between two people has been used, in general, only after both have agreed on what was said, but in some cases that has not been possible.

I have examined the findings of a Royal Commission appointed by the Federal Government into the circumstances of the bombing and, finally, have described the eventual fate of the Japanese who took part.

To thank personally all those who have helped and encouraged me to write about the first attack in history against the Australian mainland would be almost impossible. Hundreds of letters and interviews were involved.

However, I must acknowledge the debt I owe to the Japanese naval historian, Mr. Hitoshi Tsunoda; the air attack leader, Commander Fuchida; Mr. A. J. Sweeting and others of the Official War History staff in Canberra; the Director of Posts and Telegraphs in South Australia, Mr J. R. O'Sullivan; Mr E. Bennett-Bremner, of Qantas; Lieut. Owen Griffiths; Mr C. L. A. Abbott; and Mr Frank Devine, an Australian journalist in Tokyo who helped immeasurably in my approaches to the Japanese.

To the other men and women who read this book, knowing of their contribution to it with letters, interviews and photographs, or simply in checking a single fact, I express my gratitude. In most cases their names appear in the narrative.

NOTE TO REVISED EDITION

In the final chapter of this book I have discussed the report of the Royal Commissioner, Mr. Justice Lowe, who was appointed under wide terms of reference to inquire into the circumstances of the raids. I have been critical of the fact that he did not censure successive Federal governments and the Air Boards for failure to properly equip the R.A.A.F. in this forward area. It has since been pointed out to me by Sir Charles Lowe that his report stressed his inability to inquire into such matters. He had to restrict it to events which threw light upon the raid itself and measures to be taken to prevent a recurrence.

DOUGLAS LOCKWOOD

For
ARCHER THOMAS

CHAPTER 1
The Japanese Task Force

> *'Fifteen people were killed and twenty-four wounded.'*—The Minister for Air, MR. DRAKEFORD, on February 20, 1942.

> *'Approximately two hundred and fifty people were killed and between three hundred and four hundred wounded.'*—The Royal Commissioner, MR. JUSTICE LOWE, in his report, March 27, 1942.

Destruction came to Darwin in mid-morning on February 19, 1942, when war in the Pacific was but ten weeks old.

Destruction came while the sun shone, with a gentle breeze smudging a few white caps on blue waves rolling in from Beagle Gulf and the Clarence Strait.

Destruction by an enemy was brought that day for the first time to Australian soil. It came violently though not unexpectedly, with bombs and bullets and cannon shells scything through life as they splintered a fleet and a town and almost a human spirit.

Destruction and terror were such as to lead to a panic of people. Hundreds fled.

They left half smoked cigarettes, half finished drinks, unopened mail, unmade beds, incomplete jobs, open doors and caged pets.

They walked and they ran. They rode on bicycles and they rode in cars, in garbage trucks, ice cream carts, sanitary carts and road graders. Women and children, the aged, the infirm and those able bodied men who could escape detection rode in an evacuee train of cattle trucks and flat-tops that left them exposed to tropical heat.

The men who fled were not all civilians. Among them were many subject to a military discipline that was in tatters.

Those who did not flee included nearly two hundred and fifty men and women, Australian, British and American, black and white, near-black and near-white whose bodies were at the bottom of the harbour, or soaking in oil-drenched mud on the beaches, or lying shattered in inadequate shelters.

Darwin that day became Australia's Pearl Harbour, centre of a debacle in the traditional tragedy of war without equal on Australian soil. Appropriately to the analogy, the Japanese task force which wrought this havoc was part of the same force, with identical leaders, which had started the Pacific War.

The destruction was brought by the Japanese Navy, swiftly and efficiently as it had been to Pearl Harbour just seventy-four days earlier.

Pilots laughed while spreading death, gesturing crudely from the security of their cockpits and cabins, searching for opposition that might allow them, as they craved, to prove their superior skills.

That supremacy was indisputable. Knowledge of it was comforting to the air leader, Commander Mitsuo Fuchida, as the warships carrying his squadrons of bombers, dive-bombers and fighters passed from the Celebes through the Banda Sea to the Timor Sea and prepared to put an end to Australia's long history of freedom from attack.

Hong Kong, Singapore, Malaya and most of the Philippines had become part of the Greater East Asia Co-Prosperity Sphere in less than three months. Java and the rest of the Netherlands East Indies were about to fall. Japanese morale was high indeed, and for that Fuchida was largely responsible.

Nor was Japanese confidence likely to be shaken by what Fuchida and his colleagues could see around them that morning. Beneath his feet was the steel flight deck of the 36,000-tons converted battle cruiser *Akagi*, now an aircraft carrier and flagship of Admiral Chuichi Nagumo, the task force commander.

Directly behind *Akagi* at a distance of about eight thousand yards was her sister ship *Kaga*. Rear-Admiral Tamon Yamaguchi, one of the Navy's most brilliant and courageous officers, was aboard his flagship, the carrier *Soryu*, about eight thousand yards from *Akagi's* port flank. Behind, equidistant from *Soryu* and *Kaga*, was the carrier *Hiryu*. Both *Soryu* and *Hiryu* were smaller ships of 17,500 tons commissioned only four years earlier.

DIRECTION OF WIND
FOR TAKE OFF

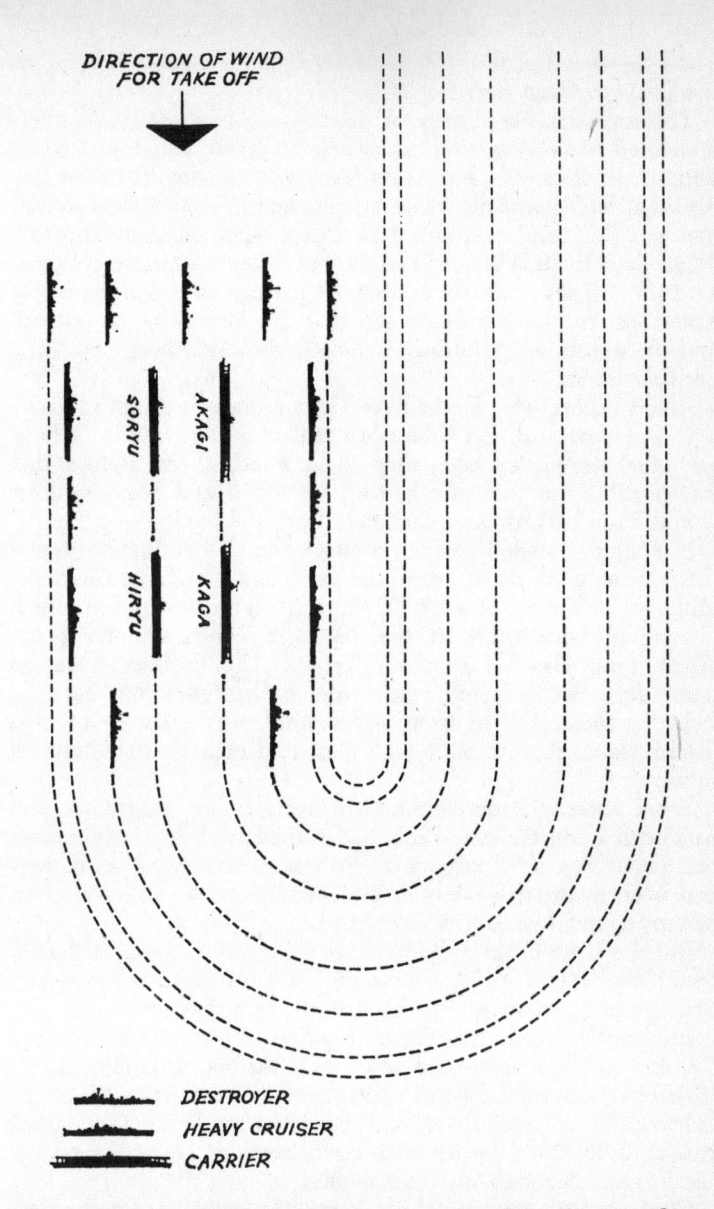

SORYU AKAGI

HIRYU KAGA

▬▬ DESTROYER
▬▬▬ HEAVY CRUISER
▬▬▬▬ CARRIER

Chart shows composition of the task force and how it turned into the north-west wind to launch 188 aircraft from the carriers.

Their top speed of thirty knots made them two knots faster than the heavier *Akagi* and *Kaga*.

The captains were service friends of Fuchida's; all were dedicated to the Emperor, the glory of Japan, and the destruction of America and her allies. Not least among them in this distinguished company was Nagumo himself, the Admiral who had led the Pearl Harbour task force. Their acquaintanceship dated back to 1933 when Fuchida was a lieutenant and Nagumo a captain. They differed in that Nagumo was a sailor and an expert on torpedo warfare whereas Fuchida was an airman and an expert on bombing, but in dedication there was little between them.

Allied sailors who might have been unlucky enough to come over the horizon in the Timor Sea that morning would not have seen the carriers or been able to approach them. Before that was possible the guns of escorting destroyers and heavy cruisers would have barked their challenge from the flanks.

If Fuchida needed further comfort, which is unlikely, it was there in the bristling shapes of the heavy cruisers *Tone, Chikuma, Maya* and *Takao*. These 12,000-ton ships, all carrying ten 8-inch guns, had been built in the 1930s in contravention of the Washington Naval Limitation Treaty. The cruisers were on point duty ten thousand yards from each of the four carriers. Between them, and in front and behind, was a screen of nine destroyers, each with six 5-inch guns and eight 24-inch torpedo tubes.

What such a force might have done to an Australian and American troop convoy which had turned back to Darwin from the Timor Sea on February 16, can be imagined. That convoy had been escorted by only one American cruiser, one American destroyer and two Australian sloops.

But the teeth in the Japanese task force were not to be denied their bite; action against most of the convoy, then at anchor in Darwin harbour, was to be delayed only by three days.

An operation order had been prepared by Commander Minoru Genda,[1] another long-time friend of Fuchida's, calling for a strike by 188 carrier-borne aeroplanes. There were to be 36 fighters, 71 dive-bombers and 81 level-bombers. The attack would be followed by 54 land-based bombers from Ambon, off Ceram, and Kendari, in the Celebes.

Fuchida was pleased to be going into action again but less

[1] When I saw Genda in Tokyo he was a leading member of the Japanese Diet.

pleased with the task he had been given. The Darwin assignment annoyed him, important though it was. The Japanese Combined Fleet staff, led by Admiral Isoroku Yamamoto, was concerned over probable Allied use of north-west Australia as a base from which to impede Japanese seizure of the Netherlands East Indies and had advanced proposals for mounting an amphibious invasion. That was flatly rebuffed both by the Navy General Staff and the Army. Combined Fleet then decided upon the best alternative, a carrier air strike to wreck the base installations in the area. Twenty years later Fuchida was still a little shamefaced about it, as though the destroyer of Pearl Harbour should not be identified with the destroyer of Darwin.

He compared it with an earlier attack on Rabaul and said: "It seemed hardly worthy of us. If ever a sledgehammer was used to crack an egg it was then."

Yet those of us in Darwin on February 19, 1942, were left in no doubt that once Fuchida was given a task he was extremely thorough in its execution, whether or not his heart was entirely in it.

Fuchida's indomitable will had been apparent since the first day of the war. As his level-bomber group had entered its run against American battleships in Pearl Harbour dark grey puffs of anti-aircraft fire concentrated around them. His plane bounced as though struck by lightning. The fuselage was holed and the rudder wire damaged. Cloud intervened at a vital moment and he missed the release point to drop his bombs. Fuchida flew back to the starting line and made another run through the flak in a damaged aircraft. This was the calibre of the destroyer of Darwin, a man known as one of the most resolute of all naval officers, a distinction not easily acquired among hundreds of others anxious and expecting to die for the greater glory of Japan. Moreover, he had a fanatical belief in the superiority of air power.[2]

[2] This view was not shared at that time by senior British staff officers. An analysis of night raids made against Germany in 1941 showed that not one bomb in ten fell within five miles of its target. Bomber Command had lost prestige. Admirals and generals scoffed at the idea that the war could be won by saturation bombing. The crowning humiliation came on February 12, 1942, when the German battle cruisers *Scharnhorst* and *Gneisenau*, with the cruiser *Prinz Eugen*, passed through the English Channel. Bomber Command put up 250 planes but could not hit targets 250 yards long on their own doorstep. One week later Fuchida and his pilots sank eight ships at Darwin and damaged others. Shortly afterwards Sir Arthur Harris, chief of Bomber Command, began mounting 1000-plane raids over Germany and restored the reputation of the aeroplane in the eyes of British planners.

Although the Navy General Staff had approved the Darwin attack in principle soon after Pearl Harbour there had been no opportunity to mount it. The first direct suggestion that the operation should be undertaken at once was made to Admiral Yamamoto by Rear-Admiral Yamaguchi on January 20. At that time Yamaguchi, flag officer commanding Carrier Division 2, had been detached with *Soryu* and *Hiryu* from Nagumo's Carrier Division 1 (*Akagi* and *Kaga*) which was attacking Rabaul. Yamaguchi pleaded with Yamamoto to let him strike Darwin alone. In the light of present knowledge it seems that he might have done as much damage with a smaller force as with that eventually used. However, there had been an argument in the Japanese high command as to whether Darwin or Ceylon should be attacked first. In late January the opinion of Commander Genda was sought. Genda, as chief planner of the Pearl Harbour operation, had an enviable reputation, and had recently come to Truk, in the Carolines, to join Nagumo as staff officer for air operations. In Tokyo twenty years later he told me: "I thought Darwin posed a threat to current and planned operations in the Netherlands East Indies and I recommended that it should be the first target. Our information showed that there had been a substantial build up of army and air forces in the area and we did not want it to be used as an offensive base against us."[3]

Permission for the attack was given by Yamamoto on January 31, but to Yamaguchi's chagrin the commander-in-chief stipulated that it must be a joint operation by Carrier Divisions 1 and 2. That meant overall command would be with Nagumo, who had already returned to Truk with *Akagi* and *Kaga*.

At 7.30 p.m. on February 9, Yamamoto radioed Top Secret Order No. 92 to the carrier fleet. This document has been made available to me by the naval historian, Hitoshi Tsunoda. It reads, in part:

"Owing to our air attacks at the beginning of February, the enemy, with its main base in Java, lost most of its naval and air strength. It is highly probable that they are planning escape to Australia, India and South Africa. It is also probable that the naval strength of Britain, the United States, the Netherlands and Australia will appear in the eastern Indian Ocean to pick them up. It appears that a part of the enemy strength is already taking refuge in the vicinity of Port Darwin. Intelligence shows that part of the U.S. air reinforcements, together with British and Australian forces, are based there.

[3] He was wrong about the air forces.

"At an opportune time the carrier task forces will conduct mobile warfare, first in the Arafura Sea and next in the Indian Ocean, endeavouring to annihilate the enemy strength in the Port Darwin area and to intercept and destroy enemy naval and transport fleets, at the same time attacking enemy strength in the Java area from behind.

"For the surprise attack on Port Darwin on February 19, the task force will advance to the Arafura Sea. After the surprise attack it will return to Staring Bay[4] for supply."

The document also details submarine operations to be carried out in the Indian Ocean, the Malacca Strait, the southern coast of Sumatra and the Torres Strait.

"The planning was a comparatively easy task," Genda told me. "We had the forces and they were well disposed. We did not expect serious opposition. We had information about Darwin's defences though I do not know where that was obtained. Darwin was a minor operation compared with Pearl Harbour. I do not think we had an elaborate spy system there, as we had in Hawaii. In the event, everything went according to plan and our losses were negligible."

Commander Fuchida stood by the wing of his Mitsubishi-built Kate bomber on *Akagi's* flight deck. He had finished a cup of bean soup and now ate sparingly from a bowl of rice and pickled plums. He accepted philosophically when told that there was neither tea nor coffee because the cooks had already left the galley for action stations; that had happened before. Fuchida put his bowl aside and gave full attention to the task ahead.

The sun was rising as Fuchida turned to his pilot and radio operator, who had breakfasted deferentially a few feet away. They were Lieut. Mitsuo Matsuzaki and Petty Officer Tokushin Mizuki, and both idolised their leader, the Navy's unchallenged top air commander. They would fly together that day on a mission whose outcome was unknown but one which, they were confident, held fewer dangers than they had faced elsewhere.

Fuchida shaded his eyes from the sun and scanned the horizon. He whistled softly at the armed might around him, still slightly incredulous, though he had personally contributed so much, that his country had come thus far in less than three months.

"It is seven thirty, Sir. We are ready when you are," Matsuzaki reported.

Since 5 a.m. the mechanical crews had been running-up engines

---
[4] In the Celebes.

and making last minute adjustments. An 800-kilogram bomb with the fuse attached had been placed in the rack of Fuchida's plane. He made a quick but expert inspection, grunted his satisfaction, then walked away to greet other crews also preparing.

First he sought out Lieut.-Commander Shigeru Itaya, a veteran fighter pilot who would lead the thirty-six escorting Zeros. Itaya was one of the most experienced pilots in the Navy with a brilliant war record and already established as an ace. He was to fighter pilots what Fuchida was to all naval airmen, a man on whom they bestowed the kind of idolatry not much less than that normally reserved for the Emperor. Itaya told Fuchida that the fighter group was as well prepared and keen for battle as it had been at Pearl Harbour. All were filled with faith in themselves as airmen and in the superiority of the Zero fighter over Allied types. Nor was that over-confidence. Western experts are agreed that at the outbreak of the Pacific War the Zero was the most manoeuvreable, versatile and effective fighter in the area.

Fuchida regretted that he could not speak personally with another old friend, Lieut.-Commander Takashige Egusa, leader of the seventy-one dive-bombers whose group headquarters was on the carrier *Soryu*. In the condition of radio silence long since imposed it was not possible to send Egusa a good-luck message and the signallers were too busy to do it by visual methods. Nor could he communicate with Lieut.-Commander Toshiie Irisa and Lieut.-Commander Takeo Ozaki who would each lead flights of twenty-seven twin-engined Betty bombers from the Celebes and Ambon in a concentrated second attack on Darwin's R.A.A.F. base.

Now Fuchida was given weather reports. Scattered cloud was expected over the target but there would be adequate visibility for the level-bombers. The dive-bombers and fighters might take advantage of the clouds by diving from behind them. Fighters could escape into them if circumstances warranted such tactics, which Fuchida doubted.

The time had come to repeat the triumph of Pearl Harbour, to again put into effect the lessons learned in twenty-one years dedicated to the Navy. The breeze freshened from the northwest, which meant the fleet must turn while the planes took off. That would be a complex operation involving seventeen warships aggregating 175,000 tons, but it was a problem belonging to Nagumo, Yamaguchi and the ships' captains. However, they had an ocean of deep water and apparent freedom from molestation. Otherwise, the launching conditions were ideal.

The about-turn, in fact, had already begun. When the fleet reached a point near 9 deg. S. Lat. and 129 deg. E. Long., two hundred and twenty miles north-west of Darwin, Nagumo ordered reversal to a reciprocal course to bring the carriers into the wind. The cruisers and destroyers turned too. The fleet was then sailing away from Darwin and would remain on that course, though at reduced speed, until the strike force returned three hours later.

Akagi completed her turn and headed full into the wind, increasing speed until velocity over the decks was equal to about 25 m.p.h. The passageways and cabins below were deserted, for every man was at his action station. The watertight bulkhead doors had been closed. The ship was in battle order, poised to strike.

Fuchida led his pilots to the briefing room under the bridge. He was at the peak of his career, a famous man with three thousand flying hours in his log book and a satisfying trail of destruction behind him. At the blackboard in the briefing room was his old Academy classmate, Minoru Genda, who planned the actions Fuchida fought. Much later I asked Fuchida about his and Genda's respective roles. He replied appropriately (for I met him in Hollywood): "Genda wrote the scripts. I directed. My pilots did the shooting."

Genda, the scriptwriter, recapitulated details of the operation which had already been thoroughly studied by the crews. When it was over he bowed to the group and wished them luck. He bowed again to Fuchida, deep and low, and the two old friends exchanged a few words.

Fuchida walked from the briefing room to his plane with his two crewmen, Matsuzaki and Mizuki. They regarded him with a devotion akin to adoration; one is not surprised for even today, with final defeat and shattered dreams behind him, Fuchida is still an intense, dynamic man of great personal charm that is evident to foreigners. His features, though clearly Oriental, are not distinctly Japanese. He has brown eyes, rather big ears and a prominent chin. His personality radiates warmth and one is instinctively attracted to him. Yet he was then a traditional fire-eating militarist, a thirty-nine years old married man with a wife and two young children. His only god was the Emperor.

As he walked towards his plane Fuchida signalled to Genda

that he was ready for the launching to begin. Almost at once imperious orders began to issue from loud speakers.

"All hands to launching stations!"

There was a brief flurry of men running to their posts and of the aircrews climbing into cockpits and cabins. Fuchida sat in the centre seat of his 3-seater Kate with Matsuzaki in front and Mizuki behind him. He gave a thumbs-up sign and heard the broadcast order:

"Start engines!"

Blue smoke and sheets of flame flashed from exhaust pipes. The stutter of discordant motors was overwhelming. Orderlies ran to Fuchida's cabin door and to the carrier's bridge to report that all planes were ready. Captain Taijiro Aoki, *Akagi's* skipper, checked instruments and made sure that the wind gauge showed the correct velocity. Satisfied, he gave the order to begin launching. Instantly Lieut.-Commander Itaya revved his engine and led a squadron of eighteen Zeros into the air to stand guard while eighteen slower and more vulnerable dive-bombers and twenty-seven level-bombers took off. They patrolled for twenty minutes before the launch was completed, thus betraying a fear that they had not ruled out the possibility of an Allied air attack against the task force.

Eight thousand yards behind *Akagi* her sister ship *Kaga* had launched her planes; so had the light carriers *Soryu* and *Hiryu*. When all were airborne Fuchida flew his group of level-bombers in single file across the flagship's bow as a signal to assume pre-arranged flight formation, a tactic made necessary by the radio silence. Fighters, dive-bombers and level-bombers climbed to cruising altitude, the fighters maintaining a protective screen above and ahead of the other planes, clearing the track and guarding against the dreaded pounce by enemy fighters. Fuchida glanced at his watch at 8.45 a.m. and brought the attacking force on to a compass bearing of 148 degrees which, with the prevailing north-west wind, would bring them over Darwin in little more than one hour.

At that moment seventy waterside workers were already on duty in the holds or alongside two ships at Darwin wharf, where twenty-two of them would be killed.

Forty-five ships were moored in the harbour, stationary targets in which one hundred and sixty lives would be lost.

The post office staff had been issued with stamps and money

orders. Of the men about to serve the public, four would soon be dead.

Five women, also to die, had fitted earphones and were at work on the town's manually operated telephone switchboard.

At the airport four miles away ten American fighter pilots were preparing to leave on a flight to Java that would take them slightly south of the Japanese and, because of bad weather, bring them back to Darwin in time to be shot to pieces.

But these people and two thousand others in Darwin were unaware of the danger. When separate warnings were given from Melville and Bathurst Islands — warnings that might have given them half an hour to prepare — they were tragically ignored.

CHAPTER 2
The Irresolute Evacuation

> *'Evacuation of women and children, the invalid and the aged, began in December, 1941, and was largely completed two months later . . . Not more than 2,500 people remained.'*
> —OFFICIAL WAR HISTORY.

> *'An Air Raids Precaution group was organised but the townsfolk were uninterested and the task was left to civil servants.'*—OFFICIAL WAR HISTORY.

The imminence of attack upon Darwin, whether by bombing raids or invasion, was recognised by the government a few days after Japan entered the war.

The mass evacuation of women, children, the aged and the infirm was ordered in mid-December, 1941 — but in circumstances containing some of the elements of a confidence trick.

There can be no doubt that the evacuation was necessary, as events were to prove. It seems equally certain that this was achieved by deluding the people into believing the Administration had statutory powers to order their removal.

While many of the evacuees were not only willing but anxious to leave, others were sent against their will after being told that refusal to do so would be an offence.

It is true that under its wide wartime powers derived from the National Security (Emergency Control) Regulations the government could proclaim a state of emergency and "do any act or thing," which certainly included power to order the evacuation of a civil population. But at the time when more than two thousand civilians were sent to the southern states the National Security Regulations, in their relation to the Northern Territory, had not yet been gazetted. Emergency Control Regulation No.

3 specified that the responsible Minister, *by notice in the Gazette*,[1] could declare that the regulations applied to a particular part of Australia. In respect of the Northern Territory that was not done until February 23, 1942, four days after Darwin was bombed.

The likelihood that Darwin would be attacked in the event of a Pacific war had been recognised as early as June, 1940, eighteen months before Pearl Harbour. Within a few weeks of the arrival of Arthur Redvers Miller as Chief Surveyor a group of prominent citizens asked the Administrator to establish a Civil Defence organisation and appoint Miller its Chief Warden. That was done. Miller zoned the town and appointed zone wardens. They included Eric Willmot, Edgar T. Harrison, (later permanent officer of civil defence), W. J. E. White, E. F. S. D'Ambrosio, L. B. Winn and the Reverend C. T. F. Goy.

Wardens had to be familiar with their zones and maintain a roll of residents, kept current by a weekly check of arrivals and departures. The organisation performed its duties perfunctorily until December 7, 1941, but thereafter with a seriousness that belied its lack of statutory authority.

On December 12, a deputation of citizens waited on the Administrator, Mr. C. L. A. Abbott, a former Minister for Home Affairs in the Bruce-Page government. His visitors were the Chief Warden, Arthur Miller, and three of the zone wardens, White, Harrison and Willmot.

The date of the deputation is significant. Although the Pacific War was then only five days old the people of Darwin had already been frightened by an air raid alert.

At 10.45 p.m. on December 11, the warning sirens sounded in earnest for the first time on Australian soil.

There was no moon. Heavy cumulonimbus clouds added to the blackness, latent with rain that had not yet fallen. Most residents had gone to bed but sleep was difficult in the leaden atmosphere and oppressive humidity, made worse by the need to lie beneath mosquito nets.

A gangster film at Tom Harris's Star Theatre was nearing its climax, which might have been the siren of a police car; instead, it was the air raid alarm. Theatre patrons, anticipating a predictable victory by the film's hero, leaped from their seats and may have panicked except for a few cool-headed soldiers in the crowd who shouted to take it easy.

They filed out quietly into the black street. A light in a shop

[1] My italics.

window illuminated women's underwear. A soldier put a brick through the glass and smashed the light globe. Chinatown was thronged with men anxious to gamble in the dingy dens of Cavenagh Street; now it was blacked out as though its switches were controlled by the sirens. Wardens patrolled their beats, advising people where to go and what to do. Hundreds walked over the cliff on The Esplanade and huddled in groups on the beach, tormented by mosquitoes and sandflies. They took blankets, pillows, and bottles of water, expecting a long wait before the hum of aeroplane engines and the crack of anti-aircraft fire heralded the start of a raid. To that extent they showed a confidence in the early-warning system not justified by subsequent events.

Two men carried sick wives down the embankment and laid them gently on the sand. One had a sprained ankle. A few shadowy aborigines assembled in segregated groups, blacker in the blackness, unable as yet to comprehend a danger that could bring white men and women from their homes at such an unaccustomed hour to the discomforts of an insect-infested beach.

Several men, expressing impatience, went back to their beds, preferring the chance of Japanese bombs to the squadrons of mosquitoes.

There was a sense of siege. An underlying tenseness betrayed the artificial calm of men and women who wondered about the significance of a bugler's tattoo, heard across the water from Larrakeyah Barracks. Was it Stand-to for the troops, or Stand-down? Not till 12.30 a.m. did the All-Clear slice into the dark stillness, muted by sighs of relief and a few wavery cheers. Enemy planes did not come and the people were not told what had caused the alarm. Thereafter they slept with one ear open, waiting for the siren. Their danger, they were to learn later, was greatest during daylight. Carrier-borne aircraft did not operate at night. For the time being, at least, they could relax and sleep.

Next morning Miller and his civil defence colleagues asked Abbott to seek from the government an immediate grant of statutory powers by the declaration of a state of emergency under the National Security Regulations.

According to Miller the Administrator demurred, saying that such drastic action might cause panic. He thought it unnecessary. Miller says he told Abbott of the conviction of all wardens that

Darwin would be bombed by the Japanese. Moreover, he insisted that if the sea lanes were cut by the Japanese Navy the town could not survive for more than two weeks. At that time there was no all-weather road to the south and then, as now, the rail termini were one thousand miles away at Alice Springs and Mt. Isa. The limited air services, provided by small 10-seater planes, could not cope with the supply situation. The town depended on shipping along sea routes that were three thousand miles long and highly vulnerable. Miller advocated evacuation of the unessential element in the civilian population.

His recollection of the conversation is that Abbott appeared not to appreciate the situation or admit the need for immediate action. Abbott, on the other hand, says that even during the life of the first Menzies government, before the Pacific War began, he had discussed the desirability of evacuation with the Minister for the Interior, Senator H. S. Foll, and was certainly aware of the dangers on that December morning.

In any event, a telegram was sent to the Prime Minister's department. Miller says it was sent only after the delegation insisted upon it. It was signed by Abbott and asked for a general grant of powers to effect the evacuation of women and children and aged persons.

The Prime Minister, John Curtin, replied the same day giving War Cabinet's approval. The evacuation was to be carried out at Commonwealth expense and with the co-operation, if necessary, of the Navy and Army. But legal authority was not mentioned.

"We bluffed gullible people into believing that we could do what we were doing," Miller says.

In mid-December a list of evacuation priorities was published, roughly in the order of women and children first. A notice was delivered to every householder[2] setting out who was to go and what they could take with them. Each person was allowed one suitcase, two blankets, drinking and eating utensils and a waterbag. They were told specifically not to take pets but to destroy them before departure. Domestic poultry was to be left as an auxiliary food supply for those remaining. Evacuation by privately owned vehicles was banned.

If authority to enforce any of this did not exist, as appears to be the case, it was taken for granted so literally that within four days the first evacuees sailed in the m.v. *Zealandia,* which

[2] Appendix 1.

returned to Darwin in time to be sunk in the first raid. *Koolama* (later sunk off Wyndham), *Koolinda* and *Montoro*, all coastal traders, were also used.

Not all of the people the government wished to evacuate went without protest. More than two hundred women either refused to go or took "essential" jobs — a term applied to telephonists, boarding house proprietresses, nurses, the Administrator's wife and her domestic servants, and stenographers and clerks employed by the government and the services. Women holding these so-called essential positions were immune from the immediate effects of the evacuation order. They were easily acquired. My wife, faced with the prospect of separation after only two months of marriage, had little difficulty in getting a typist's job with the Army. She set off each day with a gas mask and steel helmet slung nonchalantly beside her handbag. A staff car ferried her between our home and the barracks. She was well paid and made to feel that she was an extremely important part of the war effort, notwithstanding that she had only one month's typing experience. Fortunately she became convinced of the wisdom of leaving one week before the first raid.

The lack of means to enforce the evacuation of those who rebelled, or a reluctance to do so, resulted in people remaining who would be less able to look after themselves in an emergency than many of the women who went. The best example was Jack Buscall, a bed-ridden cripple who conducted a shop known as Curio Cottage. It was probably one of the first serve-yourself stores in Australia, and necessarily so. Buscall's bed was in the centre of the shop. Customers took what they wanted from the shelves to his bed. At his left hand he had wrapping paper and bags, at his right hand a cash drawer. He also had a mirror fixed to the bed in such a way that he could observe customers at the shelves behind him. He adamantly refused to move, but several days after the raids was taken forcibly.

Abbott has complained of the difficulty in getting support from the townspeople but in the circumstances it seems that they were uncharacteristically docile. The response to government pressure was so good, in fact, that enough ships to take those who volunteered for evacuation could not easily be found. Relief came unexpectedly with the arrival of a 12,000-tons American liner, the *President Grant*. She was in Manila harbour as the Japanese invasion of the Philippines appeared imminent. The captain was instructed to sail for the nearest friendly port. He chose Darwin, which he entered with the aid of a chart taken from a National Geographic Magazine. Fortunately the *President Grant* was going to the east coast and was able to take several hundred women and children. Subsequently the owners claimed £100 for each passenger, though the fare from Darwin to Sydney on Australian ships was only £25. A settlement was reached by negotiation. Later the *President Grant* sank after she struck a reef off the Solomon Islands while taking troops to the Battle of Guadalcanal.

Between mid-December, 1941, and February 1, 1942, one thousand women and nine hundred children were evacuated. In the next eighteen days another three hundred left, the latter chiefly in aircraft used to ferry reinforcement wharf laborers from Queensland.

By February 18 the population had been reduced to few more than two thousand, of whom only sixty-three were women. Darwin had become a capital city without children, or so the authorities believed. But hidden by their parents on Railway Hill were two small girls, aged five and six, who came out of hiding in their Sunday bonnets when their mother sought evacuation after the bombing. And there were thirty-five part aboriginal girls who arrived that night from Bathurst Island.

The Administration typists left by air on February 18, but still there were others who remained on various pretexts. On February 16 the Administrator discovered that Mrs Emily Young, the wife of James Young, a garage proprietor, was working as a telephonist at the post office. He saw Hurtle Bald, the postmaster, and urged that she should be sent away. Only then did Abbott learn that Bald's wife and daughter, Iris, had remained. Mrs Alice Bald was working as a telephonist and Iris had a job with the Taxation Department. There were three other women telephonists, Eileen and Jean Mullen, who were sisters, and Miss Freda Stasinowsky.

"Train your telegraph messengers to operate the switchboard," Abbott advised Bald.

"Then who will deliver the telegrams?" Bald asked.

Abbott said all telegrams could be collected by addressees at the post office. On that note, Bald agreed that he would send the women away. But he delayed doing so. Three days later Bald and all the women were dead.

Arthur Miller's civil defence organisation, though it convinced half the population to leave, was less successful in other respects. Hundreds of householders were advised to dig slit trenches but failed to do so, either because they disliked hard and sweaty work or because of an irrational belief that Darwin would not be bombed.

The New Year was just forty-five minutes old when those who held that view were reminded of the realities of war. The town's second alert in the middle of the night again lasted two hours without a raid eventuating. But in three weeks the Japanese had made remarkable advances and clearly demonstrated the ability to attack Darwin when they chose.

Moreover, the build-up of our defence forces made it apparent that the government was seriously concerned not only with air attack but the possibility of invasion. Thousands of soldiers spent Christmas and New Year erecting barbed wire entanglements along the beaches. Concrete machinegun emplacements were manned and armed. The troops, unlike civilians, had no option about digging slit trenches; they dug what they called funk-holes, super-funk-holes, and super-dooper-funk-holes according to the depth and protection they afforded.

Towards the end of January civilian morale flagged. A Citizens' War Effort Committtee was formed and at its second meeting accused the Administrator of negligence in providing for the town's welfare. Reserve stocks of food were low and workers complained of an inability to find enough in the shops. Frugal meals without fresh vegetables were being served in cafes and hotels and some had closed their doors. The committee agitated for Abbott's removal, insisting that continuity of essential work could be guaranteed only if there were continuity of essential eating.

Matters were not helped when the Minister for the Interior, Senator J. S. Collings, replied to the demands by saying he believed they were the result of public pique caused by a liquor shortage. But as early as November, 1941, beer had been available for only a few days following the arrival of the fortnightly ship from the eastern states. The military population had increased substantially, and there was resentment among civilians that their beer, which they regarded as equally essential as food in the tropics, was being served to troops who should get it in their own canteens.

A serious dislocation of defence building programmes was threatened by a shortage of petrol. Residents were forced to scramble for a few gallons as soon as garage tanks were supplied by the oil companies. Long lines of cars and trucks waited at bowsers for up to half a day. When the garages closed at noon the vehicles were left in line and the drivers walked home for lunch. Taxi operators who depended on petrol for their livelihood got as little as two gallons a week for each vehicle.

All of this led to a hoarding of food, petrol, liquor and cigarettes. In the absence of equitable rationing, allegations of corruption were inevitable. To ease the food shortage, restaurants and cafes were eventually placed out of bounds to servicemen. That created friction which led to a number of ugly incidents in the streets and one near-riot by soldiers during which almost every window in the main street was broken.

A more serious development occurred at a meeting on January 23, at which the A.R.P. wardens threatened to resign, complaining of lack of support by the government and the withholding of legal power to enforce blackout and other regulations.

The wardens alleged that in April, 1941, they had asked for sandbagged dressing stations in each zone. They had not been built, nor had a request been met that sandbags be issued so they could build the dressing stations with voluntary help. The apparent apathy precipitated the resignation of the Director of First Aid, Mr A. Brough Newell. The remaining wardens wrote to the Administrator repeating a request for legal authority. The propriety of their claim was supported by the Judge of Northern Territory Supreme Court, Mr Justice Wells, who had told Miller by letter that the organisation was without power to force anyone to do anything.

The following night a warden came to blows with a garage proprietor who would not obey his instructions and defied the warden to enforce them.

On January 26 a reply had not been received from the Administrator. The remaining wardens then resigned and advised the Prime Minister by telegram of their action. They included first aid men, stretcher bearers, firemen and demolition workers.

But there were other reasons for the wardens' disenchantment. One of the most active workers was the Reverend C. T. F. Goy, a senior chaplain who was minister in charge of the United Church — a union in North Australia of the Methodist, Presbyterian and Congregational denominations. He also ran the United Church Club which provided relaxation and entertainment for servicemen and anyone else who wanted it. In the months that followed, Chris. Goy became the friend of thousands of servicemen he helped.[3]

Goy made available the ground floor of his Manse in Peel Street as civil defence headquarters. In it were established a

[3] He was later Moderator of the Presbyterian Church in Victoria.

battery of fourteen telephones with direct lines to the Army, Navy, R.A.A.F., Fire Brigade, Ambulance, Hospital and Administration departments. The headquarters was manned, until the resignations, by chosen civilians.

Late in 1941 when war was still rather remote from North Australia the civil defence officers and representatives from the armed forces and emergency services were rehearsed in an air raid exercise. Goy was astonished to discover that volunteer helpers recruited for that day included a number of Boy Scouts to be used as runners.

The exercise took the form of a mock attack on Darwin and its defence by service units. Goy was appointed by the service commanders as an official observer and was asked to submit a written report on his findings. To lend realism to the test he was empowered to give certain orders to represent imaginary acts of sabotage, the breakdown of public services or the blocking of roads. One of his diversions and some of his observations, to say the least, are tragically ironic in the light of subsequent events.

Soon after the exercise began Goy handed a warden a note advising him that the Post Office had been bombed and the telephone exchange destroyed. He was to act on the assumption that his lines to all emergency services were cut and thereafter must use runners and motor cycle dispatch riders.

"Impossible!" the warden said. He refused to accept the condition Goy had imposed and continued to use the telephones.

Goy's memorandum had gone out simultaneously to other strategic points but as civil defence headquarters disregarded it they did too.

Another observer imposed a condition that the water main into the town had been cut. Nevertheless, Goy noticed a few minutes later that the fire brigade had a full stream of water through its hoses in controlling a mock fire.

Such inconsistencies in the exercise were noted in writing by Goy and his colleagues and sent to the Defence Co-ordinating Committee, of which the Administrator and armed services commanders were members. Goy recalled later: "I never heard of that report again."

Among other things, it pointed out that if war came any Boy Scouts in the area would be immediately evacuated, preferably before the enemy got bombers within striking distance. They would therefore not be available to act as the second string of communications.

THE IRRESOLUTE EVACUATION

Why consideration was given to sending boys on errands which would so obviously belong to men, once they became necessary, is not clear. What is clear is that on February 19 the telephone system was put out of action with the first few bombs. If the wardens had then thought of calling for Boy Scout runners they would have discovered, of course, that all boys had been evacuated.

But the civil defence organisation, as such, never did get into action. Those wardens who had not resigned, and some who had, went immediately to work when the raids occurred and did what they could to help, but their efforts were unco-ordinated and the effect was lost.

Early in 1942 Goy suggested that all civilians should be made to carry either identification discs or cards. Much of the key work on the wharves, on oil tank construction, on the railways, and at coastal artillery emplacements, was being done by civilians who stood a real chance of numbering high in the casualties if the town should be attacked. To identify the bodies of people killed by high explosive bombs might be difficult without some aid.

Goy told me his suggestion received support but was rejected by the Administrator, who thought that a system of identification was unnecessary. The aftermath of that decision is one that Goy remembers with bitterness, thus:

"As I knew personally and intimately the entire Post Office staff, I had the sad task of identifying nine bodies as they lay outside the hospital and pinning on each its first and last identification card."

CHAPTER 3
The Warnings Ignored

> *'The alarm preceded the falling of the first bomb by a very short space of time, probably seconds.'*—MR. JUSTICE LOWE.

> *'We had warning of the Japanese approach thirty minutes before they arrived.'*
> —LIEUT-COMMANDER J. C. B. MCMANUS.

For the Catholic missionaries at Bathurst Island, fifty miles north-north-west of Darwin, the day began at 5 a.m. The angelus was rung at six o'clock, breakfast was eaten at seven, and field activities by aboriginal workers followed. Three hundred members of the Tiwi and related tribes were living in the mission village. Priests and lay missionaries were understandably tense. Bathurst Island and its larger neighbour, Melville Island, stood between the Japanese southward advance and the sea approaches to Darwin, dominating Clarence Strait, Beagle Gulf, Van Diemen Gulf and Dundas Strait. It did not require too profound a knowledge of military science to appreciate that if the enemy should attempt an invasion of the Darwin area, as then seemed certain, landings on the two islands would be necessary preliminaries. In that event the undefended mission on the south-east coast of Bathurst Island would be occupied.

Apart from tenseness, however, there was little immediate concern. While the unsophisticated aborigines were aware that a war was being fought against Japan, whose nationals had frequently visited the islands in pearling luggers and cohabited with their women, few expected that it might directly affect their lives and fewer still imagined that the benevolent European civilisation they were learning to respect might be replaced by Asiatic persecution. Although often perplexed by the white man's way, and especially by his lack of hunting instinct, they were frankly astonished by his miraculous inventions, beginning with tinned food and the pedal wireless. It would have been inconceivable to any of them, if they had seriously thought about it, that the creators of these technological marvels could be defeated on the field of battle.

Nevertheless, there were several among them who understood something about the realities of war. At 9.30 a.m. all work stopped as a spontaneous alarm was raised by primitive men. High in the north-western sky, too far distant for positive identification, they saw more aeroplanes than had ever been over their islands flying towards Darwin.

Father John J. McGrath, sensing the implications of what he saw and heard, ordered the evacuation of the village which, he recalls, "immediately assumed stampede proportions." But there were some among the Tiwi who stayed to help the priest who had helped them. They included a tribesman named Paul Mangurupurramili and his wife. As Father McGrath walked quickly to the wireless room to send a warning to Darwin, Paul made what may have been the first assessment of military might by an aboriginal.[1]

"Four squadrons, Father," he said.

Father McGrath tuned the mission's transceiver to an emergency frequency always kept open by V.I.D., the Amalgamated Wireless coastal station in Darwin, and transmitted a message which should have given the defenders twenty minutes notice of what was about to happen. It was not heeded.

"Eight-S-E to V-I-D," Father McGrath said. Without repeating his call sign or waiting to make sure that V.I.D. had heard, he continued: "I have an urgent message. An unusually large air formation bearing down on us from the north-west. Identity suspect. Visibility not clear. Over."

Lou Curnock, the officer in charge at V.I.D., replied at once.
"Eight-S-E from V.I.D. Message received. Stand by."

Father McGrath could not stand by because in a few moments fighters were strafing the mission and he had to take shelter. A U.S. Beechcraft aeroplane was destroyed on the ground. When Father McGrath returned to the radio he found the channel to Darwin jammed.

Less than three weeks later a Royal Commissioner, Mr Justice

---

[1] It was by no means the last. Thereafter, until the end of the war, aborigines were used as coastwatchers and frequently reported enemy air and naval movements.

Lowe, was appointed to inquire into the circumstances of the raids and was told about the message. He reported to the government: "The A.W.A. station received the message at 9.35 and passed it to R.A.A.F. operations at 9.37. No general alarm was given in the town until just before 10 o'clock."

Nor was that the first or only warning received.

Lieut.-Commander J. C. B. McManus, senior intelligence officer at Navy headquarters, had established a coastwatching service with manned posts at strategic points westward from the Gulf of Carpentaria. One of these was on the northern tip of Melville Island, about fifty miles north of the Bathurst Island mission. The coastwatcher, John Gribble, was assisted by volunteer Tiwi tribesmen. He had a radio transmitter and a simple code by which he could instantly notify Darwin of sightings. Shortly after 9.15 Warrant Officer Bill Phaup telephoned McManus from Coonawarra naval signalling station with a message from Gribble reporting "a large number of aircraft." There were no other details, either of identification or direction of flight, but the planes could not be assumed to be friendly. McManus does not doubt that this was the first sighting of the Japanese and that if the report had been correctly interpreted the town and its defenders might have had as much as thirty minutes warning.[2]

McManus telephoned a R.A.A.F. intelligence officer, who told him the planes were probably ten American P.40s which had taken off for Java. McManus did not fully accept this interpretation. A glance at the map showed that Melville Island was north of the course of planes flying to Java.

"I was confident that Gribble must have seen something very unusual. I wanted to sound the alarm at once but was overruled. There had been a series of earlier false alarms which it was undesirable to repeat."

Gribble's report was followed a few minutes later by Father McGrath's but even with that confirmation of a large force approaching, appropriate action was not taken.

Not until McManus walked outside his headquarters at 9.58 a.m. and saw the Japanese planes with bomb bays open was a positive decision made about sounding the alarm. He went quickly into the office of the Naval-Officer-in-Charge, Captain

[2] The existence of Gribble's message is not mentioned in the Royal Commissioner's report. I have been refused access to the Minutes of Evidence by the Federal Govt., and cannot say whether he was told about it.

E. Penry Thomas, R.N., and told him what he had seen. Thomas rose from his desk, broke the glass covering an alarm button, pressed it, and sounded the sirens.

Bombs were already whistling through the air and exploded around the wharf before the alarm was heard there.

Wing-Commander Sturt Griffith, a Citizen Air Force officer, was called up for duty in the week war was declared. He arrived in Darwin as station commander on February 1, 1942, and thus had less than three weeks before the bombing in which to assess his new task.

Air-Commodore D. E. L. Wilson was North-west Area commander, with his headquarters superimposed on the station headquarters. Wilson, moreover, lived with some of his staff in Griffith's house. Griffith has claimed that rather than having a cohesive effect this proximity led to confusion and eventually to chaos. He had to live and work with officers who were senior to him in rank or appointment or both; their tasks, instead of being complementary, were simply duplicated. To make matters worse, a Combined Headquarters of the services was also located in the R.A.A.F.'s operations building. Its role was obscure. Griffith told me that North-west Area officers over-rode him to the extent that he was shorn of all authority, even in the posting of men to and from his unit without his knowledge.

In Wilson's temporary absence at General Wavell's headquarters in Java (he is believed to have gone there without Air Board permission) the North-west Area command was being administered by Group-Captain F. R. W. Scherger,[3] who agrees that Griffith had little effective authority on the base.

It is important that this should be considered if judgments are to be made on responsibility for what followed. Griffith, not unnaturally, was smarting from what he regarded as hindrance and usurpation.

"I was without authority in my own operations room so I spent my days co-ordinating a scheme of aerodrome defence," he told me. "The majority of our men had been left in Darwin beyond their normal tour of duty. Morale was low and pervaded by tropical malaise. The men showed little interest in defence and that was not improved by a shortage of weapons."

This was the situation on February 19. Griffith says he was summoned to the operations room some minutes after the warning message was received from Father McGrath. An opera-

[3] Later Air Chief Marshal Sir Frederick Scherger.

tions officer on duty, Flight Lieutenant A. Saxton, has estimated the time as between 9.40 and 9.43, though the V.I.D. log showed it had been passed at 9.37. Griffith checked and was told the message had been passed to North-west Area and also to Combined headquarters.

"It was their duty to act," Griffith says. "I was told about the American P.40s in the area but I did not agree they might have been mistaken for Japanese. In fact, I believed the alarm should have been sounded at once."

The decision to do that was delayed by doubt which should not have existed, by confusion as to whose responsibility it was, and by the absence from the station of Group-Captain Scherger, who at that moment was driving into Darwin.

Part of the delay might have been attributed to the Americans, who had previously caused false alarms. Commanders were concerned that these affected morale and resulted in an over-cautious attitude.

A false alarm had been sounded as early as January 1, and another on January 5 when a force of warships and transports was seen sailing towards the port. They were at first thought to belong to a Japanese task force about to make a landing and there was an understandably jittery period until the ships were identified as American. Major Floyd Pell caused further consternation on February 15 when he flew in unannounced with a U.S.A.F.[4] squadron of P.40s.

All these factors, taken together, contributed to the delay. But it is more difficult to explain why the alarm was not sounded at once when others are considered. Area Combined Headquarters had received the Navy report from John Gribble, the coastwatcher on Melville Island. Although the crew of an American Catalina flying boat shot down by Zeros on the way to Darwin were unable to send a warning because their radio was destroyed, there were early sighting reports from the Army. At 9.46 Major R. B. Hone telephoned from the 2/14th Field Regiment camp at Nightcliff, seven miles north of Darwin, to say that he had seen a P.40 plunge into the water and high above it a parachute open. The Official War History records that when told of this message the reply from the R.A.A.F. had been, "If this is a raid we know nothing of it." At 9.50 the same officer telephoned Army headquarters and reported an aerial dogfight

---

[4] I have referred throughout to the U.S.A.F. (United States Air Force) as it now is, although at the time it was the U.S.A.A.C. (United States Army Air Corps) or U.S.A.F.I.A. (United States Air Forces in Australia).

off Nightcliff. In spite of an apparent discrepancy in times (the bombing began at 9.58) Hone's estimate may well be correct. The Japanese made their bombing run on Darwin from the south-east although the course from their carriers was northwest. Eight minutes could have elapsed while they by-passed the town, turned, and flew back.

Nor was that all. Not far from Major Hone, Sgt. W. J. F. McDonald[5] was in charge of a detachment from the 19th Machinegun Regiment manning a concrete emplacement at Casuarina Beach, ten miles north of the town.

Trooper Cecil Burns, the beach lookout, saw planes approaching and ran to McDonald. "The Japs are here!" he shouted.

McDonald said, "They're probably our own. What makes you think they're Japs?"

"They've got bloody great red spots on 'em," Burns said.

McDonald picked up a direct-line telephone to Captain Howard Brown, staff captain at 23rd Brigade headquarters. "We've got Japanese planes," he said.

Brown, according to McDonald, replied, "Mac, I'm busy; don't play games with me. How do you know they're Japs?"

"They've got bloody great red spots on 'em," McDonald said.

Brown, also according to McDonald, telephoned Army headquarters and spoke to an officer who wanted to know how the planes had been identified as Japanese. They identified themselves a moment later with bombs on the town.

Until now it has not been generally known that the R.A.A.F. was directly warned of a big build up in enemy air activity near Portuguese Timor in time for Darwin to have been given as much as twenty-four hours notice of impending trouble. This warning, sent in code from Dili by the Australian consul, David Ross, was apparently still being evaluated when the bombs fell. Two or three days before February 19 — he is not sure of the exact date — Ross received word from Lieut. Manuel Pires,[6] Portuguese administrator of the Baucau circumscription eighty miles east of Dili, about increasing Japanese air movements. Pires said that two flights comprising forty and twenty-seven aircraft respectively had flown over Baucau from the north, gone east along the coast for twenty minutes, then returned over Baucau and north to seaward.

[5] Later Sir William McDonald, Speaker of the Victorian Legislative Assembly.
[6] Captured and executed by Japanese.

Ross had daily contact with the Department of Civil Aviation aeradio at Darwin through a Portuguese station in Dili manned by Patricio da Luz, who was later to distinguish himself in helping Australian commandos in Timor. That same evening he sent a coded signal about the Japanese flights, adding — "somewhat naively," he now says — that he suspected the presence of an aircraft carrier in the Banda Sea north of Wetar Island. Events were to prove him incorrect only insofar as he underestimated the strength.[7] Rather than take defensive action the R.A.A.F. set out to prove the reliability or otherwise of the information. Early on February 19 Ross received a signal from Darwin asking him to specify the type of aircraft, whether monoplanes or biplanes, and ending with the question, "What makes you think there is a carrier to the north of Wetar?" He could not reply because soon afterwards the R.A.A.F. radio in Darwin was destroyed. The carriers had sailed to a position off the south-east coast of Timor and given terrible proof of their presence. Ross was captured by the Japanese in Dili next morning, February 20.

On repatriation to Australia more than a year later Ross saw Group-Captain Scherger and asked why he had not acted on his report. Scherger told him he had never seen any such message.

"The intelligence boys were trying to prove what I'd told them," Ross says now. "As it turned out, that was rather a pity."

Nor was the R.A.A.F. staff at Darwin unaware of the link existing between Civil Aviation's aeradio and the Portuguese in Timor. Patricio da Luz had supplemented official coded messages with information of his own about the Japanese. The department's radio inspector in Darwin at the time, E. G. ("Ted") Betts, says the R.A.A.F. was extremely interested in Dili in the preraid period.

He recalls: "We were instructed to advise R.A.A.F. operations if the Dili station did not keep any of the regular schedules or if we had reason to suspect that the operator on watch at any time was not the normal one. In the radiotelegraphy fraternity every operator can be recognised by his brethren, with reasonable certainty, from his fist — or keying. Just as individual handwriting differs from copperplate so does the construction in time elements of Morse vary among operators. No one sends perfectly so that, in comparison with auto-machine sending, there are minor variations such as clipped or elongated dashes, square

[7] There were four, not one, and the reported position was directly on course between the Celebes and the point of launching.

or sharp dots, slightly reduced or extended intervals between elements, characters and words which the ear detects. After one operator has worked on a circuit over a short period with another, each can recognise the other's fist immediately, just as you know by the writing who a letter is from. The Darwin operators, therefore, satisfied themselves at each transmission that it was da Luz on the key and not some Japanese operator pretending to be him. Additionally, if da Luz, who was an experienced operator, were sending false messages with a bayonet at his back he would probably have been able to give us some indication without Japanese knowledge that all was not as it seemed at his end, and I think he may well have done this if the occasion had arisen. I remember reporting to the R.A.A.F. on several occasions that da Luz had missed his schedule, then having to say that he had finally come up and that we were satisfied it was da Luz."

In these circumstances it is difficult indeed to understand why a coded warning from Ross, sent by da Luz, was not passed at once to Group-Captain Scherger; it is incomprehensible, when the additional factors are considered, that an immediate alarm was not given.

CHAPTER 4

The Aerodromes: Raid 1

> *'There were twenty-odd planes of various types on the airfields. Several U.S. P.40s attempted to take off as we came over but were quickly shot down and the rest were destroyed where they stood.'*
> —COMMANDER FUCHIDA.

> *'The effects of the raid at the air station were extremely serious. The personnel, most of whom were experiencing enemy attack for the first time, were shaken.'*
> —MR. JUSTICE LOWE.

On February 12 there were just two fighter aircraft in commission at Darwin. Both were American P.40s left behind with engine trouble when the 3rd Pursuit Squadron departed for Java. The pilots were Lieut. Robert G. Oestreicher and Lieut. Robert J. Buel. Buel failed to return from convoy escort duty over the Timor Sea on February 15. That left one fighter apart from five unserviceable R.A.A.F. Wirraways and another nine at Batchelor, sixty miles away, which must be discounted. The fact that ten P.40s were operational on February 19 was fortuitous.

There had been concern in the higher echelons of Allied command at the lack of air cover for a convoy taking troop reinforcements to Timor. On February 12 the senior U.S. officer, General George Brett, then in Java, told his Chief of Staff, Brigadier General Julius F. Barnes, of the need to get a squadron of P.40s to Darwin by February 13/14 for this operation. General Barnes at first replied that sixteen P.40s were already at Darwin but later corrected himself to give the proper total of two. The squadrons available at that time were committed to other tasks and one, the 33rd, had arrived at Port Pirie on a flight across the continent to Perth. The squadron commander, Major Floyd ("Slugger") Pell, was then ordered to change his bearing and go to Darwin with the fifteen planes remaining from an original twenty-five that had left Amberley, Queensland.

He still had the continent to cross, however, and there seemed little chance that he would arrive in time to give effective cover to the convoy. His pilots were young and eager but pitifully inexperienced, some with as little as twelve hours flying in combat planes. Moreover, facilities for refuelling on the south-north route were inadequate. At one or two places the pilots had to roll barrels of petrol to their planes and hand-pump it into the tanks themselves.

Pell had ten planes left when he landed at Darwin late on February 15, only to find that the convoy had sailed early the same day. In any case, the P.40s needed so much maintenance after the long flight that Pell reported it would take seventy-two hours to put eight of them back in combat commission. To make matters worse, the maintenance crews did not arrive until late on the 16th. Nevertheless, tired as they were, Pell and two other pilots took off again that same afternoon, found the convoy in the early evening, and stayed with it for some time.

On February 16 Pell held a pilots' meeting at which Lieut. Oestreicher joined the 33rd, giving it eleven planes and eleven pilots. They were divided into "A" and "B" flights.

"A" flight was led by Major Pell as squadron commander. With him he had Lieut. Charles W. Hughes, Lieut. Robert F. McMahon, Lieut. Burt H. Rice, Lieut. Robert H. Vaught and Lieut. John G. Glover. "B" flight's leader was Lieut. Oestreicher, and with him were Lieut. Jack R. Peres, Lieut. Elton S. Perry, Lieut. Max R. Wiecks and Lieut. William R. Walker.

On February 17 the squadron flew high altitude patrols in both morning and afternoon over Bathurst and Melville Islands and escort was given to a two-ship convoy sailing towards Darwin. These patrols were continued on February 18 by planes which were awaiting or had been given maintenance. By that time the Timor convoy had been ordered back to Darwin and Pell and his squadron to Java. He held another pilots' meeting and briefed them for a dawn take-off. The American historian Walter D. Edmonds described this decision in his book, *They Fought With What They Had*,[1] as surprising.

[1] Little, Brown and Co., Boston, 1951.

"Putting aside entirely the fact that the squadron's departure would leave Darwin with no air cover of any sort," he wrote, "the Allied command was already aware that the Japanese occupation force at Macassar had weighed anchor for Bali and for three days past the island had been under such constant air bombardment that, even if they beat the Japanese to the airfield, staging the P.40s through the islands successfully would call for Providential intercession. Nothing . . . could better illustrate the desperate expedients to which the top command was now reduced."

To make the flight still riskier, radio contact with Koepang, always uncertain, failed completely on the morning of the 19th. As if that were not enough trouble, Major Pell's plane was found to have a coolant leak which caused postponement of the dawn take-off. Valuable hours were lost while an attempt was made to repair it. Finally Pell took over Lieut. Vaught's plane, told him to fly the other back to Brisbane, and led the two flights away from Darwin at 9.15 a.m. They formed behind a B.17 bomber piloted by Lieut. Clarence E. McPherson, who gave navigational aid.

At 9.30, just before the Japanese were seen at Bathurst Island, Pell received radio advice from the U.S.A.F. operations officer at Darwin, Captain Louis J. Connelly, of heavy rainstorms and a 600 ft. ceiling on the route to Java. He was advised to return and did so, undoubtedly taking into account the inexperience of pilots whose training had been cut short so that they could be thrown into action.

As the 33rd squadron came back over Darwin Pell ordered Oestreicher to take his flight to fifteen thousand feet and remain on patrol for two hours. Pell himself went in to land with Hughes, McMahon, Rice and Glover following closely behind. The exact time has never been established — in any case, watches had not been synchronised — but it was most likely between 9.55 and 9.57 when Glover, the last man in, taxied up to his dispersal point.

"B" flight formed into two 2-plane elements with Oestreicher above them as scout and began to climb through scattered cumulus cloud. The entrance to Darwin harbour was beneath them. Oestreicher reported later: "At eight thousand feet I spotted a plane diving on us from about two thousand feet above and in the eight o'clock position."

That would have been over his left shoulder. He recognised

the profile at once, saw the red roundels on fuselage and wings and shouted into his radio:

"Zeros! Zeros! Zeros!"

"On their first attack they broke our formation and forced us to dive out, dropping our belly tanks as we went," Oestreicher reported. The scattering P.40s did not include Lieut. Wiecks, No. 4 man in the flight. His radio was dead and he had not heard Oestreicher's warning. He first knew that something was amiss when he saw Peres suddenly pull out of the formation.

"I thought Peres had engine trouble and was heading back to the airfield," he told me. "I tried to catch up with Oestreicher and Perry to fill the gap left by Peres. Suddenly below me and to my right I saw that Peres was being followed by another plane. Then I saw the red circle insignia and was galvanised by the realisation that here was my very first Japanese Zero. I remember turning on my gun sight and switching my gas tanks, while all the time watching the pursuit below and trying to turn in such a way as to get in behind the Zero chasing Peres. As I turned I saw the Japanese fire his cannon. I saw shells hitting Peres, and then his plane slowly rolled over and down."

Wiecks did not see it but Lieut. Perry was shot down at the same time and plunged into the bay.

Oestreicher's formation had been broken by the overwhelming surprise of the attack and never succeeded in regrouping. Oestreicher, climbing into the sun after dropping his belly tank, was attacked and hit but managed also to get a burst into a Zero.

Wiecks remembers that he entered what he calls a "near-hypnotic state" on seeing Peres shot down. That did not last long, however, for a few seconds later Zeros were swarming over the remaining P.40s. At twelve thousand feet Oestreicher, during a momentary lull, was able to count eighteen Japanese fighters "in a lazy circle at what I would judge to be twenty thousand feet." They were apparently a reserve element sitting up top, waiting for their colleagues to break off their engagement before entering it themselves to "mop up".

Aware for the first time of how heavily outnumbered they were, Oestreicher called "B" flight and ordered his pilots towards heavier cloud at three thousand feet about five miles south of Darwin. None responded. Peres and Perry were dead. Wiecks, with a damaged radio, did not hear him. And Lieut. Walker, No. 5 in the flight, was limping back towards the airstrip with a plane full of holes and a bullet through his left shoulder. He managed to evade the Zeros long enough to land and taxi to the vicinity of a hangar occupied by unserviceable R.A.A.F. Wirraways. Walker jumped into a slit trench in time to save himself from the strafing that followed at once. His P.40 was hit by cannon shells, set on fire and burnt to a cinder.

Max Wiecks was then twenty-seven years old. He had been a pilot for less than one month and flown a fighter for only twelve hours when he arrived at Brisbane in December 1941. His last act before beginning the flight from Brisbane *via* Port Pirie to Darwin in February was to "souvenir" an Australian parachute from the operations room at Amberley R.A.A.F. base.

"I didn't have one and felt naked without it," he told me. The petty larceny was to save his life.

Wiecks recovered from his "near-hypnotic state" to find the action around him "wild and frenzied." Manoeuvre as he might, he could not escape the overwhelming Japanese force. His plane was soon riddled by bullet holes and out of control.

"I realised I was falling — not normally with the nose down, but flatly like a leaf," he recalls. "Nothing I did corrected this motion and as I was close to the water I knew I had to jump. I jettisoned the canopy and unbuckled my seat belt. Immediately I was catapulted out of the cockpit and had just opened my parachute when I heard the thud of the plane as it hit the sea. Within a few seconds I was down, too. The 'chute was filled with air and dragged me through the water like a porpoise. I realised that unless I could get clear I was in danger of being taken under and drowned. The straps had become entangled in my web belt, which also held my pistol and canteen. I had to jettison everything."

Wiecks did not yet know it but he was about ten miles from land and still in danger of losing his life. He was supported by a partly-inflated Mae West jacket and began swimming. He could not see Darwin but as the bombers went to work they started fires which raised a heavy pall of smoke above the town, making its position all too apparent.

He swam and rested throughout the day. The water was infested by sharks, stingrays and poisonous jellyfish. Rescue would have been prevented just then by the Japanese, even if rescue craft had been available and his position had been known. Moreover, the ebbing tide racing out of the harbour while it fell twenty and a half feet carried him further from land until it turned at 2.19 p.m. and began helping him back towards it, but he was unaware that he was being carried out and in like a piece of human driftwood. As darkness fell, however, the shore was close and he remembers reaching it "just as the moon was going down."[2]

Wiecks recalls: "I saw a tree ahead of me. I was exhausted but had enough strength to grab it and strap myself to it. I stayed there all night. At dawn I was able to walk to the sand. I went along a track to an Australian camp and was taken to hospital."

Of "B" flight Lieut. Oestreicher alone stayed in the air until the raid ended. After flying in cloud for some time he saw two dive-bombers and intercepted them at fifteen thousand feet. One burst in flames and crashed when Oestreicher fired; he saw smoke coming from the other as it dived into cloud. Oestreicher was told later that both planes had been found within a mile of each other and he claimed the first aerial victories over Australia. When he landed at 11.45 the left tyre and wheel of his plane were damaged by bullets and had to be replaced. This was being done by ground crews when a second raid began thirteen minutes later. No other plane was available for fighting and Oestreicher, having lived through aerial combat, now had to seek shelter in a trench as the R.A.A.F. base was thoroughly pattern-bombed and severely damaged. His own plane was destroyed.

No other plane was available to Oestreicher because all five P.40s in "A" flight had crashed or been destroyed, as had the unserviceable plane belonging to Lieut. Vaught. The squadron commander, Major Pell, and his No. 2, Lieut. Hughes, were dead. Lieuts. McMahon, Rice and Glover were wounded.

Pell had been sitting in scant shade made by the wing of his plane, deep in conversation with Captain "Shorty" Wheless, a U.S.A.F. operations officer. They were discussing the squadron's abortive attempt to reach Java and conjecturing on what orders might be passed by General Barnes when he learnt that the P.40s were not in Java as intended but back in Darwin.

The radio in Pell's plane was turned on. It crackled intermittently with static and instructions from the flight control officer in the aerodrome tower. Above these routine noises they then heard Oestreicher's voice, with its note of unmistakable urgency and repeated shouts of "Zeros!" The two men looked up and saw not only Zeros but bombers, too.

Pell jumped to his feet and ran for the cockpit, shouting to his

[2] High water was at 8.36 p.m. The moon set at 10.5 p.m.

mechanics to get the belly-tanks off. Before he could taxi out to the runway a flight of Zeros flashed across the field strafing targets at random. As Pell struggled gallantly to get into the air, with four inexperienced young pilots behind him, it was apparent to anyone with knowledge of aerial combat that they did not stand a chance.

Three Zeros swooped on Pell's tail the moment he was airborne. Unable to manoeuvre without altitude, he was a sitting shot for the highly trained Japanese. At eighty feet his plane burst into flames. Pell bailed out but his parachute had barely opened when he hit the ground. For a minute he did not move and those who watched were convinced that he had been killed instantly. Then he began slowly crawling away, trailing his parachute. An unidentified Australian, seeing Pell's distress, leapt from a trench and ran to help him. But the Japanese pilots who shot him down came back to make sure he was dead. They saw him move and strafed him as he crawled; when the Australian eventually reached him Pell was beyond human aid.

Lieut. Hughes, next behind Pell, did not get airborne. He was strafed as he gathered speed along the runway and crashed before his wheels lifted, dead in the cockpit.

Lieut. Robert McMahon had just celebrated his twenty-first birthday. He began learning to fly when only fourteen, was licensed at eighteen, and came to Australia with fourteen hours training in combat planes. After landing with Pell's flight he taxied to a dispersal area at the end of the strip and began writing in his log book a list of faults he had detected in his machine. At that moment a vehicle raced past and McMahon saw an airman waving at him frantically and pointing to something in the air. Then an American mechanic ran towards him and shouted, "Lieutenant, the Japs are here!"

McMahon saw Pell and Hughes "scrambling" their planes, Pell going across country over grass and bushes in his anxiety to get into the air. McMahon re-started his engine and went after them. Half way along the runway he had to brake suddenly to avoid a plane flown by Lieut. Walker, a member of "B" flight, who was attempting to land with a gaping hole in his arm — an arm so badly wounded that he couldn't use it and was flying "one hand." They narrowly missed colliding, but then McMahon was soon airborne and climbing towards the sun. Three Zeros were above him and to his right. "I had them just where they wanted me," he says, but the pilots apparently did not see him.

McMahon recalls: "I was flying. I got the gun sight on and

flipped the gun switches. I did a slow turn right towards the Zeros and began shooting. I wasn't within a country mile of the first one. I think I hit the second but he didn't stop. In my haste to get up I hadn't locked the undercarriage properly; now it fell down and this slowed me so much that I had no chance of mixing it. Then the Zeros got on to me. In the next few minutes I must have been hit more than one hundred times by machinegun bullets but I was wounded only slightly in one leg. Then I was over the harbour and ships' ack-ack crews began firing at me. With my wheels down they probably thought I was a Japanese. They at least drove the Zeros away for a while. The engine was on fire. Petrol was streaming from the left wing tanks and the windshield was fractured. I could see life rafts in the water, and guys swimming around everywhere, and sometimes I could see the spray of machinegun and cannon shells on the water. I did a half-roll, pointed my nose at a divebomber and began shooting tracer at him. I saw the reargunner slump over his gun but I had to pull out and did not see what happened to the plane. Then I went for the clouds. I was chased by Zeros. I wanted to get out — the old crate was like a sieve. I tried to take a pot-shot at a Zero but the guns clicked. I was out of ammunition so I went over the side. My 'chute opened at about seven hundred feet. I heard a rat-a-tat-tat behind me and a plane going by. They were shooting at me — naked I was, not wearing a plane any more, even one with holes in it. I began climbing up the 'chute-riser. The Japanese shot out some shroud lines but I got down into mangroves on the west side of the harbour. It was quiet there after all the noise. No sound at all. I didn't know which way to go. I was lost. I had no maps. I climbed a tree and could see nothing and thought I'd die there. My boots were full of blood and mud. I had no emergency kit. But I had a compress on my belt and I bandaged my leg with that. I saw that I wasn't far from the sea. I waded out, sat on my rubber parachute seat, and flailed the water to frighten any crocodiles. The current took me across the mouth of a stream. From there I could see a motor boat. It seemed a futile hope but I started yelling. They must have cut the motor because they heard me and came to take me off."[3]

[3] All ten U.S.A.F. pilots were awarded the D.S.C. Several subsequently flew in New Guinea and other theatres. McMahon was shot down during the Battle of the Bulge in Europe, suffered shrapnel wounds and broke a leg. He was taken prisoner by the Germans and released by the Russians. He is still a qualified pilot, a colonel on the U.S.A.F. reserve and a member of the U.S. Fighter Aces Assn. "I cut my teeth at Darwin," he says. John G. Glover is now a colonel and still serving.

Lieuts. Burt Rice and John Glover were last off the strip and swung sharply left when airborne. They climbed for altitude while simultaneously trying to shake off pursuing Japanese. Rice reached five thousand feet and was about to turn towards the leading Zero when he discovered that his controls, apparently damaged by machinegunning, were unresponsive. As his plane began spinning towards the ground Rice bailed out but in doing so struck his forehead on part of the cockpit with such force that he was temporarily blinded and lost consciousness. To this day Rice does not remember pulling the ripcord but he does remember landing.

He would not remember anything except for the action of "A" flight's No. 5, Lieut. Glover. While Rice swung helplessly in his parachute the Japanese became aware of his predicament. They circled as though he were a human drogue and began coming at him with machineguns blazing. Soon after he became airborne Glover had the luck to find one of the Zeros chasing Rice directly in his gunsight. He pressed the button and saw it going down. Then he saw the Zeros circling Rice and using him as an Aunt Sally. Glover abandoned his climb for altitude to break them up in what observers in the trenches on the aerodrome below regarded as a valiant but suicidal act. Glover began orbiting Rice's parachute in tight circles in an attempt to protect him but at three thousand feet his plane, critically damaged, went into a steep dive and plummeted to earth. Men watching him were convinced, when he did not bail out, that Glover himself had been hit. He had, however, been struggling to regain control. At the last instant, at the moment it seemed inevitable that he would die, the P.40 levelled off, hit the edge of the aerodrome, cart-wheeled several times in clouds of dust and smoke, and smashed into pieces that flew for one hundred yards from what remained of the fuselage.

As the dust settled, Glover miraculously crawled from the wreckage, got to his feet and began to walk along the east side of the runway. After a few steps he abruptly sat down and, overcome, buried his face in his hands. An Australian ran and dragged him to safety seconds ahead of Japanese pilots who had seen and were coming in to strafe him. Rice landed safely in a swamp and was found several hours later.

The acting North-west Area commander, Group-Captain Scherger, left the base at 9.50 to meet Air Marshal Richard

Williams[4] at the Hotel Darwin. Williams was returning to Australia from an appointment in London. Scherger had been in Darwin since September 1941, first as station commander and then as senior air staff officer to Air-Commodore Wilson. As already related, Wilson was in Java on February 19 and Scherger was acting in his place.

Scherger had driven one and a half miles from the base and was near Parap, two and a half miles from town, when he heard anti-aircraft fire. He stopped, got out of his car, and saw twenty-seven Japanese planes approaching. He is sure of the number because he counted them. Scherger got back in the car and returned towards the aerodrome without seeing Williams. Quarter of a mile from the R.A.A.F. gates a P.40 with its undercarriage dangling flew in front of his car. A few seconds later it crash landed on the strip.[5] A passing truck driver shouted to him, "One of your planes has crashed!"

"It's a raid!" Scherger said. "You'd better pull off the road and stay with me." They stood under a tree together.

Some time later Scherger tried to drive through the R.A.A.F. gates but the entrance was blocked by a vehicle parked across it. The driver couldn't be found. Scherger shouted for the vehicle to be shifted. As he did so, bullets thudded through the mudguard and boot of his car. He had believed the raid was over; it wasn't, and he had become a target of convenience for a strafing fighter. He was forced to remain at the gates until the All-Clear.

The base was heavily damaged in a second raid one and a half hours after the first had ended. That will be described in sequence later. But it was by no means ignored in the first attack. Dive-bombers and fighters, after disposing of the P.40s, went about their task unhurriedly and efficiently, selecting targets with care and then bursting upon them without opposition from the air. In a short time most of the buildings apart from the headquarters had been either machinegunned or bombed and several were in flames. The Zero pilots proclaimed their supremacy by racing up and down the airstrip at such low altitudes that their faces could be clearly seen by men in the trenches.

Nevertheless, the Japanese were not unopposed from the

[4] Later Sir Richard.
[5] Probably Lieut. Walker, who had bullet wounds and was flying with one hand.

ground. There were, in fact, a few notably determined displays of fighting spirit. Squadron-Leader A. D. Swan, a middle-aged Scot who was station adjutant, and Warrant-Officer H. W. Chapman, of Lakemba, N.S.W., manned a Lewis machinegun in one trench and fired constantly at the strafing planes. They were supported by about fifty others who manned machinegun and rifle positions. Many an airman that morning tried to shoot down an aeroplane with a .303 rifle.

One of the machinegunners was Wing-Commander Archibald Tindal, who sat on the edge of a trench and fired a Vickers gun until killed instantly by a cannon shell. Tindal was the first R.A.A.F. officer killed in combat on Australian soil. His name has been perpetuated in an R.A.A.F. base near Katherine, Northern Territory.

When the raid ended Swan and Chapman led a party which broke open a blazing ammunition store and carried explosives to safety. The station appeared to be a smoking ruin but worse, far worse, was to come later.

Darwin then had a second aerodrome at Parap between the town and the R.A.A.F. base. It was used principally by civil airliners, such as they were, flying scheduled services from Adelaide and Brisbane, and by Dutch DC3s. It was here that Ross and Keith Smith had landed their Vickers Vimy after the first England-Australia flight in 1919, to be followed, in the next twenty years, by men and women whose names are inseparable from aviation pioneering — Bert Hinkler, Kingsford-Smith, Charles Ulm, Ray Parer, Amy Johnson, Jimmy Broadbent, Scott and Black, and The Territory's own flying doctor, Dr. Clyde Fenton. When the aerodrome became too small for modern aircraft (though it was used as a fighter base by Spitfires later in the war) it was converted for use as a suburban thoroughfare with a median nature strip. It is now flanked by an olympic swimming pool and, fittingly, has been named Ross Smith Avenue.

As well as being the civil airport, it was used in 1942 as a base for a detachment of R.A.A.F. Wirraways. The Department of Civil Aviation staff were housed in a small operations building which stands to this day. They included Arthur Tarlton, Ted Betts, Bruce Acland, Ken Dalziel, Fred Riley and Len McIntosh. A separate staff led by William Wake was maintained at the flying boat base near Darwin wharf; its task was to

THE AERODROMES: RAID I

provide facilities for Qantas flying boats operating the Sydney-Singapore service, which was then being re-routed through Broome. The landline between Perth and Broome had been damaged by a cyclone during the first week of February and many lengthy messages dealing with the reorganisation, all in code, had to be handled by the aeradio network in Darwin. Tarlton and his men were working between fourteen and seventeen hours a day. They were tired and in need of a rest when the Japanese struck and their continued services became even more necessary.

At 9 a.m. Betts was wakened by Tarlton, who had been up all night. Acland and Dalziel were already on duty in the aeradio room. At 9.45, as he recalls it, Acland walked outside and saw three planes having what he thought was a dogfight over the sea north of the aerodrome. Acland felt uneasy and drew the attention of his colleagues to the planes. They watched for a few minutes but as no alarm had been sounded they did not suspect, even with a dogfight in view, that an air raid was imminent. As a precaution, however, the R.A.A.F. operations officer was asked on a direct teleprinter circuit, "Is it all clear?"

Acland's diary, compiled at the time, shows that the reply was "All clear now." He wondered about the meaning of the word "now". Had there been an earlier alarm of which the civil aerodrome staff knew nothing? His conjecture was interrupted almost instantly by the drone of many engines. He saw three large formations of aircraft and called to his mates, "Come and have a look at all the Yanks coming in. Who said we haven't got any planes?"

Simultaneously anti-aircraft guns on a site near the northwestern end of the runway began firing and the aerodrome controllers had their first indication that the planes were hostile. Acland ran to the radio room and quickly transmitted in morse $QQQ\ QQQ\ QQQ\ de\ VZDN$ — a code indicating that an air raid was in progress at Darwin. He waited for acknowledgements, which came from Daly Waters and other stations. With Dalziel and McIntosh he cut the electric power to the transmitters, locked secret books and documents in the safe, and only then went to a trench the staff had dug near their quarters. Betts and Riley were already there, Betts in pyjama pants and with his face lathered for a shave, Riley with only a towel around his waist.

"Bombs were already falling and we dived straight in on top of them," Acland recalls. He had the personal satisfaction, while the raid lasted, of knowing that word of it would already be on the way to D.C.A. interstate headquarters and, if all other means failed, the government would soon know about it.

During the thirty-two minutes the raid lasted the civil aerodrome was hit several times, chiefly by incendiaries and anti-personnel bombs (known as "daisy cutters") but also by one heavy bomb which damaged a water tower, causing a short circuit in an electrical system that started the warning siren. While bombs fell and fighters strafed the area the siren continuously sounded the All-Clear signal. It had not sounded the alert.

When the raid ended the men assembled near the administration building. The oil store and consumables stores were on fire, but so was the fire-fighting tender. The hangar, workshops and power plant were badly damaged, and a light plane owned by a part-time flying doctor pilot, Roy Edwards, had been destroyed. One end of the administration building was blown in. A ceiling fan in the radio room was lying on the floor with smashed asbestos sheets and, far worse, broken radio tubes. A small arms dump in a hut used by the R.A.A.F. had been hit and hundreds of .303 bullets were exploding.

Ted Betts remembers that the roar from fires made it impossible for anyone to be heard within seventy-five yards. A fresh wind blew flames towards the administration building which could be entered from one side only. Betts and the operators salvaged transmitters and receivers but these were unworkable because town power had been cut and an emergency unit was damaged and on fire. But a direct line to the A.W.A. coastal radio station V.I.D. was open and working. Betts spoke to Lou Curnock, the officer-in-charge, and was given permission to use his emergency facilities. He drove there in a borrowed truck and within a few minutes had transmitted a message warning all civil aircraft that they must not fly into Darwin until further notice. The D.C.A. office in Melbourne was also told about the raid. All communications affecting civil air operations were sent from V.I.D. for the next five days, though Betts and his staff established reserve stations out of town.

Arthur Tarlton later wrote an official report that included this paragraph: "Control of the situation was possible only because Betts and his operators worked like Trojans for days. Their chief concern was that Civil Aviation should not lose its invaluable communication facilities. In three days they established second and third reserve stations, in addition to normal watch-keeping and numerous other duties the situation demanded."

In the days that followed a vital contribution in maintaining communications was made by Curnock, P. J. Chapman and others of the staff of V.I.D., which not only handled communications to shipping but was the Darwin base station for the coastwatching network.

Tarlton, Betts and Acland all received official recognition of their work. So did William Wake, officer-in-charge of the flying boat base; John Waldie, coxswain of a departmental launch who rescued more than one hundred men from the wharf area, was awarded the M.B.E. . . . . We will hear more of him later.

CHAPTER 5

The Pearl Harbour Parallel

> *'The harbour was crowded with all kinds of ships which we picked off at our leisure.'*
> —COMMANDER FUCHIDA.

> *'The men of the Navy came through the attack with good spirit, particularly in the sea-going fighting ships which engaged the Japanese vigorously. The busy Japanese also turned their attention to the merchant ships. Altogether eight ships were sunk, one was beached and lost, three were beached and later refloated, and eleven were damaged.'*
> —OFFICIAL WAR HISTORY.

February the nineteenth at Darwin, as December the seventh at Pearl Harbour, was predominantly a story of Japanese naval aeroplanes attacking Allied shipping, notwithstanding other damage inflicted.

In earlier wars naval vessels mounting heavy long-range artillery stood several miles out to sea from an enemy coastline and bombarded ports and shipping. The Japanese had seen the advantage of having aircraft carriers stand two or three hundred miles from a coastline, well beyond the range of artillery, and from there accurately directing manned bombers to stipulated targets. Japan was the first nation to adopt this strategy and employ it successfully *en masse*. Its efficacy at Darwin can be judged from the fact that by the time the bombers turned back to their carriers these ships were to suffer the following fates:

Meigs, 12,568 tons, U.S. transport: Bombed, burnt and sank. Two killed.

Manunda, 9,115 tons, Australian hospital ship: Bombed and severely damaged. Twelve dead, fifty-eight wounded.

British Motorist, 6,891 tons, British tanker: Bombed, burnt, capsized and sank. The master, Captain E. C. Bates, and one other killed.

Mauna Loa, 5,436 tons, U.S. transport: Bombed, burnt and sank. Five killed.

Neptuna, 5,952 tons, Australian-owned passenger ship: Bombed, burnt, exploded and sank. Forty-five killed, including the master, Captain Wm. Michie.

Zealandia, 6,683 tons. Australian coastal trader: Bombed, burnt, and sank. Three dead.

Peary, 1,190 tons, U.S. destroyer: Bombed, burnt and sank. Eighty killed including the captain, Lieut.-Commander John M. Bermingham. Among the dead ratings was one named Rude whose Christian name was Darwin.

Mavie, 14 tons, R.A.N. lugger: Sunk by a near miss.

Kelat, Australian coal hulk: Machinegunned and sank.

Barossa, 4,239 tons, Australian freighter: Bombed and burnt. Later salvaged and two months later towed to Brisbane.

Port Mar, 5,551 tons, U.S. transport: Near-missed, machinegunned and beached with hull holed in many places. One dead. Later salvaged, towed to Brisbane, refitted, and torpedoed and sunk on her first trip thereafter.

Tulagi, 2,300 tons, Australian coastal trader: Near-missed, beached, and refloated.

Admiral Halstead, 3,289 tons, U.S. freighter: Near-missed and damaged. Her rigging shot away. The master quickly unloaded a cargo of 44-gallon drums of high-octane fuel and floated them ashore.

William B. Preston, 1,190 tons, U.S. seaplane tender: Bombed and damaged by direct hit on stern. Four killed. She also carried petrol, which did not explode. She sped down the harbour with her stern ablaze, narrowly missing the hospital ship *Manunda*, and later reached Broome.

Platypus, 3,455 tons, R.A.N. depot ship: Near-missed, machinegunned and damaged.

Swan, 1,060 tons, R.A.N. sloop: Near-missed and damaged. Three killed and twenty-two wounded.

Gunbar, 481 tons, R.A.N. auxiliary minesweeper: Machinegunned. One killed. The captain, Lieut. N. M. Muzzell, was wounded in the legs but stayed at his post.

Kara Kara, 252 tons, R.A.N. boom gate vessel: Machinegunned and damaged. Two killed.

Kookaburra, 730 tons, R.A.N. boom gate vessel: Machinegunned and damaged. Two wounded.

Kangaroo, 730 tons, R.A.N. boom gate vessel: Machinegunned and damaged. One killed.

Coongoola, 34 tons, R.A.N, motor boat: Machinegunned and damaged.

In the same action, but not inside Darwin harbour, the U.S supply ships *Don Isidro* (3,200 tons) and *Florence D* (2,638 tons) were attacked north-west of Bathurst Island. *Florence D* was sunk. Survivors reached Bathurst Island. *Don Isidro* was bombed and set on fire. She drifted ashore where eleven of the survivors died on the beach. Seventy-three were rescued.

Also in the harbour that day but not damaged were twenty-three other vessels of various types, including corvettes and sloops of the R.A.N.

On the ships alone, including *Florence D* and *Don Isidro*, at least one hundred and seventy-two people were killed or mortally wounded. Another nineteen later died of wounds on the hospital ship *Manunda*. In addition, some three hundred and thirty were wounded, more than two hundred of them seriously.

When fifty-two deaths among civilians and servicemen are added, bringing the total to two hundred and forty-three, it can be appreciated that this was one of the most devastating air raids of the war.[1]

The story is one of men rather than of ships.

Nevertheless, to put the subsequent events in perspective it is necessary to show why and how so many vessels were present.

As early as mid-January General George Brett had expressed American concern at the failure to reinforce Timor. The Australian government was then deeply involved with the New Guinea situation, the threats likely to develop against the north-west coast and Darwin, and the possibility of invasion on the north-east coast. The government's advisers thought it unwise that military strengths already spread thinly over thousands of miles of potential front line should be further vitiated by committing any substantial force to what, in some minds, was

---

[1] The Japanese sank 18 ships, destroyed 64 aeroplanes and killed 2,000 people at Pearl Harbour. Four hundred were killed during the German raid by 500 aeroplanes against Coventry on November 14, 1941.

already a lost cause in Timor. But Brett persisted and was rewarded with Australian agreement to embark the 2/4th Pioneer Battalion A.I.F., a troop of Australian anti-tank guns, a detachment of the U.S. 148th Field Artillery Regiment, and various specialist units. The Australians were loaded on to the American transports *Meigs* and *Mauna Loa* and the Americans on the Australian transport *Tulagi* and their own *Port Mar*.

The convoy began forming in Darwin on February 12 after delays caused by the discovery that it would be without air cover. By February 14 the troops had been loaded and the four transports left Darwin with an escort soon after midnight on February 15.

The escort consisted of *U.S.S. Houston*,[2] a cruiser with one of her turrets out of action; *U.S.S. Peary*, the ill-fated destroyer; and the R.A.N. sloops *Swan* and *Warrego*. When only one hundred miles from Darwin *Houston's* lookout reported that they were being shadowed by a Japanese flying boat. Next morning, not unexpectedly, the convoy was attacked by thirty-five Japanese bombers and nine flying boats. *Houston* steamed clear, drawing fire upon herself and away from the convoy. An eye-witness described it thus: "She literally spun on her keel. By superb skill in the use of avoiding action she managed to make every bomb fall in her wake. Her gunnery was magnificent. She kept the Japanese right up high. At no time was it possible to see the sheets of fire from her guns die away. The flash was so constant that she appeared to be ablaze the whole time."

Peary, Swan, Warrego and *Mauna Loa* were straddled by bombs and two men aboard *Mauna Loa* were wounded by a near-miss. The possibility of further attacks without adequate air cover and the drain upon ammunition stocks caused the convoy to be ordered back to Darwin,[3] reaching there on February 18.

The convoy's return did not escape notice by the townspeople, and for those who understood the reasons it was an omen portending graver sequels. The Administrator, C. L. A. Abbott, was well aware of them. "The return of the convoy confirmed my opinion that it wouldn't be long before Darwin's turn came," he said.

The town, in fact, had less than twenty-four hours to wait for the disaster that overtook it. Yet one cannot avoid speculating on what might have happened had the convoy proceeded and

[2] Later sunk in the Battle of the Java Sea.
[3] Ordered by Wavell from Java at 3.15 p.m., February 16.

met the Japanese task force of heavy cruisers, destroyers, and carriers bristling with dive-bombers. It seems likely that every one of the Allied ships would have been blown from the water with even greater loss of life.

It might well be asked why so many other ships were in Darwin.

The *William B. Preston* arrived in January to service Catalina flying boats. *Meigs* had been diverted from an attempt to reach the Philippines with reinforcements. These were unloaded at Darwin and the ship then became available for the Timor convoy. *Mauna Loa* was there as part of a plan to run supplies to Macassar, from where it was intended they should be transferred to small vessels and carried, one supposes surreptitiously, to the Philippines. When this scheme was dropped, she too was unloaded and became available for the Timor operation. *Port Mar* was sent to unload stores for U.S. forces already in the Darwin area. *British Motorist* and *Admiral Halstead* carried fuel to restock local storage tanks. *Warrego* and *Swan* had been detached from the 20th Minesweeping Flotilla to give antisubmarine protection to convoys between Brisbane and Darwin. The corvettes *Deloraine* and *Katoomba* were on escort and antisubmarine work from Darwin. *Zealandia* had been used by the Navy as a transport and in the December evacuation of women and children. In January she loaded supplies and reinforcements in Sydney, sailed on the 23rd, reached Darwin under escort on February 6, and was only partially unloaded on the 19th. *Tulagi* and *Neptuna* had both evacuated civilians from New Guinea and were then sent to Darwin with supplies. *Barossa* brought a load of timber for a new wharf. *Manunda* had been on the way to Singapore but was held when the situation in south-east Asia deteriorated.

Houston and *Peary*, having brought the convoy home, refuelled and left at once for the Java Sea. In the Timor Sea that night *Peary* made contact with a submarine and expended such a large amount of oil in high-speed depth-charge attacks that she again had to return to Darwin to refuel. At 1 a.m. on the 19th she anchored in the harbour at berth F-3. That same day she was at the bottom.

Peary, launched in 1920, had already seen considerable action. Only three days after Pearl Harbour she was caught in a Japanese raid on Cavite Navy Yard in the Philippines. She was hit by a bomb which riddled the superstructure, killed eight of the crew and started fires below decks. Worse still, fire began to set off torpedo warheads in a wharf workshop and she was in danger of being blown up until towed to safety. Her captain, Commander H. H. Keith, U.S.N., was wounded and relieved by Lieut.-Commander John M. Bermingham, U.S.N.

Peary's run of misfortune was just beginning. She was attacked again on December 26. On December 28 she left the Philippines for the Celebes Sea and Macassar Strait. There her radio failed and she was bombed by three *friendly* aircraft and damaged. Next morning she was attacked by Japanese bombers which dropped bombs and torpedoes. Having survived this gauntlet she came to Darwin.

At 9.58 a.m. on February 19 Lieut.-Commander Bermingham was understandably annoyed that he hadn't yet been able to refuel his ship and attempt to overtake *Houston*. He was seen fretfully pacing the destroyer's bridge. A few moments later he saw the Japanese air armada. He tensed and immediately ordered:

"Weigh anchor!"

Even while the anchor was being raised *Peary's* engines turned and she began moving towards the harbour entrance in a vain bid for the sea room that fighting ships must have to manoeuvre adequately. The crew was already at action stations and guns were being brought to bear on the attackers. But it was too late. Dive-bombers pounced mercilessly upon her. The first bomb exploded near the fantail, removing propeller guards and depth-charge racks and flooding the steering motor room. The second bomb, an incendiary, hit the galley deck house and set fire to it. The third — there were five in all — pierced the main deck and went out through the hull of No. 2 fireroom. It did not explode. The fourth bomb hit for'ard and set off the ammunition magazines, causing the second most terrible explosion seen and heard in Darwin that day. The fifth, another incendiary, exploded in the after engineroom.

Four of these hits caused fearful casualties among the crew and the ship began to sink slowly by the stern while still moving towards the open sea. One observer described her as being "like a hunted deer trying to escape while shot in the hindquarters." There were bursts of flame and spouts of water around her while dive-bombers continued the attack. Her decks were awash but she continued to fight back.

Lieut. (later Rear-Admiral) William J. Catlett, who had been *Peary's* communication and torpedo control officer, but was not on board that day, reported: "A .30 calibre machinegun and a

.50 calibre machinegun on the galley deckhouse continued firing until the last enemy plane broke off the engagement."

The crew of the steaming fireroom escaped miraculously with minor burns on the hands and feet. Only one officer apart from Catlett survived. He was Lieut. R. L. Johnson.

Lieut. Owen Griffiths, who was on board *H.M.A.S. Platypus*, said *Peary's* crew fought to the last though in imminent danger of the magazine exploding. Then it did, "and the ship disintegrated in a burst of flame which appeared to grow out and reach a height of more than one hundred feet. She finally pointed her nose to the sky and disappeared in a pall of black oily smoke, the gun on her fo'c'sle firing to the bitter end."

Lieut.-Commander Bermingham, Lieut. Arthur Gustofson, Lieut. Martin Koivisto, Ensign Phillip Joyace and seventy-six enlisted seamen were killed or drowned. For several days thereafter the bodies of dead U.S. seamen were washed up on the Darwin beaches. There were fifty-two survivors.

The 300-tons examination vessel *H.M.A.S. Southern Cross* went to *Peary's* aid. She lowered boats and picked up survivors while bombs were still falling and machinegun bullets hitting around them. Three of the survivors, badly burnt, were transferred directly to the hospital ship *Manunda*. Twelve others remained on board *Southern Cross* for two days. Lieut.-Commander C. F. Symonds, R.N., reported: "The bravery and devotion to duty shown by every officer and man, all in equally exposed positions in picking up *Peary's* survivors excludes the possibility of distinction of individuals."[4]

Of the remaining ships in the harbour three appeared to have no chance of escape, yet only one of these was sunk. They were *Neptuna* and *Barossa*, each tied by lines to the wharf, and *H.M.A.S. Katoomba*, a corvette then undergoing repairs in the floating dry dock.

On the night of January 22/23 *Katoomba* had been damaged in a collision with the U.S. tanker *Pecos* and entered the floating dock for repairs to her hull. There, trapped like a bird in a cage, she seemed to have little chance of repulsing the olive-green dive-bombers, but the pilots made the mistake of treating her as a sitting duck. She might have been sitting but she still had stings in her tail, even though some of her sailors were armed with nothing better than rifles.

Katoomba's crew was led by Captain A. P. Cousin, D.S.O., R.A.N.R., who told me: "Being caught in a floating dock during

[4] Symonds himself was Mentioned in Despatches for courage.

an air raid and presenting one of the largest targets is a most unenviable experience. But the conduct of the ship's company was magnificent. There was no panic or noticeable nervousness. Everyone was determined to put up a rare fight. This was done and the ship and dock saved."

How it was done is worth recording. Captain Cousin was in his cabin a few minutes before ten o'clock when told that aircraft were arriving from the south-east "to reinforce the R.A.A.F." He went on deck and saw a formation of planes at a height he estimated to be fifteen thousand feet. The altitude puzzled him; surely, if the planes were intending to land at Darwin, they wouldn't be flying so high. "At that moment I heard an explosion and saw a column of mud shoot skywards from the far side of the wharf, followed by other explosions. We then heard the siren on *H.M.A.S. Platypus*, the first warning given on the waterfront that a raid was beginning."

Katoomba's crew rushed to action stations. Captain Cousin instructed that bags of confidential books be put where they would not fall into Japanese hands. Depth-charges set to "safe" were lowered to the bottom of the dock and rolled as far as possible from the ship.

Official records show that *Katoomba* and her sister ships were armed with one 12-pounder high-angle gun and a 40-m.m. Bofors for anti-aircraft defence. But in *Katoomba*, at least, the Bofors had not been fitted. To supplement the 12-pounder she had Vickers machineguns mounted on each wing of the bridge, and the crew were issued with .303 rifles to use as opportunity occurred.

While watching dive-bombers attacking other ships it became apparent to Captain Cousin that two planes were assigned to each target. He told his crew that they could expect similar attention. Almost at once a dive-bomber approached from the port quarter. The Vickers machineguns, and rifles aimed from the shoulder by dozens of sailors, opened fire. When about three hundred yards from the ship, and apparently hit, the Japanese pilot turned off course and dropped his bomb in the water.

Presently Captain Cousin saw another plane approaching. From the bridge he ordered the 12-pounder crew to fire at it with a short fuse. The gun came around rapidly and fired at once. The Japanese had levelled off from a shallow dive and a second later would have released a bomb which Cousin believes could not have missed them. But the 12-pounder shell burst very close to the plane; instead of releasing his bomb the pilot climbed almost perpendicularly and did not return.

"That single shot undoubtedly saved the ship and the dock and many of our lives," Cousin said.[5] He was by then so convinced of the pattern of two attacks against each ship (there were exceptions to this, notably against *Peary*) that he told his crew: "They've had two shots at us. I doubt if we'll get more. But keep a sharp lookout." There was no further attack.

Neptuna and *Barossa* were not so fortunate. Both had sustained minor damage from the first salvo dropped by high level bombers which destroyed part of the wharf. But they were due for more particular attention. Dive-bombers swooped upon them from behind convenient cloud banks, coming in so close before dropping their lethal cargoes that it was possible to see a pilot going through the motions of aiming, pressing the release switch, and then pulling back on the controls to take him away from the destruction he sowed.

Not only were *Neptuna* and *Barossa* immobilised and rendered defenceless by the lines attaching them to the wharf; each had another vessel alongside. *H.M.A.S. Swan* had tied up to *Neptuna* fifteen minutes earlier to take on explosives. *Swan* shed the lines and got away but was near-missed and suffered casualties and damage. *Barossa*, ironically loaded with piles for a new wharf, was hemmed in by a Navy oil lighter which was refuelling from wharf installations. She had to stay alongside until after the raid.

Neptuna had gone to the wharf only that morning to unload hundreds of tons of depth-charges and other explosives. The chief engineer, John McNamara, had understood she would be riding at anchor for several days before getting a berth and had given instructions for the overhaul of one of her engines. She was able to reach the wharf under her own power but could not have left it.

Neptuna's deck cadet, John Rothery, was beginning his career as a merchant sailor. He was aged only eighteen. The ship's master, Captain William Michie, believed cadets should start at the bottom, learning as they served. In line with that policy, Rothery was chipping paint below decks, that dreary chore of all sailors, when bombs from the high level planes hit the wharf. The explosions were so violent that for a moment he believed they had been caused by the cargo of ammunition he knew

[5] The Royal Commissioner, Mr. Justice Lowe, said he had evidence that the Japanese "deliberately refrained" from attacking the floating dock.

they were carrying. He hurried up on deck and was there surprised to find the air full of aeroplanes bearing Japanese insignias.

An officer ordered Rothery to seek shelter in the for'ard part of the ship. He ran to the saloon where many of the crew of one hundred and twenty-five had already gathered. Rothery was advised to lie on the floor with his shipmates, and did so; but inability to see what was going on must have worried him for in less than two minutes he jumped to his feet and ran out on deck again. In that time the pattern of the raid had changed. The high level bombers had finished their job and now it was the turn of the fighters and dive-bombers. Rothery reached the deck just as a dive-bomber appeared from behind a cloud, aligning itself perfectly along the length of the ship as it screamed down towards him. He saw the bomb plummeting from its rack and fell flat as it crashed through the bridge and into the saloon, exploding there and killing all the men with whom he had sheltered.

A second dive-bomber came down on *Neptuna*, again hitting from behind. This bomb struck the after part of the ship and plunged into the engine room, where it exploded. Instantly fire began to rage through the stricken vessel. Rothery, showing more valour than discretion, ran down to the engine room to organise water for fire-fighting on deck. But the engine room was flooded and hoses and taps were either unserviceable or immersed. The ship was obviously doomed. Captain Cousin, knowing of her cargo, told his crew on *Katoomba* to watch for her blowing up and to seek substantial shelter against flying pieces of metal that he predicted would be as lethal as Japanese bombs.

Rothery and the others of *Neptuna's* crew who were still alive left the ship. Forty-five were dead and there were many seriously injured.[6] The survivors included sixty-two Chinese seamen. The wharf had already been cut, so they had to swim ashore. Some of the Chinese had to be coaxed and even pushed into the water. Those who couldn't swim were assisted by others who could. Their eyes were severely injured by fuel oil pouring into the harbour from broken pipelines; for some it caused blindness that lasted for weeks. Patches of oil caught fire and a few seamen were burnt to death. A number of men trapped beneath the wharf were saved only because wind and ebbing tide combined to carry burning oil down the harbour and away from them.

[6] The ship's surgeon, Dr. John Hyde, of Sydney, was awarded the O.B.E. and Lloyd's War Medal for heroism in treating the injured.

Neptuna blew up before the last survivors had reached the shore. The terrible explosion shook the entire town and will never be forgotten by those who heard and saw it. Men in the water, on land and on ships were showered with debris. Smoke and flames rose three hundred feet, topped by a mushroom cap that in later years was to become typical of the form of yet bigger explosions.

Leading Signalman Douglas Fraser was on the bridge of H.M.A.S. *Deloraine* tied up at the buoy nearest to *Neptuna*. Both the *Deloraine's* boilers had been dismantled for overhaul. The ship was immobilised and could do nothing but sit there and take what the Japanese delivered. Miraculously she was not hit — except by metal from the exploding *Neptuna*. Fraser spent most of the raid coolly taking photographs of ships under fire, on fire and blowing up. These photographs have been preserved and form part of the illustrations for this book. *Deloraine's* captain, Lieut.-Commander D. A. Menlove, D.S.O.,[7] had been taken to hospital early that morning with a heavy attack of fever. His first lieutenant, Lieut. A. C. Meldrum, was in temporary command. Menlove was put under a hospital bed during the raid but went back to duty immediately afterwards.

The Administrator, C. L. A. Abbott, had a grandstand view of the explosion from Government House on the cliff above. He recalls: "Black smoke was shot with flames as it rose. The ship was blown in halves. The stern and engines sank alongside the wharf. The bow floated for a few minutes, then turned on its side and also sank. One piece of her side plating containing two portholes with the glass still intact was found on the foreshore three hundred yards away."

Captain Cousin remembers it thus: "White hot parts of the ship flew in all directions and some heavy pieces passed right over us in the floating dock. Several parts struck *Katoomba* and one piece of white hot handrail carved a hole in our deck at the foot of the twelve-pounder gun."

The force of the explosion has also been described by Lieut. Owen Griffiths, who was in *Platypus*: "We were conscious of a low rumbling noise and knew that she was going up. We lay flat on the deck as *Neptuna* and everything in her blew sky-high with a colossal explosion which threw pieces of lifeboats, masts

[7] Menlove was decorated for his part in sinking a Japanese submarine off Bathurst Island on January 23. *Deloraine* blew the submarine to the surface with depth-charges. There it was discovered the submarine was 350 ft. long, compared with the corvette's 187 ft. She was also more heavily armed.

and debris hundreds of feet in the air in a huge cloud of smoke and flame. *Platypus* shook with the concussion. For some time afterwards ashes, dust and debris floated down to settle on everything like the aftermath of a volcano in eruption."

I was driving my car along The Esplanade half a mile away and believed the explosion meant another raid had begun. I stopped and ran for the gutter but while doing so saw the column of smoke and flames dwarfing all the other smouldering fires from burning ships and buildings that were blacking out the town. I will never forget that on top of it all, rolling slowly over and over as though it were a dumb-bell tossed by a giant juggler, there was what I took to be, and now know to have been, *Neptuna's* main mast.

An almost superhuman effort was made to move *Barossa* from her inner berth at the wharf opposite *Neptuna* only minutes before her neighbour exploded. Warrant-Officer Andrew Gibson, R.A.N.R. (S), in command of the naval tug *Wato*, sailed in at great risk, towed away a lighter, and then got a line aboard *Barossa*. But the operation had hardly begun when *Neptuna* exploded. Fires aboard *Barossa* were fought and controlled by the crew of *H.M.A.S. Tolga*, who later towed her from the wharf.

Captain's defaulters and requestmen were about to parade before Commander J. P. Tonkin, R.A.N., in his cabin on *Platypus*.

As the first man was called forward from the quarter-deck a high-angle gun on the poop-deck began firing rapidly. All hands ran to action stations and soon *Platypus* was under attack. A bomb landed by the stern but did not explode. Another burst thirty feet from the ship. A sheet of water swept across her, ripping down an awning and drenching the crew. While the gap of thirty feet saved many lives the force of the explosion sank the lugger *H.M.A.S. Mavie* which was tied to *Platypus* amidships. Petty-Officer J. Bartlett and three ratings from *Mavie* swam to *Platypus* and arrived on deck wet but grinning. They were surprised to find men on board who had not been swimming were equally wet.

Platypus was one of the luckiest ships in port. Another dive-bomber came at her but again the pilot's aim was faulty. Chief Writer R. Smith was looking through a porthole when a bomb passed his line of vision. He dropped to the deck and was shaken by the explosion that followed. *Platypus* shook violently again but the damage was slight.

Still adhering to the pattern of two dive-bombers to a ship, the Japanese pilots assigned to the troopship *Zealandia* came in to take their turn. From the bridge of *Katoomba* Captain Cousin saw a bomb strike the ship at No. 4 hatch and another crash through the engineroom skylight. Large and uncontrollable fires broke out at once and the ship gradually settled straight down, leaving only the tops of her masts clear of the water. Three of her crew were killed. The remaining one hundred and forty-two, including the master, Captain R. Kerr, reached the shore safely after waving towels and handkerchiefs to attract rescuers.

Within twenty minutes of the start of the raid twenty-two ships had either been damaged or sunk, or were sinking. More than thirty-eight thousand tons went to the bottom.

The U.S. transport *Meigs* (12,568 tons) was the biggest vessel present. She was attacked relentlessly by dive-bombers and was soon sinking. So was *Mauna Loa*. Fatalities on both ships were surprisingly few considering *Mauna Loa* was hit by two bombs in an open hatch, broke her back, caught fire, and began to go down at once, and that *Meigs*, hit several times, also caught fire and sank within a few minutes. In spite of these hard blows there were only five deaths in *Mauna Loa's* crew of thirty-eight, and two in *Meigs'* crew of sixty-six.

The master, Captain E. C. Bates, and a wireless operator, Mr. J. Webster, were killed when bombs struck the tanker *British Motorist*, but fifty-nine other members of the crew escaped. The gunnery officer, Second Officer P. Payne, told me: "Once the dive-bombers began to pick on us things went like clockwork — for them. A plane came out of the sun and scored a direct hit on the bridge where the captain and Webster were killed. The second hit us for'ard. We listed heavily to port and were on fire amidships. We decided to abandon ship." The survivors landed as blazing fuel oil raced across the water, engulfing men and rescue boats struggling for the shore. Payne remembers bitterly what he describes as "the holocaust" that ensued. "Two atom bombs were poverty-stricken reprisal for the death and destruction at Darwin," he says.[8] Seventeen years later the wreck of *British Motorist* was raised and taken to Japan by Fujita Salvage Co., of Osaka. The company also salvaged the wrecks of *Meigs*, *Mauna Loa*, *Neptuna* and *Peary* sunk by their compatriots. Crosses and a baptismal font made

[8] Payne survived three wartime sinkings. In 1944 he was one of thirty-eight who survived the sinking of the tanker *British Chivalry* in the Indian Ocean and thirty-seven days adrift in a boat. The First Officer of *British Motorist*, now Captain H. K. Wood, and the Sixth Engineer, Ted Mynott, were also sunk again and captured by the Japanese. They spent the rest of the war in prison camps. Wood and Payne, now also a captain, both still have commands with the British Tanker Company.

from metal from the wrecks were later presented as a peace tribute to the United Church in North Australia and have a permanent place in a new Darwin church.

On the morning of February 19, 1942, however, the Japanese at Darwin were neither peace-loving nor, it seemed, were they especially gallant in distinguishing between ships of war and ships of mercy. Though Japan had been a signatory to the Geneva Convention guaranteeing immunity to hospitals, hospital ships and all other places and persons carrying the Red Cross, a deliberate attack appeared to be made on the hospital ship *Manunda*, under Captain J. Garden, who won the O.B.E.

Red crosses were painted unmistakably on *Manunda's* funnel and deck. Senior officers had flown over the ship to make sure they were plainly visible. In the first fifteen minutes of the raid the Japanese pilots left her alone, and this gave rise to the belief that her immunity would be respected, though a hospital ashore had already been hit. Some witnesses have said that what subsequently transpired was caused accidentally when the destroyer *Peary* and the Catalina tender *William B. Preston* both passed close by in their attempts to escape. The accuracy of the pilots in hitting other targets does not support that view.

Captain Cousin on *Katoomba* saw a dive-bomber approaching *Manunda* from the south and directly in line with his own ship in the floating dock. He expected the Japanese to fly over *Manunda* and come at him. He was astonished, instead, to see the plane hurl its bomb at the hospital ship. It struck near the bridge and sent up a brown cloud of shattered wooden hatch covers.

In fact, that was the second bomb aimed at *Manunda*. The ship's chief officer, Captain Thomas Minto, reported that while their boats were picking up survivors from the destroyer *Peary* and other sinking vessels, *Manunda* shuddered and rolled from the effects of a near-miss. Her decks were sprayed with shrapnel from the explosion and four people on board were killed. They included Sister Margaret de Mestre, aged twenty-six, of Bellingen, N.S.W., who was hit in the back and died two hours later. The near-miss put seventy-six holes in *Manunda's* plates and, says Captain Minto, "played hell with our gear and upper works." He then adds: "We got our wind back and were carrying on when I heard a terrific roar. Debris was flying everywhere. A bomb had missed the bridge and pierced the music-room skylight, exploding at B and C decks, doing terrible damage and causing many casualties."

Twelve aboard were killed, seven were seriously injured, and fifty-one had minor injuries. The dead were Sister de Mestre, Captain Boynes Hocking who was an Army dentist, Third Officer Allan Scott Smith, Assistant Purser Robert Thom, Corporal Robert Bevir, Cook Arthur Connell, Steward John Holmes, Steward Harold Humphries, Steward Victor Kane, Steward William Spinney, Cook Richard Smith, and a ship's greaser, William McKay.

One of the severely injured was Sister Lorraine Blow, of Rose Bay, N.S.W. Since 1940 she had been four times to the Middle East as a hospital ship nurse. Her action station that day was in Ward C3, directly above the ward in which Sister de Mestre was killed. She was standing near a door leading to the deck when the first bomb missed the ship.

"I was talking, and had my arm raised, when I was hit on the side by a piece of shrapnel; but for that I would have lost my arm," she told me.

As it was, she suffered a fractured spine and perforated abdomen and spent two years in hospital.[9]

Captain Minto has graphically described the conditions on board *Manunda*: "The after end of the ship still functioned as a hospital unit and our boats and naval launches brought the wounded alongside. By nightfall we had seventy-six patients.[10] Seven fires brokes out after we were hit but we extinguished them quickly. There was one exception; one fire had to be fought for over an hour. We were then fully extended in getting the wounded on board, sounding ship and getting things working again. Bomb splinters had cut all the fire mains. Water was pouring over the gangway and approaches. We shut down while the engineers made temporary repairs to stop the worst of the holes but the water had to be turned on again on two occasions to put out fires. What had been a well-appointed lounge on B deck was stripped bare and only debris remained. A grand piano could be recognised only by twisted wire. Steel bulkheads were blown out and pierced in dozens of places. Steel decks were blown up and blown down. The medical officers' quarters were

[9] Sister Blow was attended to on board by Dr. Keith Bowden, later Victoria police surgeon. She resumed nursing after the war and was for eleven years in charge of the casualty department at Prince Alfred Hospital, Sydney.

[10] In this respect *Manunda* acted as a floating Casualty Clearing Station, treating the wounded and dying fresh from the field of battle. Her operating table was in full and continuous use by doctors who worked without pause.

wiped out. On C deck the purser's office could be identified only by the safe and some papers. Bathrooms were reduced to porcelain chips and blocks of cabins where the nurses lived were levelled. On D deck heavy pillars were driven downwards. Overhead lighting in what was once a firstclass dining saloon was hanging in a mixture of wood and plaster. On the promenade deck heavy glass windows an inch thick were simply vacant frames. Glass was everywhere. The after end of the bridge was blown away along with our wireless equipment, the direction-finder and the echo-sounder. The chart room was adrift and ready to break up. The compasses were all to hell. The military people had a watching brief until the first bomb hit us. After that they worked all the hours God sent treating the terrible wounds and burns with never a moment to themselves for hours on end. All ranks did a great job of work, particularly the nurses. The crew also did exceptionally well. The Deck department was exposed without cover during the greater part of the raid, manning boats, carrying stretchers, fighting fires and hoisting the wounded on board. Two stewards helped to man a boat. The engineroom department effected temporary repairs to the fire mains and permanent repairs to the steering gear controls which were badly cut by shrapnel."

The coolness and competence of the medical staff was the result of months of training for just such an emergency, but that this should have been so in the chaos described by Captain Minto reveals an outstanding example of devotion. Matron Claire Schumack, of Rockdale, N.S.W., was the first matron appointed to a hospital ship. Although shaken by blast she supervised nursing of the wounded and dying, often in thick smoke from fires on board which threatened their own safety and created an atmosphere of uncertainty. She was later awarded the Royal Red Cross.

The difficulties on board were compounded by the fact that the lifts between decks were out of action and patients had to be carried up and down companionways by orderlies.

Next day *Manunda's* complement of wounded and sick rose to two hundred and sixty-six with the embarkation of one hundred and ninety men from civil and military hospitals ashore. In spite of severe damage to her navigation instruments and the depletion of her staff, the ship left Darwin at 11.30 p.m. on February 20 and reached Fremantle safely.

The dead were taken ashore before the ship sailed but others died on the way. In the early stages of the voyage she hove-to daily for a burial service. Later the state of the engines was such that this task had to be performed without stopping. Nineteen had been buried at sea before *Manunda* reached Fremantle.

That a hospital ship had been in Darwin at all to help cope with the emergency was entirely fortuitous. She was on her way to Malaya when the situation there deteriorated; this and the subsequent turning back of the *Houston* convoy and all it implied had caused indefinite delay. Thus it was that she was on the spot to give the most effective aid when it was most needed. The problem of evacuating seriously wounded patients was solved quickly. How they might otherwise have reached base hospitals in the south where specialist facilities were available is a point that doctors who were present do not care to contemplate.

The view that she was attacked accidentally or mistakenly is insupportable, and it is a matter for surprise that some medical and military historians have conceded that to be the case. It is beyond belief that a stationary ship of 9,115 tons — the second largest present — could not have been avoided if the pilots had genuinely wished to do so. The attack leader, Commander Fuchida, excused it this way: "We did not want to hit the hospital ship and I was surprised when I heard what had happened. It was the fault of the dive-bomber crews. I questioned them and they said they did not see the Red Cross, though I did."[11]

Few of the forty-five vessels in the harbour escaped attention of some kind. Fortunately the number of bombs carried by the Japanese was limited and they were reserved for the best targets. But they did pick their marks at will; the pilots gave the impression of enjoying their work, demonstrating their supremacy by alternating strafing sweeps with others during which they simply observed or waved at the people below, as much as to say "Well, how did you like that last burst?"

The U.S. transport *Port Mar* was beached near Channel Island leprosarium after it was found that her hull had been holed in many places. So was the Burns Philp motor vessel *Tulagi*. Both were later refloated. *Admiral Halstead* had near-misses but did not sustain serious damage. Ordinary Seaman H. J. Shepherd was killed when *H.M.A.S. Gunbar* was machine-

[11] After Pearl Harbour the Emperor summoned Fuchida to Tokyo and inquired about injuries to non-combatants. He was anxious to know whether any hospital ships had been hit. Fuchida assured him that no such mistake had been made.

gunned and the skipper, Lieut. N. M. Muzzell, was wounded in both legs. The boom defence vessels *Kara Kara, Kookaburra* and *Kangaroo* all suffered casualties when strafed. Petty-Officer F. Moore and Leading Cook F. B. Emms were killed aboard *Kara Kara*. The boom vessels, and their sister ships *Karangi, Kiara* and *Koala* steamed around in the thick of the fighting giving assistance to stricken crews. So did the auxiliary minesweeper *H.M.A.S. Tolga*. For courage and devotion to duty Able Seaman C. D. Scott, of *Koala*, was awarded the D.S.M. *Kiara's* engine broke down while she was engaged in rescue operations and she had to anchor near the wharf. A patch of burning oil was seen drifting towards her while she was immobilised. *H.M.A.S. Yampi Lass*, a lugger, steamed up and towed her away. When the raid began *Yampi Lass* was tending the well-known deep-sea diver J. E. Johnstone, who had distinguished himself by recovering more than one million pounds worth of gold from the lost ship *Niagara* off the New Zealand coast. Johnstone was about to dive in an attempt to recover a sunken barge and had actually received the traditional "good luck" pat on the top of his helmet when the first bombs fell. He was on a ladder with his feet in the water when hauled back and his helmet removed. On seeing what was happening Johnstone lost no time in removing his heavy diving suit.

The Royal Australian Navy did much that morning in helping defend the port and in rescuing survivors. The behavior of the sailors was exemplary and forms one of the most creditable aspects of the overall story. Official sources show that a few merchant seamen deserted and others refused to work in daylight. The master of *Tulagi*, Captain J. Thomson, had to call on survivors from *Neptuna* to form a crew when his vessel was refloated. Three of his officers had been evacuated with shock but three European and thirty-one Chinese seamen were listed merely as being "ashore." Among the disciplined fighting men of the naval service, however, there was no indication of any lack of steadiness under fire.

Nor were the activities of the Navy confined to ships. Indeed, the City of Darwin today owes more to the ancillary duties of the senior service than most people realise. One of two pipelines which bring Darwin's water forty miles from Manton Dam was laid as a naval project and financed with naval funds. It cost nearly four hundred thousand pounds. Although the amount was never repaid the Navy pays rates to N.T. Administration for water that comes along its own pipe. Moreover, the Navy protected the vital water supply by installing a boom — a double anti-torpedo net — thirty feet from the concrete retaining wall of Manton Dam. This was installed by Commander A. E. ("Chook") Fowler, R.A.N., and a detachment of army engineers. Fowler's major task was to install an anti-submarine and anti-torpedo net across the entrance to Darwin harbour, a distance of six miles. That became operative in 1941. Fowler had an independent command of six vessels, twenty officers and four hundred ratings, with headquarters in buildings near Fort Hill.

Shortly before ten o'clock on February 19 he was at his desk. His window faced east but the front door opened to the south towards the main wharf. His secretary, Lieut. William Burke, R.A.N.R., was in an outer office and Able-Seaman Arch Lewis at a nearby telephone switchboard. Fowler heard Burke and Lewis talking about a large number of planes they could see. Burke entered Fowler's office to tell him but at that moment the area was shaken by an explosion. Fowler reached his door to see other bombs striking the wharf and falling into mud only one hundred yards from him. Almost immediately a third "stick" from high level planes fell on the town behind him.

Fowler recalls: "We did not know it at the time but that salvo hit Government House and the post office. This meant that all my men working in the open and my headquarters were straddled by bombs which fell fore and aft of us. We suffered no damage and no loss."

Fowler hurried back to his office to telephone Navy headquarters for orders. But one of the bombs which flew over his head had hit the telephone exchange and the lines were dead.

The harbour was soon a sea of burning oil and struggling men. His duties, and those of his staff, were immediate and obvious. Further orders from operational headquarters were unnecessary.

His men and his craft were used to take survivors from sinking and burning ships and to rescue others from the water. The ebbing tide, flowing from the direction of the wharf, carried dead and wounded to the small promontory on which the boom establishment was situated. Fowler and his sailors were thus among the first of the rescue parties, helping ashore men who were horribly burned and wounded, and recovering the bodies of others beyond help.

Burning fuel oil which covered the harbour from the boom defence area to the outer anchorages was swept towards the entrance at about three knots, drawing into it many survivors from sinking ships. Among the rescuers there were men who, more than twenty years later, are still revolted by the smell of fuel oil because of its association with burning human flesh.

The grim task of recovering dead and wounded continued for several hours. The badly wounded were sent to Darwin hospital at once for treatment. The dead were put on a hand cart and taken to the hospital mortuary.

Fowler recalls that one of the men recovered from an area of blazing oil was a chief stoker who, all agreed, was dead. He was put on the handcart on top of six other bodies and sent to the hospital. Fowler expected never to see him again but in a Melbourne street two years later he was waylaid by the stoker, who thanked him for his rescue. He was still receiving treatment for burns but was otherwise well.

"Even then I didn't have the heart to tell him what we really thought when we sent him up on the dead-cart instead of with the wounded," he said.

The story of the Navy and the merchant ships is not quite complete. Indeed, it ended on a note of high drama and tragedy that took at least another fifteen lives, and perhaps more.

On February 18 the Filipino supply ship *Don Isidro*, of 3,200 tons, was attacked by a Japanese plane north of Wessell Islands in eastern Arnhem Land. She escaped serious damage and continued on her way in an attempt to reach the Philippines with a cargo of ammunition and supplies. This was obviously a vain hope for the Japanese had already occupied most of the country. The captain may have changed his mind about going there; if not, he was certainly proceeding by a circuitous route. On February 19 the ship was a few miles off the north-west coast of Bathurst Island and there was seen by the Japanese returning from the strike on Darwin. She was an irresistible target and was soon on fire as the result of five hits by bombs. The crew abandoned ship, believing that *Don Isidro* was sinking. Instead, she drifted ashore and burned there for several days. In all, eighty-four survivors reached the beach after being in the water for ten hours. Eleven died and were buried there. Seventy-three others were rescued by *H.M.A.S. Warrnambool* and brought to Darwin, where two more died. During this operation *Warrnambool* was bombed by a Japanese float-plane. For distinguished service in attending to the wounded Sick Berth Attendant D. E. Shelley was awarded the British Empire Medal.

A similar fate overtook the U.S. supply ship *Florence D*, of

2,638 tons, also with a Filipino crew. The same force bombed and sank her twenty-five miles north-west of Point Deception, Bathurst Island.

Shortly before the attack a U.S. Navy Catalina flying boat circling the ship was "jumped" by nine Japanese fighters and forced down. The pilots, Lieut. (later Admiral) Thomas H. Moorer and Ensign W. H. Mosley, though both wounded, made an emergency landing after much of the aircraft had been shot away. However, the pilots and all six other crew men survived in a rubber boat. They were picked up half an hour later by the *Florence D*, which carried ammunition. At noon the ship was bombed and strafed by a float plane but not severely damaged. At 3 p.m. nine carrier-based dive-bombers returned, scoring four direct hits and five near misses. *Florence D* was abandoned and sank immediately, but when it was seen that her stern was still above the shallow water some of her crew returned aboard. Of the eight men who had been in the Catalina and were rescued by *Florence D*, then forced to abandon ship, only one was killed. Forty survivors from the flying boat and the ship reached Bathurst Island. There they were seen two days later by the crew of a R.A.A.F. search plane. Some were rescued by boats from H.M.A.S. *Warrnambool* and others by Brother Andrew Smith in the mission lugger *St. Francis*. Brother Smith picked up Commander Carmelo Lopez Manzano and ten others, four of them badly burnt, and took them to Darwin. Two days later he returned to find that twenty others had arrived at the mission, having walked across the island. Two who were badly wounded had been carried thirty miles by colleagues.[1]

[1] This story is told in detail in Appendix III.

CHAPTER 6
The Much-Maligned Wharfies

> '*I led the main strength of my level bombers in an attack on the harbour installations and I dropped our first bombs on the single pier.*'
> —COMMANDER FUCHIDA.

> '*The wharflaborers had knocked off for the ten o'clock smoke-oh and were bunched at the elbow of the jetty. A bomb hit nearby, hurled a locomotive into the sea and took away an entire span, effectively trapping the surviving workers.*'—OFFICIAL WAR HISTORY.

The roll of those who were to die on the wharf was governed by chance to a degree that has never ceased to mystify some of the survivors, especially the former members of No. 4 gang of the waterside section of North Australia Workers' Union.

By December 1941 Darwin's wharflaborers had a reputation for irresponsible militancy that was shared elsewhere only by the most extreme left-wing unions. They were famous, or infamous, depending on one's political attitude, throughout Australia.

News stories which began "The Darwin wharf is idle again today" had ceased to be worthy of space, even though this was our most forward port of war, simply because they were no longer news.

The result was that when certain foodstuffs were unavailable in the shops the waterside section became a public Aunt Sally. Although the stoppages were not always their fault, "blame the wharfies" was soon a convenient excuse for storekeepers who wished to explain to customers why they had no potatoes, or whatever it might be. Previously the reason had been "It's on the boat" — a reference to the fortnightly shipping service which rather imputed blame to the shipowners for their irregularity. Seldom was a businessman heard to admit to his own ineptitude or insolvency for not carrying adequate reserve stocks.

Whatever the truth of this situation might have been, an objective researcher cannot overlook three salient and creditable facts about the behavior of the wharflaborers after December 7:

1. Nobody was conscripted to work on the wharf. After air raid alerts and the rapid southerly advance of Japanese forces it was apparent that Darwin would either be bombed or invaded. In that event, the men on the wharf could have been under no illusion about the danger of their own exposed position. The popular belief, following several night alerts, was that when the raiders came it would be in darkness. To anyone with the slightest susceptibilities the wharf must have seemed a hot spot indeed. There were no safety precautions, no local defence, and it shone with a blaze of lights that could be seen for miles.

2. On December 11, following an appeal by the Federal Minister for Labor, the late Mr E. J. Ward, the wharflaborers began working stretches of up to twenty hours a day in tropic heat in an attempt to speed up unloading. When that did not meet the situation, Ward flew to Darwin himself and prevailed upon the union to agree to the importation of more than one hundred and sixty additional watersiders. These men were flown to Darwin within the next few days and became known as "The Flying Wharfies." At the same time, the Minister said of the delays: "They have happened because the wharf seems to be nobody's business."

3. On February 19 the civilian death toll was thirty-seven. Of that number, twenty-two were wharflaborers. Some of the survivors subsequently remained in town to offer their services usefully at a time when the road leading south was carrying most of their highly vocal detractors.

None of the foregoing has been made clear by contemporary writers and some who had scant knowledge of the facts were unfairly critical.

The Administrator, C. L. A. Abbott, has castigated the wharfies. He has said that their agreement to importation of the flying-wharfies was "reluctant", that they objected to losing overtime, and that the delays they caused contributed materially to the loss of valuable ships during the raid.

Yet he has also said: "In spite of all the defence activities . . .

there was an insuperable bar to the prompt unloading of cargoes. This was the Darwin wharf itself. Nothing had been done to make it an efficient working unit . . . It ran out on steel and wooden piles from Stokes Hill. When it got into deep water it took a right-angled turn. It was along this turn that the ships were berthed, there being room for one ship on the outside and for a smaller vessel at the inner berth. All unloading was done with the ship's winches and, since the rise and fall of tide averaged twenty-two feet, there was a period at low tide when it was extremely difficult to swing cargo out of the holds on to the wharf."

Nor was that all. The right-angled turn midway along the wharf was too sharp to be negotiated by railway trucks pushed by a locomotive. Therefore a turntable operated by a donkey engine had been installed. Two trucks at a time were shunted on to the turntable and then eight trucks were pushed by hand, one at a time, to the ship's side. When they were full they were pushed back, again by hand and one at a time, to the turntable.

If the designer of this jetty had been told, "The government wants facilities that will compound the difficulties and increase the delays," a better job could not have been done.[1]

Even so, the wharf in 1942 was a vast improvement on what it had once been. As late as 1940 no provision existed for motor vehicles to approach a ship's side. Unfortunate passengers had to walk nearly three-quarters of a mile along a narrow path before they could obtain any kind of transport for themselves or their luggage. In that year the road was extended to the neck of the jetty and the surface decked to take motor vehicles.

Abbott described the man who stoked the donkey engine and operated the turntable as the Croesus of the Northern Territory. Work on the wharf then began before 8 a.m. and finished at 8 p.m., sometimes later. In order that the donkey engine would have steam up when required it was necessary for the operator to light his fire about 3 a.m. That was paid for at overtime rates and, according to Abbott, the man's wages fluctuated between eighty and one hundred pounds a month. Similar hours today would bring in an equal amount in a week.

Nevertheless, the shipping situation must have given the Administrator constant worry. Harbour congestion worsened alarmingly after the Pacific War began with the arrival of

[1] A new wharf built after the war overcame the problem by the simple expedient of replacing the right-angle with a curve, a solution that might not seem too difficult to a layman. That eliminated the need for the turntable, the donkey engine, and the shunting of trucks.

American transports, freighters and warships whose captains were accustomed to the best berthing and refuelling facilities in the world and expected them at Darwin.

The delay in recovering cargoes was particularly galling to the American base commander, Colonel John Robenson, who had handled shipping on the U.S. west coast where a notorious Australian, Harry Bridges, had controlled the longshoremen for many years.

Brigadier-General Julius Barnes complained bitterly to the Prime Minister, Mr Curtin, when a ship containing the guns for two American field artillery regiments had to wait three weeks before unloading.

The American historian, Walter D. Edmonds, has said: "The wharfies had their own ideas of hours, pace and weather conditions, war or no war, under which a man should work. They would refuse to work at all if American troops were put on the job with them. In four days they barely dented the holds of the first ship at the Darwin pier. Twenty-five more came crowding into the bay to await their turn and offered a rich target to the Japanese. At this stage Colonel Robenson, a tough old cavalry officer, decided to disregard the pleas of the Administrator and the Australian military commandant, both of whom feared political repercussions. He posted guards and machineguns along the pier, put his troops to work on a ship, and in a few days had ironed out most of the difficulties."[2]

Eighteen gangs were registered at that time with fourteen men to a gang. By February 18 three shifts of six gangs were working around the clock. The chairman of the waterside section of the union was Joseph ("Yorky") Walker, a gruff but amiable communist who was as militant in fighting for the rights of workers as anyone had a right to be. The secretary was John Edward Hynes.

As a member of No. 4 gang, Walker was rostered for the day shift on the 18th. It was his duty, before knock-off time, to find out how many gangs were wanted on the same shift next day. He asked the wharf supervisor, Reginald Erickson, and was told that five would be enough.

"I was surprised and delighted," Walker recalls. "I've always had a constitutional reluctance to get out of bed in the morning.

[2] Edmonds' statement is inaccurate. Wharflaborers did work alongside American troops. It was for this very reason that some men who might otherwise have died were off duty on the morning of February 19.

Number four gang was the sixth in line for day shift. That meant we would not be rostered until the following shift."

Walker telephoned Hynes at the union office so that he could draw up a list of the gangs and display it there. Walker posted a similar list at the wharf. When Hynes got the news that only five gangs were needed for day shift he exploded.

"What the hell's wrong with Erickson . . . only ordering five gangs! I thought there was supposed to be a war on and that we were being blamed for the slow turn-around?"

Walker pacified him, concerned momentarily that Hynes, if he made an official complaint to Erickson, might destroy his chance of sleeping in.

"He's supposed to know what he's doing," Walker said. "I've no doubt he reckons tomorrow will be another mess up like today. We've hardly done a tap of work . . . we couldn't move for Yankee soldiers . . . they've been off-loading the convoy the Japs chased back."

Hynes grumbled again but accepted the five gangs for work at eight o'clock next morning. They were Numbers 17, 18, 1, 2 and 3, a total of seventy men. Hynes was in No. 3 gang. Six days later he died at sea in the hospital ship *Manunda* from internal haemorrhage caused by concussion in the water. The first stick of bombs killed Erickson.

Instead of being on the wharf, Walker, true to his promise to himself, was still in bed in a bungalow behind the Victoria Hotel. The town's main air-raid siren was on a water tower nearby; he was thus in a good position to give an opinion on the argument that has gone on ever since — which came first, the siren or the bombs?

"Although in bed I was not asleep," Walker recalls. "I heard the two together. The siren wound up to a peak of noise. People in the town could hear it but they couldn't have done so on the wharf. They must have had bombs before they heard the alarm."

Subsequently the union was criticised for failing to quickly provide an accurate list of the men who were lost. Several months later the fate of some was still unknown and worried relatives could be told no more than that. The list Walker posted on the wharf contained only the numbers of the gangs and not the names of the men rostered for duty, many of whom were "flying wharfies" and new to the job. The only list of that kind was in Hynes' pocket when blast threw him into the sea.

Besides Hynes, four others of No. 3 gang were killed. They were Johnny Cubillo, Domingo Dominic, Catalina Spain and

Andrew Dejulia. All were working *Neptuna*, Hynes and Spain on the wharf itself, Dominic in No. 1 hold, Cubillo as a midship winchman, and Dejulia as a shunter, a term that meant nothing more than that he was one of several men who pushed the railway trucks by hand to and from the ship's side.

George Tye, another member of No. 3 gang, had been working on the wharf since 1940. He lived in a house at Frog Hollow, a low-lying section behind the town that in other cities might have been described as being on the wrong side of the tracks. It was a shanty-town of shacks and tents inhabited mainly by itinerants. Tye was an exception; he had been in Darwin for eighteen years and occupied one of the few respectable houses in the quarter. For many, there was no reticulated water supply; they drew it in buckets from a community tap and tried to cope with millions of mosquitoes and sandflies which every night invaded from their bases in nearby mangrove swamps.

On February 19 Tye forgot that he was rostered for daytime work, his gang having recently changed over from night shift. He was still in bed at eight o'clock when his mate, Johnny Cubillo, called. Tye wanted to stay there but Cubillo persuaded him to get dressed by saying that No. 3 gang was short-handed. They arrived late at 8.40 and began shifting paravanes, an anti-mine device, from the port to starboard deck of *Neptuna*. The gang had opened No. 1 hatch and was about to knock-off for morning smoke-oh when Tye saw aeroplanes high overhead. He said to Cubillo, "Yankee reinforcements at last! That makes me feel better." The planes were approaching from the southeast. Then the bomb bays opened and they saw and heard bombs screaming down towards them.

Tye and Cubillo ran from No. 1 hatch to the crew's quarters for'ard in *Neptuna*. They heard the explosion of the first bomb in the water a few dozen yards away and then direct hits on the wharf itself and on *Barossa*, tied up at the inside berth. The explosions unnerved them, especially when Robert Stobo, a seventeen-year-old *Neptuna* cadet, said, "I hope they don't hit number three or number four hold; they're full of T-N-T and depth-charges." Stobo died a few minutes later.

Tye recalls: "I came up on deck with Johnny. I jumped over the side of the wharf into the water with a lot of others, wharfies and ships' crews, but Johnny kept running along the wharf. That was the last time I saw him alive. Then the dive-bombers came at us. Thank God they were straight . . . they hit what they wanted. I was swimming under the wharf as bombs were hitting it and the ships alongside. I made my way towards the elbow of the wharf. That had already been hit, and the shed where men were gathered for smoke-oh, and it had all gone . . . just disappeared."

Tye recognised Alan Byers in the water. He was struggling to keep afloat. Then Tye saw that his right eye had been shot away and his left leg was severed. He supported Byers while other men under the wharf tied him to a pile with ropes until he could be taken to an ambulance. Byers died on *Manunda* six days later. Jack Hynes, also to die on *Manunda*, was in the water near Tye. He was a normally reticent man and Tye did not think it unusual that Hynes was silent. He could not know that the wharf section secretary had sustained fatal internal injuries.

Catalina Spain, also of No. 3 gang, floated past face downwards in the water. Jack Rogers, his closest mate, turned him over and saw that he was dying. Although wounded himself, Rogers supported Spain in the water until, in a few minutes, he died.

Gus. Brown, of No. 1 gang, was blown into the water by the blast that wrecked the recreation shed. Tye saw him swimming back towards the wharf, apparently uninjured. Then another bomb hit the decking, tearing out several huge planks as though they were splinters. One fell on Brown's head, killing him instantly.

The dive-bombers, Tye saw, had delivered mortal blows to *Neptuna*. A plate had been blown out of the side of No. 2 hold and the ship was settling gently in the water in an upright position. Tye could not know, at the time, that her end would be much more violent.

Oil pipelines along the wharf had burst and in some places had caught fire. Patches of oil on the water were also blazing. Tye was fifty yards from that kind of danger but needed no urging when a rescue launch owned by the Department of Civil Aviation, and manned by John Waldie, came by and offered him a lift ashore.

"By the time I got to Stokes Hill the *Neptuna* was getting hot and beginning to rumble,'" Tye recalls. "I knew then that this could be an unhealthy spot. At that moment a man named Johnny Wilkshire arrived in his truck. He jumped from the cabin, rushed into the water and began helping the wounded ashore."

Tye says that as he did so Wilkshire shouted, "Anyone fit enough to drive a truck take mine and get these wounded chaps to the hospital. I'm going after others." Seconds later he was in a commandeered launch and heading out into the harbour toward stricken ships.

Another who forgot he was rostered for work was Ricardo ("Cardo") Conanan, a Filipino. He wasn't as lucky as Tye. Conanan was a hatch man whose gang was also short-handed. A man was sent to his lodgings in Cavanagh Street to find him. He was still asleep but dressed quickly and arrived half an hour late. One of the first men he saw on the wharf was James Yuen.

"What's the matter, Cardo?" Yuen asked. "You look as though you're still half asleep."

"Gawd, I'm crook," Conanan said. "I had a heavy night on the grog."

For that reason, perhaps, he was one of the first to knock-off for smoke-oh. He hurried from *Barossa* to the recreation hut at the elbow of the wharf. A few minutes later he saw the planes and heard bombs falling towards him.

"Good-bye boys," he shouted. "I'll see you in the next world." Seconds later he was dead.

Geoffrey Dangerfield, a wharf foreman employed by Commonwealth Railways, lived in a house on Railway Hill with Geoffrey Moss, a Public Works Department clerk. Having cooked and eaten his own breakfast he saw that Moss was still in bed asleep.

"Get up, you lazy bastard!" he shouted. "You'll be late for work." "Bastard" was a strong word for Dangerfield, an Englishman.

Moss sat up and rubbed his eyes as Dangerfield walked to the door on his way out.

"What's your hurry?" he asked, and, as a parting shot, "Watch out the Japs don't get you."

Dangerfield did not answer.

Two hours later Moss was with the Director of Works, E. W. Stoddart, in the Public Works office near the railway yard when he heard the sirens. Stoddart appeared not to have heard and carried on with his work.

"The sirens have gone, Mister Stoddart," Moss said.

"Yes, I heard them," Stoddart replied. "Let's wait a minute, Mister Moss, and see what happens."

They did not have a minute to wait. Bombs fell simultaneously on the wharf. Moss thought of Dangerfield, then ran for a drain near Railway Hill which was rapidly filling with men. He lay down with stinking effluent flowing into his face. He recognised Police Sergeant William Littlejohn among others taking refuge nearby.

"Good-day, Bill," Moss said.

"Good-day, Geoff," Littlejohn said, as though passing the time of day in these circumstances was a necessary politeness.

At lunchtime Moss walked up Railway Hill to his house and prepared a simple meal. He made a pot of tea and sat down to wait for Dangerfield.

"I'm still waiting," he says. "He was blown to bits." Dangerfield's car, registered number N.T. 13, waited too — until it was impressed by the army.

On his way to work Dangerfield had stopped for a moment to chat with an old friend, Ossie Jensen.

"Have you made your will, Ossie?" he asked. Jensen said he had. "I want to make one and I don't know how to go about it," Dangerfield said. Jensen advised him to see either Brough Newell or Dick Ward, then the only solicitors in town. He said he would do so when he finished work that day.

On arrival at the wharf Dangerfield spoke to a colleague, James Yuen.

"I don't like our chances today, Jimmy," he said. "That convoy's back because the Japs chased it back. They know it's here and they'll come duck shooting."

Prophecy and fact were separated by less than two hours.

Dangerfield was on a span of the wharf that disappeared completely when hit by bombs. No trace of him was ever found. His widow, Betty, wrote to his family in England and told them of his death. After the war she went there and married her late husband's brother, Harry.

Jimmy Yuen was one of six Chinese wharfies. The others were Alf Jan, Claudie Shang, Peter Ng, Yetti Jan and Fan On. Yuen and Fan On, as members of No. 17 gang, were the only two rostered for duty that day.

Yuen, then twenty-four years old, was the son of a storekeeper father who had migrated to the Northern Territory last century. He was educated at Darwin Convent School and worked in Fong Yuen Kee's store in Chinatown until the evacuation of women and children created unemployment for shop assistants. He then transferred to the wharf.

On February 19, in the home he still occupies, Yuen cooked a breakfast of chicken soup for himself and four of the five other Chinese wharfies. All but Fan On lived with him. Appropriately, one feels, the chicken had belonged to members of a Japanese Club who had been interned.

"There were no Japanese left to look after the chickens, so we took that duty upon ourselves," he recalls with a grin.

Yuen rode his bicycle to work and by eight o'clock, as a winchman, was helping unload timber from *Barossa*. At 9.55 he left for the morning smoke-oh in the recreation shed. If he had gone there directly Yuen would almost certainly have been among those killed; instead, he crossed the wharf to the outside berth and began talking to Foo Hee, the Chinese chief cook from *Neptuna*.[3] He did not know that Darwin was about to be attacked until a bomb burst in the water nearby. He looked up, saw the planes, and realised that his mates were already running. Then a bomb hit the rightangle of the wharf. A locomotive, six railway trucks and several men were hurled into the sea. They included Geoff. Dangerfield, Ernie Hodges, Francisco Chavez and E. ("Whitey") Shores, all of whom were killed instantly.

Yuen was only thirty yards away. He was knocked down by the blast. By the time he got up the locomotive, trucks and recreation hut were in the water and a huge gap in the decking had cut off his escape to land, and of all the wharfies and seamen who were beyond that point.

Yuen's erratic behavior in the next few minutes was typical of many. At first he ran to the far end of the wharf and climbed beneath the decking. But when more bombs fell nearby he decided the position was too exposed. Perhaps he could see too much of what was happening; in any case, he liked it even less when Japanese fighters began machinegunning the area. Yuen then climbed back on top of the wharf and ran along it to *Neptuna*, going aboard and crouching in a corridor leading to the passenger cabins, apparently believing irrationally that if he could not see the Japanese they would not see him. However, he stayed only briefly — until a bomb landed in No. 1 hold where Tye and the other members of No. 3 gang had been working. Fire broke out at once and soon the skipper, Captain Michie, gave the order to abandon ship.

"I heard him give that order and I reckoned it included me and I took his advice," Yuen says. "I ran off with the purser, Joe Floyd. We went to the seaward end of the wharf because the landward end was cut. Some badly wounded men were struggling around in the water. Floyd and I rolled a dozen empty

[3] Yuen is himself a notably good cook.

THE MUCH-MALIGNED WHARFIES

petrol drums over the side to help those who seemed to be in trouble."

Having done that, Floyd said, "Let's dive in; this is getting too hot."

They dived together, ten feet from the top of the wharf to the water. The tide was running out. Yuen and Floyd swam together for a while but then parted company. Yuen struck out for open water and the boom wharf two hundred yards away, trying to get around patches of blazing oil. He had been in the water twenty minutes and was almost exhausted when a launch came along and the crew began to pick him up.

Then one of them said, "Hey, this is a bloody Jap! Let's throw him back or knock him on the head."

Yuen shouted: "Fair go, mates! I'm a bloody wharfie." They believed him.

"Gee, it was funny," he says now.

Yuen was put ashore in the boom wharf area, shocked and covered in oil. He was sitting on sand at the edge of the water, with the boom wharf itself as a shelter, when *Neptuna* blew up.

Yuen recalls: "Although I was a few hundred yards away the explosion lifted me two feet off the ground, like I was a feather, and dropped me back with a splash in the water. I thought my ribs had been cracked. Parts of *Neptuna* were coming to earth for several minutes. It was terrible . . . terrible! . . . these huge planks and masts thrown hundreds of feet like matchsticks . . . they landed on the foreshore and on the town and on the ships . . . hundreds of yards away."

Yuen walked up Kitchener Drive to the town and was given a lift to the hospital. He arrived to find dozens of Chinese seamen seeking treatment for burns and wounds and he was asked by the nurse in charge of casualty, Sister Elizabeth Cousin,[4] to act as interpreter. With Yetti Jan and other Chinese wharfies Yuen left town the same day, without food or water, to join hundreds of men waiting at Adelaide River for evacuation or enlistment.

On the wharf the men on the footplate of Commonwealth Railways shunting locomotive NF6 were Driver Mick Dempsey and Fireman Barry Andrews. The bomb which destroyed a section of the wharf tossed the engine over the side like a discarded toy. It was never recovered. Twelve rail trucks were destroyed or damaged. Dempsey and Andrews were both thrown

[4] Her brother-in-law, Captain A. P. Cousin, was on *Katoomba* in the harbour.

into the sea. Neither had time to speak. Andrews' lungs were injured by the blast; he suffered haemorrhage and shock and was evacuated on *Manunda*. Dempsey was severely shocked when helped from the water and had to be evacuated. The two men became separated in the water and neither knew the other had survived. An hour after the raid when Andrews was seen by another railway worker, Bob Pender, he was dazed and repeated a single question, "Where's Mick?"

Bob Pender had been on night shift and was in bed at Railway Hill. As soon as he heard the bombs he left the house by climbing through a window instead of walking through the door and has no idea to this day why he did so. He hid under a small tree, hoping the Japanese would not see him. Two parrots in the branches were so startled by the noise that they remained within a foot or so of his hand, quite silent. "But their feathers were shivering," Pender says.

Pender was in the railway yard when *Neptuna* exploded. "I knew that what went up must come down so I dived under a railway truck with a driver, Jock Sutherland. And just in time! We were no sooner there than iron and timber and bits of the ship's plates began to fall around us like hailstones." Presently Pender saw an unrecognisable man walking towards him.

"Bad show, Bob," the man said.

"Who are you?" Pender asked.

He was Ian Bell, a shunter, and one of Pender's best friends. He was covered so completely in oil that only his eyes seemed free of it. Bell had been under a rail truck when it fell into the sea as the wharf collapsed, and swam through several acres of fuel oil then gushing on to the water from fractured pipes. Pender told Bell, who lived at some distance, to go to his house nearby for a shower and a change of clothes. When Pender returned later in the day he found a dirty towel and saw that a shirt and pair of shorts were gone. Bell was evacuated and Pender, who remained, did not see him again for five years. When they met Bell said, "Bob, I owe you some clothes."

The launch driver who rescued James Yuen and threatened to throw him back was John Waldie, the twentyfive-year-old coxswain employed by the Department of Civil Aviation on its flying boat facilities near the wharf.

Waldie remembers seeing Yuen in the water and being unable to decide whether he was Japanese, Chinese or Filipino. Oriental seamen were everywhere. Sixty-two of *Neptuna's* survivors were Chinese, and there were another thirty-one from *Tulagi*. Forty-eight Lascars had escaped from *British Motorist*. "I couldn't tell who they were," Waldie recalls. "Many I picked up were smothered in oil and I could distinguish only that they were human beings."

It is not possible to estimate the exact number of men who owe their lives to Waldie but he is known to have rescued more than one hundred. The officer-in-charge of the flying boat base, William Wake, has attested that Waldie remained in his launch from the time the raid began until long after it ended.

Wake himself was knocked flat near the D.C.A. control building at the wharf approach by blast from the first bombs but remained in the area. Waldie was working on the engine of launch C.A.22 near steps used by flying boat passengers. Above the noise of the engine he became aware that a mate, Percy Gordon, was shouting at him from the top of the steps. Waldie could not hear what Gordon was saying so he climbed up towards him. When half way to the top the first bombs landed in the sea and on the wharf.

Instead of seeking shelter, Waldie returned to C.A.22. Within a few minutes he saw the vital need for a rescue vessel beneath the wharf, where men were dying and being threatened with incineration. With a D.C.A. boathand, Ray Crocker, he went out to help them. Waldie estimates that thirty men immediately clambered into the launch, which was in danger of capsizing. One man's foot had been severed. He took them ashore while further bombs dropped and fighters strafed the area. His memory of how many trips he made is hazy but on April 15, 1942, William Wake made an official report to the Director-General of Civil Aviation in which he wrote: "Crocker remained with the launch for two trips and Waldie then carried on alone for at least another three. On each trip the launch carried more than thirty men, besides towing in five crowded lifeboats. When everyone had been evacuated from beneath the wharf Waldie took two Qantas pilots, Captain Crowther and Captain Hussey, to a flying boat which had survived the raid. They were able to get it away to Groote Eylandt. He then took me around the bombed ships in the harbour to pick up other survivors."

An aeradio operator, C. W. Vincent, confirmed Waldie's efforts in a report describing him as the leading spirit in rescue operations, and pointing out that he worked under bombing, machine-gunning, and in the vicinity of an ammunition ship that was on fire.[5]

[5] Waldie was awarded the M.B.E.

Several other men acted with supreme courage in the rescue operations, notably Lieut. Ian McRobert, R.A.N.R. (S), who was the Navy's assistant harbourmaster; Leading Seaman E. M. Ericsson, of *H.M.A.S. Platypus*, and John Wilkshire, a civilian. These three formed themselves into a hastily organised rescue squad which became responsible for saving dozens of lives.

Wilkshire and a friend, Don Bergin, were loading sand on Wilkshire's truck at Mendil Beach, more than a mile away, when the raid began. They realised the sand might be useful in fighting fires so they drove instinctively, and without thought of their own safety, towards the oil tanks and the wharf. Bombs were still falling as they arrived. Sailors without ships and wharfies without a wharf were being helped ashore by Waldie but others in the water were beyond his immediate reach. Wilkshire saw that it was here he could do the most good. As the wharf laborer George Tye has already related, Wilkshire shouted for anyone able to drive a truck to use his as an ambulance in getting wounded men to hospital. He then went into the water and in the next few minutes helped more than twenty wounded and exhausted seamen ashore. While there he was strafed by Japanese fighters. He could see the planes coming in towards him and the spurts of water as machinegun bullets hit close by. He handed the men over an embankment to Don Bergin, who directed them to the truck and other vehicles then arriving.

Wilkshire was soon covered in oil himself. He recalls that he swallowed mouthfuls of it; the taste remained with him for days. Soon after he had helped the last wounded man to safety Wilkshire and Bergin overheard a naval officer calling for volunteers to man a launch in picking up survivors from ships stricken in the bay. This was Lieut. McRobert who, with Ericsson, had already rescued a number of them. Wilkshire and Bergin offered at once. They took a second D.C.A. launch, C.A.2, and a hitch-hiking passenger, Lieut.-Commander Etheridge Grant, U.S.N. captain of *William B. Preston*. Grant, ashore when the raid began, did not yet know that his ship had been hit, that her stern was ablaze, and that she was trying to escape through the boom; that part of the harbour was obscured from his view by a promontory of land, Fort Hill.[6]

As the five men moved towards the launch they were warned

[6] *Preston* got through the boom at 25 knots and reached Broome next day. There the first-lieutenant sent a Catalina back to Darwin to recover the captain. The ship proved an exceptionally tough customer for the dive-bombers. This was later explained; the crew had salvaged .50 machine-guns from a number of unserviceable flying boats and had them in use.

by watersiders that *Neptuna* was about to blow up, and that to put to sea anywhere near her would be extremely hazardous. Nevertheless, they did so, and had gone only one hundred yards before the predicted explosion came.

Wilkshire recalls: "The launch was blown clean out of the water. It was the most terrible explosion imaginable, yet I saw little of the destruction until it was over because of what happened to us."

He was thrown bodily into the water, sustaining a broken finger and shrapnel wounds in the legs. Fortunately he was able to grab the gunwale of the launch, which had settled on an even keel, and climb aboard again. Grant was also in the water. Wilkshire called to him but he did not answer; instead, he began swimming towards a buoy which he reached and clung to until rescued. McRobert was lying unconscious in the cabin and Bergin had been thrown across the engine and burnt. Wilkshire took the tiller, headed the launch for the middle of the harbour, and in a few minutes McRobert revived.

"I remember coming to and finding Wilkshire at the wheel; we were going flat out," McRobert told me.

Wilkshire says: "First thing he did was to take off his steel helmet and hand it up to me at the wheel. Then he came out and introduced himself for the first time. We shook hands all round."

This strangely assorted and self-appointed rescue party steered for *British Motorist*, the tanker which was burning and sinking. As though they had not had enough when a ship loaded with T.N.T. exploded almost on top of them, they were now moving towards a burning tanker, with all that implied. Disregarding the extreme danger of being enveloped in blazing oil, the rescuers went alongside, only to find that the crew had already been taken off by *H.M.A.S. Tolga*. But McRobert and his mates saw that one man was still aboard. Mahommed Hussein, suffering from pneumonia, had been left behind in his bunk when the remainder of the crew were rescued. *British Motorist* slipped to her side and sank soon after they had taken him off. As the launch moved away McRobert saw, nearby, a man sitting alone on a raft. He was drifting unconcernedly on the tide to the harbour entrance. He had erected a large beach umbrella, was surrounded by bottles from which he drank frequently but alone, and adamantly refused to be interrupted.

While they were taking survivors from *Mauna Loa* and *Meigs* the launch broke down and could not be re-started. They were taken in tow by a Navy vessel and, at the end of a rope, completed the evacuation of stricken ships. On the way back to the wharf, and when still one hundred yards from it, their towboat was fouled in debris and stopped. McRobert and Wilkshire swam ashore to get help and were assisted from the oily water at the boom defence depot by Commander Fowler.

One of the vessels still floating when the raid ended was half boat and half aircraft — the four-engined Qantas flying boat *Camilla*. Heavy smoke from burning ships had screened her from the Japanese pilots; she was a target they would not otherwise have neglected.

Camilla was swinging on her moorings in a slight north-west breeze about two hundred yards south-east of the wharf, dangerously close to *Neptuna*. She had arrived the night before and was being held at Darwin while clarification of the military situation in the islands to the north was awaited. On January 30 *Camilla's* sister ship, *Corio*, had been shot down near Koepang while on a special flight to evacuate women and children from Sourabaya.

If any reminder were needed of the extreme danger in taking slow flying boats through air space already dominated by the Japanese it was provided by Captain Aubrey Koch, *Corio's* skipper, who was at that moment a patient in Darwin hospital with severe bullet and other wounds. Of eighteen crew and passengers, seven escaped from the sinking craft and five eventually reached the shore by swimming five miles. Koch, with bullet wounds in the arms and legs, was one of them.[7] They were three hours in the water. Koch had been admitted to hospital in Koepang. Every day he was there the town had been raided by Japanese planes. He was still a stretcher case when brought to Darwin in a R.A.A.F. plane. Seven days later he had recovered sufficiently to be able to crawl out of his hospital bed during the first attack on Australia.

By February 19 the air route through the chain of islands to eastern Java and Wavell's headquarters had been abandoned and arrangements made for a shuttle service between Broome on the north-west coast of W.A. and Tjilatjap on the south coast of Java. Thus it was that several Qantas crews under Captains H. B. Hussey, W. H. Crowther and C. R. Gurney were being held in Darwin.

[7] The others were Mr. Frank Moore, Mr. John Fisher, Lieut. B. L. Westbrook, R.A.N., and First Officer Victor Lyne.

These land-based Betty bombers were among 54 that took part in the raid on Darwin

A Betty bomber releasing its load over Darwin.

Vice Admiral Chuichi Nagumo

The explosion from the first bombs ever to land on Australia. They can be seen exploding in the water alongside the m.v. Neptuna *and* H.M.A.S. Swan, *not far from the Qantas flying boat,* Camilla

m.v. Neptuna *hit and on fire, the smoke becoming denser*

U.S.S. Peary, *a destroyer, exploded and sank. This dramatic photograph was taken by Signalman Douglas Fraser from H.M.A.S. Deloraine. H.M.A.S. Katoomba is in the floating dock and the hospital ship* Manunda *at right*

The tanker British Motorist *with propeller clear of the water and still on fire*

The pilot on the right of this group of U.S. airmen is Lieut. Robert Oestreicher who gave the warning 'Zeros!' from aloft

The remains of a U.S.A.F. P.40 fighter destroyed on the ground by Japanese fire after crash-landing

Only the shell remains of this store at the R.A.A.F. base

Damage to hangar and remains of aircraft at R.A.A.F. station

Ruins of R.A.A.F. equipment store

The R.A.A.F. nursing staff with the R.A.A.F. doctor (Sqdn. Leader D. C. Howle, centre) at Daly Waters, N.T.

Sir Frederick Scherger, in the uniform of Air Commodore

THE MUCH-MALIGNED WHARFIES

When the alert sounded Captain Hussey was awaiting his turn in a barber's shop in Smith Street, the main thoroughfare. Soldiers being shaved were occupying the two chairs, but the siren had such an effect on the hands of one barber that his client jumped from the chair and quickly finished the job himself. Hussey abandoned his shave. He walked out of the building and through the yard of Victoria Hotel looking for open space. He hurried towards the new Hotel Darwin on The Esplanade, intending to seek shelter below a nearby cliff. Bombs were already exploding on the harbour and wharf. Near the Club Hotel corner in Mitchell Street, Hussey was joined by Captain Gurney and Mrs V. Hansen, a Qantas employee. As a second formation of Japanese planes released its bombs the two captains and their blonde companion dropped into the dirty gutter outside the hotel, there to be spattered by flying debris from the post office one hundred and fifty yards away. Presently Captain Crowther arrived with his shirt front open and soap around his ears. It was evident that he, too, had been trying to get a shave.

As thick smoke poured up from the harbour area and settled over the town Hussey and Crowther became convinced that *Camilla* could not have escaped destruction. When the attack eased Mrs Hansen drove them to the flying boat base. Smoke from *Neptuna* and *Barossa* was blowing straight over *Camilla* but she was still afloat and from that distance appeared to be undamaged. The jetty leading to the wharf had been severed and men were struggling out of the water and being brought ashore in launches. From them Hussey and Crowther learnt that *Neptuna* had a cargo of depth-charges and would inevitably explode. In that event, they were sure, *Camilla* would be blown from the water. They decided she must be saved.

They ran down the flying boat passenger ramp just as John Waldie was landing his last load of survivors. He took them at once to *Camilla*. Before going aboard the two captains quickly but thoroughly examined the flying boat, finding only two small shrapnel holes in the elevators. These would not prevent her flying.

Fortunately the shore batteries were coupled in, giving ample power to start the motors. While Hussey engaged switches Crowther tried the starters and found they worked normally. They checked the fuel gauges and saw that all tanks were full. Crowther got the engines going and Hussey went below to cast off the mooring rope, allowing the north-westerly wind to blow them away from the burning ammunition ship. Fearing that near-misses on ships and the wharf may have damaged submerged plates Hussey lifted the floor boards and examined the bilges. There was no excessive water.

On returning to the flight deck Hussey found that all engines were going. Crowther taxied across the harbour while Hussey recovered mooring ropes and secured the hatches. These tasks would normally have been done by other members of the crew, but this was no time for a captain to quibble about getting his hands dirty.

Crowther turned *Camilla* into the wind; then he opened the throttles and with Hussey in the first officer's seat the lumbering machine gathered speed, stepped up on the water and took off. Almost immediately three explosions were heard and for a moment they feared an anti-aircraft battery might be treating them as a target. That was followed by a loud bang which appeared to come from a lower deck. Hussey investigated and found a pantry window had blown open.

Three minutes later, and not more than eight minutes after *Camilla* had left her moorings, *Neptuna* blew up. A Qantas passenger launch, *Halcyon*, and other small craft near her were sunk by the explosion. *Camilla*, had she still been there, would almost certainly have shared the same fate.

Having got the flying boat into the air the question was what to do next. Hussey and Crowther could not be sure that Japanese fighters were not still in the area. They had to expect attack at any moment. In fact, a second raid shortly occurred, but by then *Camilla* was safe. Crowther flew south for twenty-five miles, then east towards the Alligator Rivers flowing into Van Diemen Gulf from the western borders of Arnhem Land. They decided to attempt a landing in the estuary of one of these rivers. The East Alligator, one hundred and fifty miles east of Darwin, was sufficiently wide for their needs. However, realising that the refuelling barge at Darwin might have been damaged, and that wireless communication would be difficult, they turned instead and set course for the fully equipped flying boat base at Groote Eylandt, four hundred miles away in the Gulf of Carpentaria. There they refuelled and waited until four o'clock before returning to Darwin to evacuate the remaining crews, staff and passengers. Being unable to borrow a radio operator from the Groote Eylandt base they arranged for a signal to be sent to the aircraft at half-hourly intervals to let them know whether Darwin was being attacked. Hussey and Crowther guessed correctly that an arrival just before dark would be safe. The All Clear signal was received regularly and the return flight went according to plan. Nevertheless, it must have been a strange experience for two senior captains, accustomed to flying with a full crew and complement of passengers, to be alone over the empty wastes of Arnhem Land with no guarantee that they would reach their destination safely.

At Darwin they worked until one o'clock in the morning arranging their load and for the transfer from hospital to *Camilla* of their colleague, Aubrey Koch. For a few hours before dawn they tried to sleep in chairs in the foyer of the otherwise abandoned Hotel Darwin.

At 5.30 a.m. they went with passengers and crew to the damaged D.C.A. control building near the wharf to find that they had no means of reaching the moored flying boat. John Waldie alone remained to operate the launch but he was home in bed. Most of the rowing boats had been sunk. At dawn Hussey saw an overturned dinghy beneath the surface of the water near the jetty steps. This was salvaged, as was another washed in with the tide. Crowther and Hussey rowed out to *Camilla* to prepare her for take-off. Passengers and their luggage were taken out later, with Koch on a stretcher, and in a few minutes the boat was on its way back to Groote Eylandt and Sydney. More than a year later — on April 22, 1943 — Koch swam away from *Camilla* near Port Moresby as he had from *Corio* near Koepang. The flying boat sank there after a crash landing in bad weather. On that occasion eighteen survivors, including Koch, swam throughout one night and until three o'clock the following afternoon before being rescued.

CHAPTER 7

The Militia Tested

> *'Anti-aircraft fire was intense
> but largely ineffectual.'*—COMMANDER FUCHIDA.

> *'The only defence to the enemy raid over the
> harbour and the town was by means of anti-
> aircraft guns. The batteries operated efficiently
> and the personnel performed very creditably in
> their baptism of fire.'*—MR. JUSTICE LOWE.

The noise made by Japanese bombs and bullets was equalled by the detonation of anti-aircraft guns, first as shells were fired and then as they burst near the planes some seconds later. The most vivid impression of many people who survived the day is of difficulty in sleeping through the nights that followed against involuntary recollection of jagged sound.

If there were any justification for describing the foregoing events as The Battle of Darwin, meaning combat by equivalent forces as distinct from the invincibility of one, it would rest with the anti-aircraft batteries.

The gunners were men trained to fight. They had the means to fight. They were chiefly young militiamen irked by the stigma of "choco"[1] and determined to prove their resolution to others as well as themselves. They were unit-mates of long standing with young officers who had risen from the ranks — *their* ranks. They maintained an intense barrage that was respected even by the disrespectful Japanese although, as Mitsuo Fuchida says, their fire was largely ineffectual.

Two heavy anti-aircraft batteries were present, the 2nd and the 14th. The 14th consisted chiefly of young men from N.S.W.

[1] Most Australian militiamen were known as 'chocos' (from chocolate soldiers). It was originally a term of derision but, like the Rats of Tobruk, it eventually became a name of which many militiamen were proud.

THE MILITIA TESTED

who had been in Darwin for more than a year. It had well-established detachments of 3.7-inch guns at strategic points in the town and on its perimeter. No. 1 detachment, with four guns, occupied Darwin Oval on the cliff overlooking the harbour, the Post Office, Government House and Hotel Darwin. Most of the men were less than twenty years old. They lived in tents and huts but crew quarters were also built into the 12-ft earthen revetments around each of the guns. These had been made comfortable with beds of bush timber and items of furniture which, according to one bombardier, were simply "acquired."

As in most artillery batteries, the anti-aircraft gunners did their training at the double, with the result that all the twelve-man crews were sharp and keen. Their well-disciplined training sessions were comforting to those citizens of Darwin who did not understand the limitations of widely dispersed anti-aircraft fire.

Lieut. Graham Robertson was a twenty-year-old bombardier when he arrived with the 14th Battery late in 1940. His commanding officer was Major D. H. Vose. The 2nd Battery was commanded by Major Nigel Sutherland and Major F. F. ("Doggy") Mooy was over-all commander.

Robertson was one of several men commissioned from the ranks. He had been promoted to lieutenant only five days before the raid and on that morning was in charge of the Oval detachment. He remembers that towards the end of 1941 the unit's one hundred and fifty men were disconsolate and disillusioned. While it is true that they were equipped with four 3.7-inch guns they had no fire control instruments. The guns were therefore unserviceable. Supplies of ammunition had also been inadequate even for training. Dozens of the young militiamen had applied for transfer to the A.I.F., but had been refused as a matter of policy because the battery was classified as essential to home defence. During the year the gunners were visited by the Governor-General, Lord Gowrie, who asked if they were happy. The unit spokesman was more direct than diplomatic and detailed a list of grievances. Gowrie was told the guns, while splendidly maintained, were useless because other units allotted the comparable tasks of guarding Sydney and Melbourne had higher priorities for fire control instruments. What part His Excellency played in the subsequent events is not known, but soon after his return to Canberra the Darwin units had what they needed. Trenches then had to be dug across the Oval, in solid rock, to bury cables carrying fire control data from predictors to the four guns. These cables, although connected, were still exposed and vulnerable on February 19; all guns might have been neutralised by a single cannon shell in the trench. On that day, also, the guns had been proof fired but the crews were unpractised.

"Our very first shoot with live shells was in deadly earnest," Robertson says.

On the night of February 18 all anti-aircraft officers were warned by Major Mooy of the possibility of Japanese attack within twenty-four hours. The *Houston* convoy had steamed up the bay past Larrakeyah army barracks and had anchored directly below and a few hundred yards to the west of No. 1 detachment's positions. The significance of its return was apparent to the anti-aircraft commanders. They checked their ammunition. The guns were manned for a dawn Stand-to. Then the men went to breakfast and returned to work on the cable trenches and revetment walls.

At 9.55 an air sentry looked through a telescope and sounded a local alarm, heard only by the unit. The crews took post on their guns, as they had done repeatedly in the past weeks. Robertson entered his command post and went to the telescope, expecting to see friendly planes. That had happened earlier in the morning when six Hudson bombers flew in from Koepang, and again when the American P.40s took off. This time, instead, he saw more planes than he could count, and the silhouettes were such that he could instantly recognise them as Japanese. For a split-second, though knowing it to be true, Robertson could scarcely believe what he saw.

Then he shouted to his men: "This is no drill! This is fair dinkum!"

Gunner Leslie Lewis, of Pymble, N.S.W., was layer-for-line on No. 1 gun. He had just turned twenty. Lewis's seat was on the left side of the gun. Breakfast had been brought to him there from the section kitchen on the northern side of the oval. Then, because he felt unwell, he had gone to lie on his bunk inside the emplacement. That prevented him keeping an appointment to visit a friend on board *Neptuna*. At 9.56 he was still lying down. A few seconds later Bombardier Jack Mulholland ran to the bunk, tipped Lewis to the ground, and shouted, "Righto, Lewis! It's on!" The urgency in his voice made Lewis realise that this was more than another exercise;

what the young gunners had been trained to expect was there in fact to be repulsed. Lewis reached his seat on the gun clad only in a pair of shorts as Robertson issued his warning.

Readings from height and range finders were already pouring into the command post and within two minutes, as the first Japanese bombs were still in the air, Robertson gave the order: "Fire!"

An anti-aircraft shell was on its way, to burst at fourteen thousand feet, as the first bomb exploded and the sirens sounded. Thereafter the guns fired without pause until the raid ended. At that stage each was reduced to its last two or three rounds of ready ammunition. Fresh supplies were quickly brought up from a bulk dump beneath the Oval grandstand.

The gunners deserved better success than they achieved. Robertson believes they may have shot down one high level bomber but it was not confirmed and the Japanese have not since admitted the loss of any such planes. They did get one at low altitude. A dive-bomber was seen attacking the *British Motorist* on a course that would bring it towards the Oval. Bombardier Mulholland, on No. 1 gun, waved his bare arms and shouted directions to his layers and fired by sighting along the barrel. As the plane came out of its dive the shell hit it on the nose and the crew saw it plunge into the harbour. Mulholland and the rest of the crew flicked pouring perspiration from their faces and eyes and went on with the job.

Surprisingly, the Oval emplacement was not heavily attacked. Sporadic strafing by fighters was ineffectual and there were no casualties. It is difficult to understand why dive-bombers operating almost over the barrels of the guns did not attempt to put them out of action; they were obviously a prime military target.

Sergeant Laurie Huby, assistant to Lieut. Geoff. Barnard in a detachment at the northern end of Fannie Bay civil aerodrome, went into action wearing only a steel helmet, respirator, boots and soap.

The Fannie Bay detachment had distinguished itself two hours before the raid by firing warning shots across the bows of unidentified planes approaching from the north. The planes were six R.A.A.F. Hudson bombers returning from their base at Penfui, near Koepang. All were heavily laden with servicemen being evacuated from untenable positions in Timor. Recriminations between the R.A.A.F. and the Army followed the shots but that didn't worry Huby or Barnard; they didn't have adequate identification; they were tired of guessing; and they, too, had seen the *Houston* convoy come back and understood the reasons.

After the gun which fired the warning shots had been cleaned Huby had walked to the showers. He was naked and lathered with soap when the alarm sounded. He jumped into his boots, grabbed his helmet and respirator and ran to his post. He stood naked on top of sandbags to give fire signals to his gunners, but had to move when seen by a Japanese pilot who, perhaps affronted, dived and strafed him. Bullets struck the sandbags, one hit a predictor, and another struck Lance-Bombardier Michael Brennan in the leg. He had to be evacuated. But Huby was missed and not until the raid ended did he get his pants on.

A detachment of two 3-inch guns at Elliott Point, Larrakeyah, fired on the Japanese but did not observe any hits. These guns were not attacked, for which the officer commanding, Lieut. E. J. Hanley, was thankful; a large ammunition magazine had been built about one hundred yards from his guns, and painted white. Hanley had asked permission to camouflage it but that was refused because damage was feared to sensitive shells and cartridges by the higher temperatures the camouflage would induce. After the raids Hanley supervised the work without permission.

Perhaps the least enviable anti-aircraft position that day was occupied by a light-machinegun troop commanded by Lieut. Donald Brown,[2] then aged twenty-one, who had been commissioned nine days earlier. His ten Lewis guns were mounted in pairs surrounding oil storage tanks on Stokes Hill overlooking the wharf and, as bombers fly, only one hundred yards from it. The tanks were another seemingly obvious target; if they were hit the defenders would be in danger of incineration.

The gun posts were commanded by Brown (in the command post), Sergeant Tom Fraser, Bombardier Jack Ryder, Bombardier "Doc" Halliday and Lance-Bombardier Fred Wombey. They fired continuously at planes strafing the ships and wharves. Brown does not claim that his guns shot down any of the Japanese but they are credited with having saved the oil tanks. Their fire was such that the Japanese stayed away. The gunners' lives were threatened by fragments of *Neptuna* after she exploded. Pieces of red hot steel, lengths of rigging with pulleys

---

[2] Now Major, and still serving in the Regular Army.

attached and part of the splintered main mast landed on Stokes Hill. The blast buckled a galvanised iron fence with its steel supports on the seaward side of the gun positions.

"Bits of the wrecked ship made the entire area highly lethal," Brown remembers.

On the southern and northern perimeters of the town other anti-aircraft units were in constant action. One of these was a troop from headquarters squadron of 19th Machinegun Regiment consisting of thirty militiamen from the Horsham district in the Victorian Wimmera. Most of them had been schoolmates in the small township of Natimuk, and among them there was a comradeship rare even for Australian army units. Their officer, Lieut. Rex McRae, had attended the state school with his troopers. They included a father and son, Corporal Charles and Trooper Bill Ellifson.

The unit arrived at Darwin with advance sections of the regiment in January and moved into Winnellie camp six miles south of the town. It was equipped with Hotchkiss light machine-guns adapted for anti-aircraft work. In an atmosphere of tenseness and expectation the men were sent straight to previously prepared gunposts within an hour of arrival and spent their first night in Darwin ready for combat. As it happened, they were attacked only by mosquitoes.

The four gunposts, one in each corner of the headquarters area, were circular pits built of sandbags to shoulder height. The unit's task was to defend its own headquarters against enemy air attack. They were to do better than that.

After the first few days of excitement the novelty of their new situation dissipated and the troopers, like thousands of others, became bored with endless training in the fierce tropical heat.

Early in the morning of February 19 Sergeant Wallace Woolmer took the troop to the centre of the camp for instruction in Morse signalling, leaving one man on duty at each gunpost. It was a subject for which they had little appetite.

Woolmer had been talking for a few minutes when Trooper Alan ("Runky") Knight said, "Christ, Wal, do we have to learn this bloody crap?" Such freedom of expression was common in the unit, built on the base of mateship at school.

Woolmer replied, "It's on the syllabus and I've got to ram it down your necks whether you like it or not."

At that moment they heard the roar of engines and saw

planes flying in perfect formation high above the town.

"It's about time we got some bloody planes," Knight said, as bombs began to fall.

The anti-aircraft training manual, leaving nothing to chance, specified that in these circumstances the troop commander should give the order, "Aircraft! Prepare for action!"

Instead, Woolmer shouted to his squad, "Man the bloody guns!"

The drill had been practised frequently and the guncrews ran to the pits. Three guns were commanded by corporals. Woolmer was in charge of the fourth. With him were Corporal Athol Wade, Trooper Jim Cutchie and Trooper Bert Emmerson. Trooper Alf Schmidt was in reserve in an adjoining pit. His duty was to handle ammunition and spares. They wore shorts, shirts and steel helmets.

A few minutes after the first bombs fell a single Japanese fighter flew low over Winnellie camp, situated near the southeast end of the R.A.A.F. runway. It was identified as a Zero on reconnaissance but it did not attack.

Bert Emmerson, No. 1 on Woolmer's gun, said, "Say the word, Wal, and I'll into the bastard!"

Woolmer directed that the fire be held, not wishing to disclose their position to a plane that was not attacking. But they were seen. The Japanese pilot turned and flew directly over the spot. As he banked for a better view Woolmer saw his face clearly through the perspex canopy of his cockpit. He also saw the Japanese give him a rude thumbs-up sign.

"He'll be back with his mates," Woolmer said, realising that he had disappointed impatient gunners. "You'll get your chance."

Sure enough, the plane returned in a few minutes with several others. The gunposts were strafed and camouflage netting was shot away, literally from around the ears of the crews.

Trooper Bill Ellifson, on another gun, was firing from a position requiring the left arm and elbow to be raised. A Japanese bullet passed under his armpit and into the sandbags inside the gunposts. The troops disregarded personal danger. They were vulnerable but enraged at this Japanese audacity. As the strafing became more intense fire orders were shouted constantly. Even so, there was time for levity.

"Just like duck opening day at Clear Lake," Bert Emmerson said.

"Yeah, but this time the bloody ducks are shooting back," Woolmer said.

THE MILITIA TESTED

The barrels of the air-cooled guns were soon smoking hot. In Woolmer's pit Corporal Athol Wade picked up a spare barrel and prepared to fit it. Emmerson released the hot barrel and tossed it quickly into the ammunition pit.

"Here, Schmitty, cool this off!" he shouted.

Trooper Alf Schmidt saw it coming and instinctively caught it. "You bastards!" he shouted, as his hands blistered.

The strip-fed Hotchkisses were loaded with tracer, armour piercing, ball and explosive bullets, a lethal mixture if the lightly protected Zeros were hit with a burst. To improve performance the troopers had adjusted gas regulators beyond the recommended safety level to produce a faster rate of fire.

"This was a highly illegal practice that caused barrels to overheat and which only the troops knew about," Woolmer recalls. "We would all have been court-martialled if caught."

The four guns continued to exchange fire with the planes without success on either side. But when blood was eventually drawn it was Japanese. A Zero flying in from the northern side of the camp approached a gunpost manned by Corporal Allan ("Patsy") Weidner, Trooper Max Grant, Trooper Alan Knight and Trooper Roy Jones.

Grant, Number 1 in the crew, opened fire. As the Zero swept over the pit he quickly traversed the gun through one hundred and eighty degrees, knocking Knight down in the process.

"Watch what you're doing, you crazy bastard!" Knight yelled.

But Grant's movement enabled him to fire a prolonged burst into the Japanese plane from the rear.

Weidner saw what was happening and gave some rather informal encouragement. "Up his arse! Up his arse!" he shouted. A few seconds later there were cheers and cries of "Got the bastard!"

Smoke began pouring from the Zero, which was then also fired upon by other guns. It was seen crashing in flames half a mile away. The pilot was killed.

Although they had been in action for nearly thirty minutes and tracers had shown bullets entering the fuselages of other Zeros, this was the only plane they saw go down. Several hours later, when they had cleaned their guns, the troopers were taken to see the wreck. On mantelshelves in several homes in the Wimmera today there are pieces of metal and instruments from one of the first Japanese planes shot down on Australian soil by anti-aircraft gunners. Only a few months earlier these men had been wheat farmers, woolgrowers, grocers and mechanics. The most frustrated man in the troop was Corporal Charles Ellifson, an Anzac veteran. Instead of looking along the sight of a machinegun, as he had at Gallipoli, he was on guard duty when the action took place. He consoled himself by acquiring the guardhouse ammunition and firing at the fighters with his rifle.

CHAPTER 8

The Silent Lines

> *'The explosions marched inexorably shorewards along The Esplanade to the Post Office, the police barracks and government offices.'*
> —OFFICIAL WAR HISTORY.

> *'We have no record of the town being attacked. Our pilots had strict orders not to attack cities but only ships, wharves and military installations. At Pearl Harbour we concentrated on such targets. I am surprised to learn that the town of Darwin was bombed.'*—HITOSHI TSUNODA, Japanese Navy historian, in an interview with the author.

Of all the tragic events of this terrible day none is more poignant than the story of what happened at Darwin Post Office where ten people lost their lives, six of them women the Administrator had urged to leave. Two of the women were mother and daughter whose husband and father was also killed. Two others were sisters. All had stayed in Darwin in circumstances that were courageous but foolhardy.

The Postmaster-General's Department was housed in a complex of buildings that occupied almost an entire block between the new Hotel Darwin and Government House, with frontages to The Esplanade and Mitchell Street. They included the Post Office, the telegraph office, the telephone exchange, cable company offices, stores, residences and staff messes. The more substantial buildings were of local stone. A new Post Office entrance was being erected in Mitchell Street in concrete but was incomplete. The private homes were chiefly of timber and iron with slatted bamboo walls designed for maximum air circulation in the humid climate.

Dozens of Darwin people went to the Post Office that morning between nine o'clock, when the doors were opened, and nine fifty-eight, when they shut forever. I was one of them. Few lingered under the verandah protecting the private mail boxes; there was an air of tension, as though the men and the few women going about their business were subconsciously aware of imminent tragedy.

The postmaster, Hurtle Clifford Bald, had already made his daily issue of stamps to the clerks when the doors opened. Several dozen people seeking attention were at the small general delivery counter but they gradually dispersed and by 9.45 the flow of traffic was normal. Bald sat in an office so badly lit that he kept a window and door open. This was his second term in Darwin. In 1928, as a young man, he had come north from Kapunda in South Australia and stayed for six years. In 1934 he returned to S.A. to serve as postmaster at Kadina, Port Lincoln and Glenelg. His work brought him under official notice and he was promoted. Darwin, meanwhile, had become a military outpost and as the situation in the Pacific deteriorated its importance was enhanced. The naval and air bases were reinforced. New Army barracks had been built and several thousand troops sent to the area. It was the point at which the overseas cable from London reached Australia, and both the last and first ports of call for flying boats operating the empire airmail service between Sydney and Singapore.

In 1940 Bald, then forty-seven, volunteered to return as postmaster. His wife, Alice, and daughter, Iris, aged nineteen, went with him. All took a keen interest in the town's social and sporting life. The only member of the family not in Darwin was a fifteen-year-old son, Peter, who was completing his educcation at Prince Alfred College, Adelaide. His fare had been paid on a Guinea Airways flight that would take him north to his family for the Christmas holidays. A few days before he was due to leave an airline official telephoned to say that the plane had been commandeered by the Army. It was arranged that he would be put on a later flight. While waiting, Peter Bald went to a sheep station at Hallett, S.A., to stay with an uncle and aunt, Mr and Mrs R. K. Tiver. In that period the military situation worsened rapidly; civilians were being evacuated from Darwin and the young man was told that he would not be allowed to go there. Within a few weeks he was to be the sole surviving member of his family.

Archibald T. R. Halls, one of two supervisors, was in charge of the day shift in the telegraph office. He had been in Darwin exactly five days, having arrived from Stirling, S.A., where he lived with his wife and four children.

A few minutes before ten o'clock Halls was testing the telegraph circuit to Adelaide. Heavy traffic was on hand, including priority military messages, and there had been some technical difficulties in clearing it. Halls was "speaking" on the circuit with the chief transmission engineer in Adelaide, Francis P. O'Grady, who later became Director-General of Posts and Telegraphs.

At two minutes to ten Halls broke off the "conversation" with this telegraphed message to O'Grady:

"*Sec.* (meaning wait a second).
There's another air raid alarm.
I'll see you shortly."

He never did. That was the last message sent from the Darwin Post Office. Within a minute or so Halls was dead.

As we have seen, the first bombs fell on the wharf and shipping but probably less than two minutes elapsed before the police barracks, Government House, the Administration offices and the Post Office were being attacked. At least six bombs each weighing more than one thousand pounds fell in this area. One excavated a crater twenty feet deep and forty feet in diameter in almost solid rock.

Of the ten people killed at the Post Office, nine were crouched in the postmaster's garden in what was thought to be the safest shelter in the vicinity. They were Hurtle Bald, Mrs Alice Bald, Miss Iris Bald, Mrs Emily Young, Miss Eileen Mullen, Miss Jean Mullen, Miss Freda Stasinowsky, Mr Archibald Halls and Mr Arthur Wellington. A bomb landed almost on top of them and completely demolished the shelter. They died instantly.

Iris Bald, then aged twenty, had arranged that in the event of a raid she would go to a trench at the Taxation Office where she worked. It was an accident of fate that she was at the Post Office when the raid began and quite naturally took shelter with her parents.

Jean and Eileen Mullen had been living at the Victoria Hotel in Smith Street but had transferred that morning to a vacant departmental house on The Esplanade. Soon after she began duty Jean Mullen answered a call into the main switchboard and recognised the voice of Dennis Connors, who had been sharing a table at the Victoria with them.

"What's the right time please, Jean?" Connors asked.

"Oh, is that you Dinny?" she said. "It's right on nine-forty. By the way, we won't be seeing you for lunch. Eileen and I have moved into our new home."

"I'll send you a couple of chickens as a house-warming present," Connors said.

"Thanks, Dinny. You do that, and then come and help us eat them."

Twenty minutes later she and her sister were dead.

Freda Stasinowsky, aged thirty-five, was the fourth child in a South Australian family of nine. She had volunteered for work in Darwin in 1941. Just before leaving she went to Morgan, on the River Murray, to say goodbye to her mother and father. She was in high spirits and excited at the prospect of a long trip across the continent.

At 9.30 a.m. Constable Robert Darken, a tall handsome grey-eyed man with the sharp angular features of the fondly-imagined "typical" Digger, went to the public library from the police station one hundred yards away. He intended to borrow a book.

One of the other borrowers in the library was Iris Bald. Darken remembered that he had promised to lend her a novel.

"If you walk back to the police station with me I'll get it for you now," he said.

Iris Bald couldn't spare the time. "I'll come for it later today," she said.

They left the library together and walked towards the Post Office. Iris crossed Mitchell Street at about 9.45 and walked through the public entrance on the way to her home next door. Darken turned left and went back to the police station. He was standing on the verandah when he heard the planes and realised instinctively that the engine noise was not that of Wirraways, Kittyhawks, Hudsons or any of the other types he could recognise.

Darken's first thought was for his mate, Constable (now Sergeant) Dave Mofflin, who had been on night duty and was in bed asleep. Darken ran to his room, pulled him out of bed bodily, and was pushing him through a rear door of the police barracks when bombs began falling in the area.

Blast from the first bomb on the police barracks itself blew both Darken and Mofflin under a cement tank stand near the door. A three-thousand gallons tank, full of water, was on the stand. By the end of the raid it had disappeared and Darken never saw it again.

Surrounded by the fury of war and of falling masonry Darken asked Mofflin if he was all right.

"I think my leg's been hit," Mofflin said. "Maybe it's paralysed; I've got no feeling in it at all."

"I think I've been hit too," Darken said. "I've got a sharp pain in the leg." They were lying close together beneath the stand. Darken looked down and saw that Mofflin was pinching a leg to establish "feeling" — but Darken's rather than his own. Later Darken recovered the mattress Mofflin had been sleeping on from the branches of a tree fifty yards from the room, which had been blown to pieces.

While lying under the tank stand Darken thought of Iris Bald. When the raid ended he went to the Post Office and was in time to help police colleagues lift her dead body and those of her parents on to the tray of a truck that would take them to the morgue. A garage proprietor, James Young, arrived and found the dead body of his wife.

Earlier in the morning Iris Bald had made a date to attend the Star Theatre that night with Leslie Penhall,[1] an eighteen-year-old clerk in N.T. Administration. Soon after making the date Penhall was sitting behind his desk in the Administration offices on The Esplanade. Nearby were two other young clerks, Jim Pott and Con Parker, who both still live in Darwin.

Shortly before ten o'clock Pott looked out of a door facing south and saw the sun shining on silver metal aeroplanes. Then he heard the engines.

"Come and see these kites," he said.

Parker and Penhall joined him at the door. As the planes were flying from south to north across the town none suspected that they might be Japanese — until a few seconds later the wharf erupted.

"They're not ours!" Penhall shouted.

The three men began running, each in separate directions. Penhall went back through his office, out past the police barracks and across Mitchell Street, intending to seek refuge on the face of a cliff which sloped one hundred feet from the south-western side of The Esplanade to the beach below. To do that he had to run between a tennis court and the Post Office. Several bombs had already hit the area. Penhall noticed that

[1] Later Assistant Director of Social Welfare in Central Australia.

two had landed on the tennis court, one on either side of the net. As he was about to run down the cliff a bomb landed squarely in the Post Office yard less than ninety feet from him. The blast precipitated his leap but not before a piece of shrapnel had torn a hole in the sleeve of his shirt and caused a superficial wound in his left arm.

"I reached the bottom of the cliff on my face," Penhall recalls.

While there he thought of Iris Bald, who was already dead. He lay beside a log while Japanese fighters strafed the anti-aircraft battery on the Oval. Penhall was directly in the line of fire as the pilots pulled out of their run. Bullets splattered on the rocks around him but he wasn't hit. Nor were any of about twenty other men, mainly postal workers, sheltering there with him.

Reginald Rattley, then a twenty-six years old telephone mechanic, is one of few survivors who has a fixed opinion of the exact time of the bombing that differs from others.

"The Post Office clock stopped at nine-fifty," he says. "It had been going a few minutes earlier. I know because I checked my watch by it. The blast just about knocked it off the wall but the hands were undamaged and I reckon it proves the time the bombs fell."

Most people, including the Royal Commissioner, are agreed the raid began at two minutes to ten. Military time was not synchronised between the R.A.A.F., Army and Navy and no accurate record was kept. My own watch showed 9.58. But I have spoken to people who are adamant in their divergent opinions fixing the time at 9.30, 10.15, 10.30, 10.45 and as late as 11 a.m.

A few minutes before the raid Rattley had been in the telephone exchange where he talked with the Mullen sisters, Freda Stasinowsky, Mrs Bald and Mrs Young. The telephonists were all extremely busy; the manually operated switchboard was jammed with calls from military and civilian subscribers. Nevertheless, they found time to greet Rattley. After checking his watch by the master clock he walked from the exchange to the telephone technicians' office where he talked with Walter Rowling, his foreman.

"What do you think of our chances today?" Rattley asked.

Rowling was pessimistic. "We're going to get it in the neck," he said. The night before they had been on The Esplanade together and watched the Timor convoy return. "What hope have we got with that target to tempt the Japs?" Rowling had said then. "You can't tell me they won't follow them in."

When the sirens sounded Rattley said to Rowling, "Probably just another alert."

"Alert be damned!" Rowling said. "I'll bet this is fair dinkum." They were among his last words.

The two men went through the door of the technicians' office and saw and heard the first salvo of bombs. Rattley ran towards a trench he knew had been dug in the yard of the postmaster's residence but Rowling went elsewhere.

Rattley saw that Bald, his wife and daughter, the telephonists, and Halls and Wellington, were already in the trench. He managed to get in, too, but left again at once.

"It was like a rabbit warren," he says.

For a few moments he walked around aimlessly, wondering where to go. Then he went back to the exchange for no other reason than that it was home, the place he was used to, and there he felt a sense of quite unwarranted security. The first bombs had burst and the switchboard was abandoned. A few seconds later another stick straddled the block occupied by the Post Office and the cable company.

Rattley then believed he was in a prime target area. He ran through the door, crossed The Esplanade, and jumped for the edge of the cliff as another bomb struck. He was lifted bodily by the blast and hurled to the bottom. He came to rest near Penhall, temporarily unconscious.

Rattley remembers hearing the All-Clear. He climbed the cliff and reacted quickly when he saw the shambles that a few minutes earlier had been the post office and telephone exchange. He knew that people were dead or dying and he could see that nobody would have been able to phone for medical aid.

A truck came by and Rattley asked the driver to take him to the hospital, a mile away, to get help. There he found a young naval doctor willing to return with him to the Post Office. He does not remember the doctor's name. But he does remember that when they reached the Post Office the senior engineer, Harry Hawke, said: "There's nothing you can do here, doctor. They're all dead."

Rattley picked his way through the debris to the home of David O'Brien, a line foreman with whom he lived. O'Brien's car, an old sedan which had been parked in the yard, was now lying with its wheels in the air in the garden of the house next door. A crater covered the area where it had been. That was convenient, because Rattley discovered a need to use O'Brien's lavatory, a pan type which had stood in the yard. It had disappeared without trace so he used the crater.

As shock subsided Rattley realised there would be much work for skilled hands. The town's telephone circuits were silent. He would be needed to help in the restoration. He saw a red P.M.G. vehicle on the street. The cabin had been blown off so cleanly that neither the steering wheel nor the seat were damaged. He pressed the starter and the motor worked. With a load of other postal employees aboard he drove to a temporary Post Office already being established in Cavenagh Street and reported for duty.

Constable (later Sergeant) Eric McNab had been on plain clothes duty at the police station. With Constables Victor Hall, Bob Darken, Ron Brown and Sergeant (later Inspector) William McKinnon he was in the first police party to reach the Post Office when the raid ended.

After finding the remains of the nine men and women and having them identified, McNab saw shrapnel-riddled curtains flapping gauntly in the breeze in what had been the Balds' living room. He tore them down and wrapped them around dead women whose bodies had been stripped of clothing by blast. He took the keys of the postmaster's safe from a trousers pocket on Bald's body and handed them to A. A. ("Tom") Mansfield, of the postal section, who then became responsible for £26,000 in cash, stamps, money orders and other securities.

At 9.58 Mansfield was in the mail section sorting airmail into private boxes and general delivery. As the bombs fell he dropped the mail and went to a trench with Harold Nuttall, a postal assistant. Seconds after one bomb burst Walter Rowling, the telephone foreman who had been with Rattley, fell into the trench and said, "Oh, my bloody back; I've been hit." Mansfield and Nuttall wiped blood from his mouth and when the raid ended assisted him from the trench. He died on *Manunda* next day.

Mansfield returned to the Post Office to find mail and telegrams scattered like feathers. One of these had been addressed to Ralph Shepherd, a Public Works Department employee, who had come to the Post Office a few minutes before the raid expecting just such a message. The telegram with its glad news had been in the racks awaiting delivery but now was lost. Shepherd went back to work not knowing that his wife, in Perth, had given birth to a baby daughter. In the confusion that followed he did not learn for another six weeks that he was a father.

After discovering that he was the senior surviving postal clerk Mansfield and Albert Taylor, another clerk, cleared the counter tills, put the money in mail bags, identified each with the name of the appropriate clerk, and took it to his residence in Smith Street. He also collected money and securities from branch Post Offices at Larrakeyah, the R.A.A.F., Winnellie army camp and Vestey's depot, a total of £32,000. For several days he had sole responsibility for its custody.

Harry Hawke, the senior engineer, was sitting at his office table in a building adjacent to the postmaster's residence. With members of his staff he ran to a trench five yards from the office. He remembers seeing several bombs falling towards them, then hearing a rush of air "like the tearing of linen" as they approached. One exploded thirty yards from him at the rear of the linemen's store, and that was followed by several simultaneous eruptions.

"For about twenty seconds the area was completely blacked out as debris flew skywards and then fell around us," he recalls. "Our heads and shoulders were covered with dirt and small stones."

As Hawke, temporarily dazed, regained his composure he looked up and saw one of the main telegraph poles. The crossarm was broken in the centre and each half hung suspended at an agle of about thirty degrees. The wires had snapped and tangled and Hawke knew at once, even before the raid ended, that Darwin's telegraph connection with Adelaide and the rest of the world had been cut.[2]

Perhaps unwisely, Hawke left his trench while Japanese planes were still attacking shipping in the harbour. He was concerned for the telephonists and walked towards Bald's home where he believed them to be sheltering. A domestic water tank was tilted on its foundations and water poured from it. Beyond that he saw the remains of Bald's house. The rear walls and roof had gone. The lounge room was fully exposed with a piano and console radio standing against the one remaining wall.

Hawke climbed over the rubble and found a bomb crater at the spot where he had seen Bald personally excavating a shelter. Lying there were the broken remains of eight men and women. Hawke did not know until later that a ninth body had been blown into the fork of a tree. He was the first man to reach

[2] There was no interstate telephone service at that time.

them but they were beyond all human aid. He called for help in removing debris from one body in an endeavour to identify it; before he was able to do so dive-bombers came in dangerously close and Hawke and his colleagues were forced to return to their trench until the All-Clear.

Hawke then left the police and wardens to remove the dead and set about the vital task of restoring communications. The telegraph office was badly damaged. Part of the roof had fallen in. All window frames and door frames were blown out. The instrument tables were covered with debris, although little of the equipment appeared to be destroyed. In the telephone exchange, Hawke found, the ceiling had collapsed. The main distributing frame and switchboard were undamaged but were covered by inches of dirt. In spite of the mess it seemed likely that the telephonists might have survived the raid if they had remained in this exposed position instead of seeking the shelter of a trench.

The linemen's store had been wrecked by a bomb which struck a corner of the building. Tools and line stores were scattered over a wide area. Heavy cable drums were flattened or collapsed by concussion and blast. One drum of cable three feet in diameter and weighing four hundred pounds was lifted out of the yard and over an adjacent house to land in the street one hundred yards away.

Hawke had taken care for several weeks to ensure that his precious fleet of five vehicles was not needlessly congregated. At night they were dispersed. Yet four were near the Post Office that morning and all were badly damaged though useable; they were driven for days thereafter with broken hoods, windscreens and bonnets.

The postal hall was a shambles of rubble, having received the full blast of a bomb. But the engineroom and battery room and their equipment were intact apart from damaged windows. Hawke removed electrical fuses to prevent fire, then took a Morse key and sounder and a Morse relay and batteries and drove about one mile to the Lands Department offices in Cavenagh Street, where emergency telegraph lines from the main route had previously been installed.

One of the men with Hawke was William Duke, who was A. T. R. Halls' opposite number as telegraph supervisor on the night shift.[3] Duke had sheltered in a trench screened by sandbags and emerged with the All-Clear to find that the home

[3] Duke, Mansfield & Constable McNab were awarded the B.E.M.

THE SILENT LINES

he had occupied before his wife's evacuation, and most of their worldly goods, had been reduced to a pile of rubbish. He joined Hawke, lineman Herbert Page, telegraphists W. J. Hayles, Arthur Thompson and John Lyons in establishing an emergency link with Adelaide.

At that time Duke's wife and two small children were nearing the end of an eighteen hundred miles road and rail journey to Port Augusta, her home town in South Australia. As she stepped on to the Port Augusta station platform at noon Mrs Duke was told by relatives of a news flash that Darwin had been bombed and that nothing was known of casualties or survivors. She was then one of several thousand women scattered throughout Australia who waited anxiously for days and even weeks before receiving word from or about their relatives. But Peter Bald did not have long to wait for news of his parents and sister, Iris. He was roller skating on the verandah of the homestead at Hallett, S.A., when summoned by his aunt, Mrs. Tiver, and told that he was an orphan.

Emergency power was supplied to the temporary office at the Lands Department and the Morse apparatus connected. All lines on the Darwin side of that point were ordered by Hawke to be cut. Technical adjustments were made along the line to Alice Springs and the first message since Halls' 'Wait a second' to O'Grady was flashed to Adelaide forty-five minutes after the first raid ended. Hawke dictated while Duke operated the key:

> Hawke and Duke here. We have just had bombing raid which appeared centred on and near postal buildings causing much damage. Several officers' lives lost many injured. Post Office and PMs residence completely wrecked. Telegraph office and phone exchange appear intact but covered with much debris. Line shop and quarters occupied by O'Brien wrecked. Damage to motor vehicles. Regarding staff cannot locate postmaster but saw bodies what appeared to be his daughter and female telephonists. Will confirm loss life when wardens ascertain. Bombing commenced before air raid alert had ceased. Most officers caught at their posts. [There follows a list of names of survivors who had been seen, including the fact that Rowling was injured and in hospital.] Would like instructions as buildings not habitable and area vicinity PO too dangerous for staff or equipment to remain owing ships and oil tanks on fire, and centre of bombing targets. Staff must disperse widely at once. Can I use discretion regarding maintenance communica-

103

> tions and location temporary offices. Postal business will be impossible several days. All staff badly unnerved and do not desire remain in quarters near PO. Will endeavour billet them wherever possible. The scene of destruction at PO is most nerve wracking. Will remain here at Lands Office. Stations please keep lookout for us. Sec . . . getting more details survivors . . . Mrs Bald not seen . . . Nil of Bald family . . . Afraid Bald family and telephonists were in the shelter which received direct hit.

After sending this message Hawke realised that the building was not big enough to accommodate all his staff. Moreover, it was built of timber. Having seen the effects of bomb blast on stone it is understandable that he was worried about damage to vital equipment if the wooden building should be hit, either by high explosives or incendiaries. He was faced with the additional responsibility of restoring the local telephone service. The exchange switchboard was intact but all the female operators were dead. Nevertheless, the pressing need for telephone communication, especially between the armed services, seemed obvious. Yet when Hawke asked the Army to make available switchboard operators from the Signals Corps he was told that the exchange could be closed. The services would rely on their own field sets.

Meanwhile a second Japanese raid had taken place, concentrated on the R.A.A.F. aerodrome four miles from town. The main telegraph pole route followed the road and railway at a point close to the aerodrome, where wires were broken. As this was a military target likely to be subjected to further attacks Hawke decided to move the telegraph office far enough away to avoid continuous interruptions. He selected an abandoned fettlers' hut near the railway ten miles from town and moved for the second time that day. The Army agreed to give him food and tents for his men.

During the afternoon about fifty linemen, mechanics, telegraphists and other postal employees went back to the battered Post Office to retrieve what they could from their rooms. Most of them managed to find a stretcher, a mattress and a mosquito net, and with those they seemed reasonably content. They had a "home". The cooks salvaged enough pots and pans and other Mess equipment. When the first raid began one of the cooks, George McCarthy, was preparing a large saucepan of stew for the evening meal. He recovered it intact and watched it carefully during the ten-mile journey on the back of a truck; that

THE SILENT LINES

night the postal workers were among the few in Darwin who ate a hot meal. John Garth, a cook in another postal Mess, wasn't so fortunate; bomb blast wrecked his kitchen and a batch of scones which would have been eaten a few minutes later at the morning smoke-oh.

At 3 p.m., four hours after the message from Hawke and Duke, the telegraph line was again restored.

"I felt disappointed that we had been out of touch for so long at such a vital time but this was a matter beyond our control," Hawke reported.

By 5 p.m. a steady flow of traffic was being handled but military priorities ensured that Press messages written by three newspaper correspondents[4] were not accepted. These reports were sent on a Morse key from Katherine, more than two hundred miles away and thirty hours later, after the correspondents had reached the town by evacuee train to lodge them. Any value in the stories not destroyed by the passage of time (official announcements had been made and eye-witnesses had already reached Brisbane on the Qantas flying boat) was attended to by the military censors.

[4] Axel Olsen of *The Argus*, Melbourne; Merton Woods of *The Daily Telegraph*, Sydney; Douglas Lockwood of *The Herald*, Melbourne.

CHAPTER 9

Death and Escape at Government House

> *'I personally gave orders to the pilots not to attack the town.'*
> —COMMANDER FUCHIDA.

> *'Machinegunning harried the town more than the bombs.'*—OFFICIAL WAR HISTORY.

The Administrator, C. L. A. Abbott, and his wife, Hilda, were at breakfast on the louvred verandah of Government House when *Neptuna* weighed anchor and began moving up to the wharf.

Beyond the bougainvillaea, the frangipani, the bananas, papaws and coloured crotons growing profusely on the cliff overlooking the bay the Abbotts had an uninterrupted view of the ships at anchor, among them the white hull and red cross of the hospital ship *Manunda*. The morning was clear, but oppressively humid. Mrs Abbott might have wondered how long it would be before her husband's immaculately starched white shirt and trousers were limp with perspiration. She was not to know that within two hours cleanliness would be one of her smaller worries.

Charles Lydiard Aubrey Abbott, then aged fifty-five, was a World War I army officer who had risen from the ranks and been wounded on active service. He entered Federal Parliament in 1925 and in 1928-29 was Minister for Home Affairs in the Bruce-Page Government — the Minister then responsible for the 523,000 square miles of the Northern Territory that he would control as Administrator from 1937 until 1946. It was said of Abbott that he was far too strait-laced and insistent upon the proper observance of protocol to be at ease in Darwin's rather rebellious pre-war community. He was heartily disliked by unionists and Abbott let it be understood that the feeling was mutual. Those he wished to impress or regarded as social equals found him charming and affable; those he did not thought of him as stand-offish and a bit of a snob — a judgment that was natural enough in a cosmopolitan town whose residents resented government from Canberra and the controls exercised upon their lives by a man who had quasi-viceregal status. There was no Legislative Council, Administrator's Council or even a Municipal Council to advise and help him, nor did the people have access to him through any civic organisation that might have been regarded as expressing a unanimous view. He did not have the close contact with people that contemporary Administrators enjoy, a fact that contributed to distrust and dislike. But it cannot be said the fault was on one side more than the other, and in retrospect it appears that Abbott's term was no less successful than that of some of his predecessors and successors.

As he sat at breakfast with his wife on that fateful morning his military training must have alerted him to the imminence of air attack and perhaps invasion. Indeed, he had already arranged that in the event of an air raid the staff at Government House should shelter under his office in the western grounds. The office was strongly built, abutting from the side of a slope with reinforced concrete pillars supporting a concrete floor. Beneath the floor was a concrete strongroom with a thick iron door. Abbott sought expert engineering advice on the suitability of this under-floor area as a shelter and was told that it was safe against anything but a direct hit.

Abbott had a walk of only thirty yards from his private verandah to the office, a walk made pleasant by the beauty of tropical shrubbery and the harbour spreading below him to its western shore six miles away. His first appointment was with the chief accountant, Alex Fyson, who had been instructed to get his staff away to Alice Springs that day. Fyson was still with the Administrator when the sirens sounded. Abbott told him to return to his own office and Fyson left, but on his way across the hundred yards or so between Government House and the Administration headquarters he was flung to the ground by blast from a bomb. He reached safety and was later treated at the hospital for bruises and abrasions. Although badly shocked and suffering violent headaches he took his account books and ledgers to Alice Springs, a five-days journey. There he agreed to go to hospital and was found to have a fractured skull.

Meanwhile Mrs Abbott, her servants and the Government House staff hurried across the lawn with small bags of necessities to take shelter under the office. Those present were Abbott and his wife; Elsie Kilmartin, a part-aboriginal maid; Daisy Martin, aged eighteen, also a part-aboriginal maid; Charles See Kee,[1] a young Chinese who was Abbott's personal secretary; a Russian chauffeur, Nicholas Kampur, and his wife Katherine, who worked as Government House cook; Billy Shepherd, a part-aboriginal gardener and his aboriginal wife, Lucy; and Leo Goodman (or Midwei Alinggudum) of the Marananggu tribe, a young aboriginal who swept the verandah and grounds.

Abbott directed that they should all go as far as possible under the building for maximum protection. Almost at once a bomb burst in the grounds only fifteen yards from the office. He recalls: "The entire office structure seemed to rise in the air. The concrete floor above us lifted and the reinforced pillars snapped like dry sticks; then it settled down amid the crash and rumble of falling masonry and grey dust. The bomb obliterated one half of the office, making a crater twenty feet deep and thirty feet wide. The walls and floor were blown in and a huge block of concrete fell on Daisy Martin, burying her from head to waist and killing her instantly. I remember seeing her legs twitch and stop. Leo Goodman was pinned by one leg and called out in fright. The driver and I were half an hour trying to extricate him. My wife and the others hurried down the face of the cliff to take shelter and stayed there until the raid was over."

On inspecting the ruins of the office later Abbott realised that they would all have been crushed under the collapsing concrete floor but for the steel door of the strongroom which had been swung open by the blast and jammed under one corner of the floor, holding it up.

Nor was this the only attention the Japanese gave Government House. Fighter pilots machinegunning men on the ships and in the water became aware that the Australian blue ensign was flying from the flagstaff on the lawn. This appeared to infuriate them and they fired at it continuously in an attempt to shoot it

---

[1] When See Kee joined the others under the office he left on his desk an engraved Parker pen he had bought in Shanghai. The pen was lost in the rubble of the office and See Kee, who shortly afterwards joined the R.A.A.F., forgot about it. In 1945 he returned to Alice Springs to resume work. A desk had been allotted to him. Lying on the fresh blotting paper was the pen he had lost three years earlier and one thousand miles away.

DEATH & ESCAPE AT GOVERNMENT HOUSE

down. But while riddled with bullet holes (the large white star was completely shot away) the flag continued to fly.[2]

The road to Government House was almost impassable, being piled high with debris scattered by the bombs. Abbott's first visitors included the government secretary, L. H. A. Giles, who had blood dripping from a wound in his forearm; Major-General D. V. J. Blake, the military commandant; and the chief of police, Superintendent A. V. Stretton. Abbott instructed Stretton to mobilise the police and arrange with the Railways to prepare an evacuee train.

Mrs Abbott left by road for Adelaide River the same afternoon. She drove her own car with the Russian cook, Mrs Kampur, beside her. In the rear seat was Elsie Kilmartin and Leo Goodman. That night they all lay down together on a tarpaulin in the garden of Mt. Bundey station homestead near Adelaide River. Next day they joined an evacuee train to Larrimah, then resumed driving and five days after the raid reached Alice Springs. Her fellow travellers included Mrs C. E. Herbert, of Koolpinyah station, the eighty-four years old widow of Judge Herbert, who had been Administrator from 1905 to 1910; the Bishop of Darwin, the Right Reverend Francis Xavier Gsell; Dutch doctors and their wives who had been flown to Darwin from the Netherlands East Indies; an American consular official; Catholic nuns, and thirty-five part-aboriginal children.

Among them, too, were the Bleeser family, who conducted a store in Darwin; and the wife and twenty-years-old daughter of Lieut.-Commander J. C. B. McManus, the Navy intelligence officer who had received the first warnings of the raid. Florenz Bleeser had given a lifetime to the N.T. He was a naturalist who spent every spare moment collecting botanical specimens. He died during a cold winter in the south, heartbroken by the news that his carefully annotated specimens, zoological and botanical books and indexed photographic plates, the result of fifty years work, had been thrown out of his home by looters and trampled and destroyed in a day.

[2] Abbott realised that this was the first flag damaged by enemy action on Australian soil and as such had historical significance. Another was found for the flagstaff; the damaged one was lowered and has since been preserved in the War Memorial at Canberra. On the day peace was celebrated the flag flew behind the Governor-General, then the Duke of Gloucester. It had noble company, being flanked by others that had flown at Villers-Brettonneux in World War I, and by the flag from *HMAS Sydney* when she sank the Italian cruiser *Bartolomeo Colleoni* in the Mediterranean.

Arthur Miller, the chief A.R.P. warden, was living in the Administration officers' mess at Myilly Point near the civil hospital. The cook, Billy Byers, gave him eggs and bacon for breakfast. Miller then said goodbye to him and prepared to leave for work at the Survey Office in Cavenagh Street. Byers was resting on his bed. "Goodbye, Arthur," he said, "I'll give you a good stew for lunch."

For several days Miller's Survey Office staff had been packing vital records dating back to 1863. With land titles which had already been sent to Alice Springs the records filled more than one hundred wooden cases.

The North Australia Railway operated three hundred and forty miles of narrow-gauge track between Darwin and Birdum. It was plagued by a shortage of rolling stock to cope with increasing military traffic and by a loss of skilled employees to the fighting services. These were among the reasons why the survey records were still in Darwin in danger of being destroyed by enemy action.

Miller, however, had prevailed upon the railways manager, Keith McDonald, to get them away on condition that men from the Survey Branch went to the station yard at ten o'clock on February 19 to help with the loading and also to help *push* rail trucks into a siding.

At 9.58 Miller was waiting outside his office for Cecil Goodman, an employee who was to drive him to the station. He looked up and saw aeroplanes and bombs dropping from them. The chief warden ran into the main office and shouted, "Get to your shelters! The Japs are here!" Then he heard the siren.

As chief warden, Miller had a demonstration slit trench at the rear of his office. It was big enough to accommodate the fourteen members of his staff but when they reached it not one of the men who had helped with the digging could get in.

"It was overflowing with cuckoos," Miller recalls.

He walked around the side of the building to the front fence and there saw Alf Shepherd, a veteran of the Battle of Mons, sitting unperturbed on the steps, watching planes diving and bombs falling as though at a cricket match.

"You get a good view from here," he said.

Miller stayed with him while a fighter machine-gunned Daly Street nearby. They saw a man run and throw himself into long grass just as a dog at his heels was hit, rolled over and lay still.

When the raid ended Miller and Goodman went to the A.R.P.

headquarters in Mitchell Street. A number of wardens had reported for duty. They included Ray Foskey, who says that at the height of the raid, in the infernal din made by bursting bombs and shells and the roar of aircraft engines, he said to a colleague, "What a hell of a noise!" The warden replied, with a finger to his lips, "Sh-h-h; they might hear you."

Miller pinned a red and blue armband on his khaki shirt and left at once for the Post Office, aware of hostility in the stares and manner of civilians and servicemen who had already gathered to watch bodies being taken away. This was explained when a man shouted at him, "Get out, you military copper bastard!" His khaki clothes and the A.R.P. armband made him look like an M.P.

Miller saw the chaos and the death that had been brought to the Post Office and knew that, in that place, his armband was useless and he was helpless. War had come there with devastating ferocity. He looked at the body of Hurtle Bald, a close friend who had died quickly but with terrible violence, and was aware of the futility of his task.

After attending to the needs of shipwrecked seamen and visiting the police station to get casualty figures he drove more than a mile across town to the vicinity of the hospital, which had also been hit. A house in Lambell Terrace opposite the hospital had been wrecked and the Administration officers' mess, where he had breakfasted, was badly damaged.

Miller searched in the rubble outside and inside the Mess for Billy Byers. He called his name but received no answer. Meat and vegetables were set out on the kitchen table ready for the promised stew. At the door of Byers' room Miller saw that the iron bed on which he had been lying that morning was no longer there. It had been driven through the wooden floor by a boulder he estimated to weigh five hundred pounds. This had been thrown up in one piece from a crater next door and hurled through the roof to land squarely in the middle of Byers' bed. The floor caved in and the bed, with the boulder still on the mattress, now lay beneath the splintered timbers. But no trace of Byers could be found.

The downstairs lavatory had been shattered and fluid leaked from shrapnel holes in the pan. Two punctured tanks were spurting rainwater. The Mess kept its own poultry — a few Black Orpingtons and Rhode Island Reds. All were fast asleep on their roosts. Miller lifted a hen into his arms and spoke to it soothingly. "What's happened to you, old girl?" The hen clucked contentedly, was put back on the perch, and again fell asleep. Miller assumed they were either suffering from shock or the pall of smoke from the harbour made them think night was falling.

Several hours later Billy Byers was seen walking aimlessly down the main street. He was dazed but otherwise unhurt.

Abbott's chief responsibility as Administrator was to evacuate the remaining civilians. At noon he ordered Miller to send away all women, wounded and old men. He has recorded that apart from nurses there were then only four or five women in the town and no children. There were in fact sixty-three women and thirty-five part-aboriginal children.

The evacuees were to be put aboard a freight-train, mainly of flat-top trucks and cattle trucks. Miller made his evacuation headquarters at Parap police station, two and a half miles from town. His assistants included Mr Justice Wells, of Northern Territory Supreme Court, and Constables Lionel McFarland and Ron Brown.

Shipwrecked sailors had been arriving at Parap since noon. They had no food, no money . . . nothing except the clothes they wore.

"Which way is Adelaide?" one asked McFarland.

"Straight down that road," McFarland said. "Two thousand miles down the road."

Many of them were undeterred and began walking south. Later in the day Judge Wells sent a truck to bring them back to Darwin. They came without protest and were billeted in homes that had suddenly become vacant.

Miller sent civil defence assistants to collect food for the evacuees on a proposed journey by rail and road one thousand miles to Alice Springs that would take at least five days.

"Where do we get it?" Ted D'Ambrosio, one of the wardens, asked.

"I don't care. Find it," Miller said.

"How do we pay for it?"

"Charge it to that well known Chinese gentleman, Mister ARP."

On orders given without legal power by wardens patrolling their sectors, women and old men began to arrive for embarkation. They included many who had previously defied the authorities with "We are not leaving our homes." Now they asked, "How soon can we go?" They were beaten and frightened. They included two coloured children in Sunday bonnets who had been hidden by their parents when evacuation was ordered in December and had been kept in hiding since. But they did not include the part-aboriginal girls, who were taken by road to Adelaide River and joined the train there.

One of the women was Mrs John Taylor, wife of a doctor who treated wounded throughout that day and night. Mrs Taylor had remained in Darwin to operate the hospital switchboard. During the raid she was struck on the knee by shrapnel and was one of her husband's first patients. She had to be carried aboard the train. Another was Miss Ena Dalton, a twenty-five-years-old teacher who had taken an essential job in order to remain in Darwin through the evacuation. She ran the kitchen at Parap police station, recruited a staff of volunteer women, and began preparing tea and sandwiches for the journey. Many of the evacuees had not eaten since breakfast.

An air raid alert sounded before the train was ready to leave. Those who were able began to run for shelter. If a raid developed the train would almost certainly be a target. A Chinese girl screamed in panic. Miller hit her across the face with his open hand and told her to "shut up." She did.

"Keep your places on the train or you'll be left behind," he shouted to the others. "It's probably a false alarm." He was guessing, but the bombers did not come.

Several young men tried to get on the train and some had threatened Miller when he refused permission. He realised that if the numbers grew two or three policemen might have difficulty controlling them. He was also concerned that the train would become overcrowded and the meagre food ration inadequate. So he sent to Larrakeyah Barracks for armed protection. Two soldiers arrived with Tommy guns and asked Miller for instructions.

"A live burst at the feet of any young man who tries to get on this train," he ordered. "But don't kill anyone." There was no more trouble.

The name of every evacuee was taken. Soon after four o'clock, with about seventy passengers sitting and standing exposed on the flat-tops and in cattle trucks, Miller gave permission for the train to leave. Then he was told that an unexploded bomb had been found buried in the centre of the line near the aerodrome, and he had to make a dreadful decision. Heavy casualties were inevitable if the bomb exploded while the train was passing over it. Yet he knew that a train had come into Darwin since the raids without disturbing the bomb. Delaying departure until it was removed could be equally dangerous if the Japanese returned.

"Go now," he told the traffic officer. "Tell the driver to take it quietly past the aerodrome."

A contributory factor to the confusion that still exists over the exact time of the bombing was that the Darwin Court of Summary Jurisdiction was in session and one case had already been heard when the first bombs fell. The Court normally sat at ten o'clock but the Stipendiary Magistrate, Mr C. K. Ward, began that day's hearings by a clock that was twelve minutes fast.

Richard C. Ward, a young Melbourne barrister who had come to Darwin to join A. Brough Newell in a law partnership, was defending Patrick Murray, a client charged with keeping a common gaming house.

Deric Thompson was sitting at the court clerk's table and Joseph Wesley Nichols, a big man weighing more than twenty stones, was waiting to relieve him. The court clock showed ten past ten when the Magistrate imposed a fine of ten pounds. Defence counsel rose and asked for time to pay . . .

"How much time does the defendant want?" the Magistrate asked.

"Twenty-four hours, Sir."

At that moment Dick Ward heard the sirens, looked out the court window, and saw bombs falling on the wharf. The defendant did not know it yet, but he could have had more time than he asked to pay the fine.

"This Court stands adjourned . . ." the Magistrate said, rising with what dignity could be mustered in the urgency of the situation. The formal announcement of an adjournment seemed unnecessary when bombs were already falling on adjacent buildings, but legal tradition dies hard.

The Magistrate, counsel and several members of the staff ran to a trench at the rear of the courthouse which had been dug only a day earlier by Nichols, Thompson and an aboriginal named Tipperary. Two of the occupants were girls employed by the Crown Law Department, Miss Florence Wright and Miss Ella Cheong. Florence Wright subsequently married Richard Ward. Their romance might be said to have started in a trench during the first air attack on Australia. Ella Cheong was the bridesmaid.

When he appeared that morning as counsel for the defence

DEATH & ESCAPE AT GOVERNMENT HOUSE

Dick Ward[3] was actually Lance-Corporal Ward R.C., a member of the Australian Army. Although an able lawyer and brilliant advocate the army needed him. He was put to work as a clerk in the records section at Larrakeyah Barracks. His job was to rule column lines on pieces of paper. The columns, presumably, would later be filled with figures by sergeants and staff-sergeants but he did not have to worry about that; with only three weeks' experience as a soldier he was thought to be capable of ruling lines and nothing more.

On February 19 he was given leave to defend Murray. His partner, Brough Newell, had been commissioned in the army. The town's other lawyers had gone and Ward alone was available to help civilians in trouble. On each occasion the army had to be consulted.

Ward remembers that as he followed other court officers to the trench Murray ran out the front door and was wounded in the arm by shrapnel from a bursting bomb. In spite of that, he returned next day and the court record shows he paid the fine at a time when most other civilians had left town. One must assume that he regarded the fine as a gambling debt and therefore one of honour. The page of the court record book dealing with events of that day contains no reference to the precipitate adjournment, but is superimposed by the imprint of a muddy boot, apparently made by someone in a hurry.

Near the hospital later in the morning Ward saw James Wingham, an old-time resident who was obviously shaken. Although he knew the town well and was only a block from it he asked Ward to direct him to the hospital.

"Did you get hurt, Mister Wingham?" Ward inquired.

"N-n-no," Wingham said. "I just want to see if they'll give me something for a bad case of dysentery."

Ward returned to Larrakeyah Barracks. There he found more interest in digging slit trenches than in ruling paper. His pen and ink were exchanged for a shovel and crowbar. But the work was hot and before long he wanted a drink. He asked permission to go to his home in Daly Street on the pretext of protecting it from looters. Although the looters were chiefly soldiers like himself, he was allowed to go after explaining that the house contained valuables. What he did not explain was that the valuables, in large quantities, were predominantly the produce of breweries and distilleries. No one could doubt that

[3] Later he represented both Alice Springs and Darwin as a member of N.T. Legislative Council.

115

with a war on and the hotels closed his hoard amounted to priceless treasure. A welcome guest in the days that followed was a neighbour, Bill le Rossignol, who proved in the best way possible that his reputation as a sly-grog peddler was not unwarranted. For the first time in months le Rossignol did not have to fear police raids. On the contrary, Ward provided the roof and le Rossignol the victuals for what might have been called The Police Mess. The regular guests included constables who later achieved some eminence in the force. And there were wharf laborers, seamen and a couple of journalists. The house stood on top of piers eight feet high. Ward thought it wrong that his friends should have to run downstairs when the air raid sirens sounded so he installed a ground-level bar within easy reach of the slit trenches, taking care that bulk supplies were protected from possible bomb blast.

One day an army officer came to the door and asked if Ward was ready to rejoin his unit.

"Oh, yes, I think the place will be all right now," he said. "My mates will look after it."

He went back to the war . . . and just in time, too, for the records section, now fifty-six miles from town, had exhausted its supply of ruled paper.

Judge Wells was in his home on The Esplanade during the raid. His first act afterwards was to cross the Oval near his home to congratulate the young anti-aircraft gunners on their valiant fight.

Wells then walked to the Supreme Court where he directed Nichols and Thompson to save the records and a library of thousands of volumes of legal books. To Nichols, this was just another task. He already had twenty-six separate appointments; so many jobs, in fact, that he wrote letters to himself. As Sheriff of the Northern Territory, for instance, he often received instructions from the clerks of Supreme Court, the Court of Summary Jurisdiction, the Local Court and the Licensing Court — himself in each case. He was also Electoral Registrar and Registrar of Births, Deaths and Marriages, and it was in these capacities that his and Thompson's work in the next few hours was vitally important. The records included the registration of all births, deaths and marriages in Darwin since the 1890s.

Every register and every volume of the library was manhandled into trucks and taken ten miles out of town. At a lonely spot in the bush they were unloaded on to sheets of galvanised iron and covered with tarpaulins. There they remained for three

DEATH & ESCAPE AT GOVERNMENT HOUSE

weeks, at the mercy of the tropical monsoon, until arrangements were made to take them to Alice Springs.

It happened that while Nichols and Thompson were unloading one truck of books an American army officer who had been a lawyer stopped to ask what they were doing.

"We're putting a law library here," Nichols said.

The American shook his head in disbelief. "It's the first time I ever saw one in bushland," he said. "And a damn strange time to be doing it."

After seeing the Administrator, Wells went to Fannie Bay gaol and released thirty prisoners he had sent there from his court, some for capital offences. They included several aborigines to whom the Judge found it necessary to say: "Among you there are men I sentenced to long gaol terms for killing Japanese pearlers. I am letting you go. From now on you can kill as many Japanese as you can find. Instead of a gaol sentence the government will probably give you a medal." One can only assume that simple aboriginal minds must have been thoroughly perplexed by this change in the judicial attitude to killing.

The gaoler at Fannie Bay, Robert ("Jock") Reid, was sitting in the gaol office typing a report when an aboriginal prisoner, Stockman Jimmy, who had been sweeping the yard outside, came to his door and said, "Big mob aeroplane come high-up." Reid went out, saw the planes, and thought they were Japanese, an opinion confirmed by bombs within moments.

Instantly Reid ordered all dividing gates and doors within the gaol to be opened to allow free movement in the event of damage to the cell blocks. He then ordered prisoners and guards[4] to keep under cover and out of sight. But two prisoners at the rear yard gate with Guard Albert Orton were seen by a fighter pilot who had been strafing the civil aerodrome adjoining the gaol. The pilot turned, perhaps mistaking the guard's uniform for a soldier's, and came back with his guns firing. Bullets were embedded in the internal walls, one narrowly missing Reid's head.

All prisoners except one were now under cover. The exception was a native who had been washing the floor of the gaol hospital. He came out to cross the yard and join the other prisoners in the cell block, and Reid paused outside to usher him in. At that moment another fighter streaked over the gaol with guns blazing. Cannon shells ripped holes in the corrugated iron wall of the

[4] They included Tas. Pickersgill, later Chief Gaoler.

kitchen and one went through a bucket the native was carrying. The prisoner fell at Reid's feet, terrified but unhurt. He was trembling from toes to finger tips and pleaded, "Boss . . . Boss . . . let me go bush."

Reid tried to reassure him. "You stay with me Tiger and you'll be all right."

One might be pardoned for thinking that Tiger[5] would be made of sterner stuff, and immune to a little blood. Tiger had already served ten years of a life sentence for murdering two white prospectors named Koch and Stevens. He was an immense Brinken tribesman from the Fitzmaurice River district on the north-west coast of the Northern Territory. He was six feet four inches tall. His muscles rippled in the sun. He wore plaited rush bands on his arms. In tribal life he had been a naked warrior whose matted hair was bound with a headband of brilliant parrot feathers. His aspect was fearsome and it seemed unimaginable that he could be less than a man of unquenchable personal courage. In the face of Japanese bullets, however, he turned to jelly.

After being released, Tiger was first of twenty aborigines and ten white men to pass through the gate and he began running the moment he was free.

"He was overjoyed and I've no doubt reached his tribal country in record time," Reid says.

One only seemed reluctant to go. This was Stockman Jimmy who said to Reid: "Boss . . . more better I stay along you . . . you no-more got Missus now . . . you got nobody to look out for you . . ." Reid was touched by this demonstration of loyalty but persuaded Jimmy to leave after convincing him that he could be of more assistance by helping the police in his own country at Daly River.

Among the white prisoners was a young soldier who had received a heavy sentence a few months earlier. On being freed he reported to civil defence headquarters. After learning that he was trained in first aid Abbott ordered that he be put on the staff. He gave excellent service and his conduct was brought to the notice of the government. Later he received a free pardon.

[5] Tiger was a brother of Nemarluk, a crafty multi-murderer who killed three Japanese pearlers. When Nemarluk was arrested after one of the longest chases in N.T. police history and sentenced to life imprisonment (he died in gaol) his title as King of the Wilds was inherited by Tiger. He was to die violently himself — speared to death in 1953, almost in sight of the spot where he had killed Koch and Stevens. His murderer was a man who coveted Tiger's young wife.

DEATH & ESCAPE AT GOVERNMENT HOUSE

Meanwhile, beneath the cliff on the Fannie Bay foreshore two Greek contractors were working a stonecrusher. They were enclosed by small points of land, and the top of the cliff was thirty feet above them. Their view to seaward was obscured by the crusher, which clattered deafeningly. At noon they climbed to the roadway, mounted bicycles and began riding towards town. Then they saw black smoke rising above the town and were puzzled by it. At a road junction they passed dozens of vehicles of all kinds moving southwards. Finally one of the Greeks asked a countryman the reason for it all. Only then did they learn that they had lived and worked through two air raids without knowing that either had taken place.

A remarkable feature of the raid is that although more than two hundred and forty people were killed only fifteen were civilians working in the town itself, and ten of those died at the Post Office. A few incendiary bombs among the densely populated and poorly constructed buildings of Chinatown might well have doubled the total casualty list. This may lend substance to Japanese claims that pilots were instructed not to bomb the town.

Two men died alone. William Bowen, a Welsh laborer, lived in a camp at Frog Hollow. When strafing began he ran from his tent and sheltered behind a small tree. Apparently believing that since he was out of sight he was also out of danger — a belief quite commonly held — he decided to steady his nerves with a drink from a bottle of rum he had brought with him. Bowen was pulling the cork when a fighter pilot began machine-gunning the area at random. His body was found three days later. It had a bullet through the heart, a bottle in one hand and a cork in the other. Sidney de Mills is believed to have died in the same strafing run. He was a fifty-years-old fish trapper who also lived alone at Frog Hollow. Two bullet wounds were found in his body.

Most of the cafe proprietors left their premises when the All-Clear sounded, abandoning everything they contained. The Administrator sent Captain A. C. Gregory, a master pearler, to "raid" shops and cafes for potatoes, onions, vegetables, tinned and fresh meat and any other food he could find. Volunteer cooks were recruited by Superintendent Stretton and within an hour large pots of stew were being prepared for the shipwrecked and the homeless. Gregory visited Koolpinyah Kool Stores where the manager, Dennis Connors, told him: "Business as usual, Greg. We're staying open." Steaks were lying in sawdust on the floor. The front window was shattered. There was no electricity for the refrigeration plant. But Connors was as good as his word. With Jack Hayles, George Reid and Johnny Lopez he kept the butchery and iceworks operating without interruption until the end of the war.

While Connors and Gregory were talking the chief engineer of *Zealandia*, Bill McNamara, walked past with other members of the crew.

"I thought you'd be getting your ship away," Connors said.

"We haven't got a ship," McNamara replied, "and that goes for a lot of others. And we haven't got anywhere to camp or eat."

One of Connors' visitors that day was Lou Curnock, officer-in-charge of the wireless transmitting station V.I.D. He walked through the broken shop window and said to Connors: "You know, Dinny, Father McGrath told us the Japs were on the way and I relayed the message to the R.A.A.F. at once. I got it at nine thirty-five and they had it two minutes later. But I don't think they took it seriously; they thought McGrath was a bit of an old woman."

Keith Jarvis, then aged twenty, was a cashier at Gordon's Don Hotel, known affectionately as The Bloodhouse. Like the three other hotels The Don had exhausted its supply of beer. The entire stock consisted of a few bottles of cheap spirits and liqueurs, previously unsaleable. The manager, George Adams, had opened the bar door before breakfast[6] and one or two hardy drinkers were lamenting the beer drought which had continued intermittently for several months. Broken bottles, papers, and rubbish lying in unswept gutters added to the stench from the hotel's open drains and the unsewered premises of Chinatown.

Jarvis heard the sirens and walked downstairs. As the bombs fell he ran behind a corrugated iron lavatory. Adams was on the floor inside. But theirs wasn't necessarily the most unpleasant refuge. Several men emerged from an unspeakable half hour in the Chinatown gutters. They went straight to the bar and gave their orders.

"A double creme de menthe."

"Cherry brandy, George. Make it a double-header. I've got to get rid of this stench somehow. Haven't got a drop of rum have you?"

"Gawd, could I do a beer! Did you smell that gutter!"

[6] Licensed hours were then 7 a.m. to 10 p.m.

DEATH & ESCAPE AT GOVERNMENT HOUSE

"I've got the Joe Blakes, George; give us a shot of somethin'. Anythin', long as it'll calm me nerves a bit and help get rid of that stink."

An hour or so later the hotels were closed by the police on orders from the Administrator.

Others who sheltered in gutters that day included Michael Paspalis and his wife, Chrissie. Paspalis is now a multi-millionaire and one of Australia's richest men. On February 19, 1942, they were running Roslyn Court, a new rooming house they had built in Smith Street. They were also catering for Qantas flying boats; this was regarded as an essential service and for that reason Mrs Paspalis had been able to remain in Darwin. Both ran from Roslyn Court as the bombs fell and lay in the Smith Street gutter, and there they stayed until the All-Clear. They had plenty of company. The Smith Street and Cavenagh Street gutters were almost fully occupied. That same morning Paspalis drove to Adelaide River, hoping he would be able to get his wife away. But from there the road was impassable so he returned to Darwin. That night he saw Captain W. J. Crowther, of Qantas, who agreed to take them both to Sydney on the flying boat early next morning. The food eaten by the passengers and crew on the long trip was prepared by Paspalis and his wife.

Roy Edwards was one of few men in Darwin that day who had been born there. It was principally a town of itinerants. His father was a pearling master who had employed Japanese divers, one of whom, Jiro Muramats, subsequently died in internment. An interest in aviation was nurtured by the pioneer aviators of the 1930s. When Hinkler, Kingsford Smith and others landed after long flights from England, Edwards was there to greet them. He won his own flying licence in 1935 and by 1941 was flying on emergency aerial ambulance trips. He now owns Newcastle Waters cattle station, a property of four thousand square miles.

Shortly before ten o'clock on the day of the bombing Edwards walked along a lane behind Jolly's store on his way to the Post Office. Near the public library he met L. R. McKenzie, secretary of the local division of the Red Cross. They stopped to chat. They were joined by Mrs A. M. Bleeser on her way back from the Post Office. Edwards asked her if many people were waiting there to be served.

"It's no good going now," she said. "There are so many people you'd wait quarter of an hour."

McKenzie and Edwards continued their conversation. Two minutes later they heard aeroplanes. For Edwards their arrival was significant and fortunate. He was already a substantial property owner.

"Thank God, the Yanks are here at last," he said. "We'll be all right now. If the Japs hear of this lot they'll think twice before attacking."

McKenzie said, "What are those silver-looking things they're dropping?"

Edwards said, "Good God! They're Japs. Go for your life!" Simultaneously a siren wailed.

Edwards ran one hundred yards to what he thought would be the best air raid shelter in town, a reinforced concrete coldstore behind Koolpinyah butchery, of which he was part-owner. Not only was it adequate against anything but a direct hit but had the advantage of also being climatically pleasant on a torrid day. He settled down there to sit out the raid in comfort. His only companion was a young iceworks employee, Alf Brown.

"This is a good spot, Alf," Edwards said.

"I don't think it is," Brown said, "and we'll have to get out of here. What if a bomb breaks an ammonia pipe? We'd be suffocated." He had remembered that the network of pipes around them contained ammonia gas.

While bombs crashed down Edwards and Brown ran fifty yards to the rear of Wing Cheong Sing's store in Bennett Street. One member of the Wing family had recently returned from a part of China which had been under Japanese attack and had urged them to build a shelter. It was the only one of its kind in Darwin — an underground room of reinforced concrete with an air intake pipe — but at that moment it seemed to be the haven of every second Chinese in town.

As Edwards and Brown ran down the steps they were told by an Oriental voice: "No-more come in here . . . too many . . . too many."

"We pushed ourselves in," Edwards recalls. "There wasn't room for anyone to fall over. The shelter was twenty feet by twenty-five feet and there must have been two hundred people inside. Somehow there seemed to be safety in numbers. Alf Brown was much happier with a big crowd than he'd been with me alone. One thing I discovered is that in an air raid racial prejudice disappears instantly. A human being who might die next moment isn't interested in whether his neighbour is

European, Chinese or aboriginal. His heart beats heavily and he lives every beat because each might be his last."

Edwards was the only man in Darwin who owned a private aeroplane and therefore had no evacuation problem, or so he thought. For that reason his wife Ash, a former Matron of Darwin hospital, had stayed. During the raid she was alone at their home on The Esplanade except for an aboriginal factotum, George Mungalo. But when Edwards took his wife to the civil aerodrome to fly her to safety he found the plane riddled by machinegun bullets. They had to go on the evacuee train.

Two other Australian aviators were then ten thousand miles away in Washington, D.C. There the noted American poet and Librarian of Congress, Dr. Archibald MacLeish,[1] broke the news of the bombing to the wife of this country's first Minister to the U.S., Mrs. R. G. Casey.[2] He spoke to her of Australia as "your immaculate country." One assumes he used the adjective in its context of "never having been molested." It may have been the first time Australia was referred to in such terms. If so, it would certainly be the last.

Father William Henschke had come to Darwin in 1915 when Chinese merchants were using water buffaloes to haul carts along the unmade streets. He was Catholic parish priest and vicar-general.

On February 19 he rose at 5.30, observed his devotions, and at seven o'clock said a Mass in the modest wooden church in Smith Street. Henschke had been disturbed by reports of Japanese reconnaissance planes over Darwin but that morning his worry increased to alarm. He knew the lugger *St. Francis* was bringing nuns from a west coast mission at Port Keats but, worse still, the group of thirty-five part-aboriginal girls had arrived the night before from Garden Point, Melville Island. They were being cared for by Mother Adrian and four sisters.

After breakfast Father Henschke drove to the Post Office and spent half an hour on parish affairs. One of his self-imposed tasks was a daily visit to Jack Buscall, the crippled owner of Curio Cottage store. He arrived there at 9.45 to pick up Buscall's bank deposit, one of the kindnesses the priest did every week for the bedridden man. Buscall gave him a pay-in book and two hundred pounds in cash. Henschke left with the money at five

[1] *The Irresponsibles, A Time To Speak, A Time to Act, Freedom is the Right to Choose.*
[2] Later The Lady Maie Casey, wife of Lord Casey, Governor-General of Australia.

minutes to ten in order to be at the bank doors when they opened. He did not like holding such a large sum for longer than necessary.

"But I had a presentiment that something was wrong," he recalls. "Instead of going to the bank I turned in the opposite direction and drove back to the presbytery with all that cash."

As Henschke passed through the gates he was met by a group of the Garden Point children who were pointing skywards and shouting, "Look, Father! Look, look!"

"Run for your lives!" he shouted. "Get inside at once."

The girls and one three year old boy, Johnny Greddon, had been brought from Garden Point by Sister Annunciata, Sister Eucharia, Sister Antoninius and Sister Alfonso. An equal number of boys remained there and were cared for throughout the war by Father Connors, Brother Bennett and a part-aboriginal woman, Mrs Tom Liddy.

The girls and Johnny Greddon had been due to leave Darwin early that morning but at the last minute transport could not be found. After they had been sent running by Father Henschke **they were put under beds** on the ground floor of the Sisters' quarters and mattresses piled on top of them for protection.

Immediately after the raid the American army commander, Colonel John Robenson, provided trucks to take the children to Adelaide River. They were accompanied by the four Sisters from Garden Point, Mother Adrian, and Sister Gabriella. The Sisters wore blue working habits. Each child had a sugar bag containing a change of clothes and toilet articles. They were given half an open coal truck in which to travel.

Father Henschke returned to Curio Cottage after the raid and found Buscall still in bed. "I couldn't run; I couldn't go anywhere," Buscall said. "Did you get that money to the bank?"

Henschke admitted he hadn't and returned it to Buscall. "I don't think the banks will open today," he said. He was right, for they were closed by government order and the staffs and money evacuated.

Buscall adamantly refused to leave Darwin, in spite of the disappearance of most of his customers. Finally the Army insisted and he could not resist when lifted, bed and all, on to the tray of a military truck. He was driven around the streets to see his demolished town and then to an aerodrome sixty miles away for a flight that would take him out of The Territory forever. He died a year or so later.

CHAPTER 10

"All Patients Under Beds!"

> *'Large bombs caused damage to the Darwin civil hospital. An Army hospital at Berrimah was shot up. The R.A.A.F. hospital was bombed and damaged.'*—OFFICIAL WAR HISTORY.
>
> *'I did not know that hospitals were bombed and I am very sorry to hear of it.'*—COMMANDER FUCHIDA.

Darwin's only public hospital in 1941 was a ramshackle building of iron and concrete overlooking Doctors' Gully, which derived its name from the off-duty romances of young medical officers and nurses. It was ill-equipped and unsatisfactory. Moreover, the gate to Larrakeyah army barracks, an obvious target if war came, was only a few hundred yards away. The slightest miscalculation by bomber pilots might cause the hospital to be hit instead of the barracks. Work began that year on a new 130-bed hospital which cost £165,000 and opened in January, 1942. The building combined practicability with the most modern tropical hospital design; there were wide corridors and big open wards that could be made to accommodate many more than planned in an emergency. The operating theatre and obstetrical wards were said to be among the best in Australia. More than eleven thousand moveable fibro louvres had been used in the walls to ensure maximum air circulation. The hospital was segregated. Aborigines and part-aborigines, the latter known as half-castes but then treated as full-bloods, were confined in a special ward.

While taking all these factors into account the designers overlooked or ignored one of the vital reasons for relocation — to get away from Larrakeyah. The site chosen at Myilly Point on Kahlin Bay was no further from the military installations, as the bombs fly, than the old one had been. We shall never know with any certainty, therefore, whether the Japanese bombed it intentionally or were really aiming at Larrakeyah. The fact is that six heavy bombs fell near the hospital, causing extensive damage; the barracks across the bay were not hit at all.

On February 19, Surgeon-Commander Clive James, R.A.N.V.R., was scheduled to begin an appendix operation on a sailor at ten o'clock. The anaesthetist was to be Surgeon-Lieutenant A. James. The two were not related. Sister Audrey Jaffer, who had come from the Australian Inland Mission hostel at Alice Springs, was assisted by Nurse J. Palfrey in preparing the theatre.

Two minutes before ten o'clock Nurse Palfrey left the theatre to get the patient from the male surgical ward. On the way she heard the sirens and saw Japanese planes dropping bombs on ships in the harbour. She ran back to the theatre and said to Sister Jaffer, "Sister, the Japanese are here and dropping bombs."

Sister Jaffer had a pair of theatre lifters in her hand and was about to take swabs from a steriliser. She went with Nurse Palfrey to the verandah and was in time to see bombs falling around the hospital.

"My heart stood still," she recalls. "I ran to our quarters where I shared a room with Sister Eileen Elcock. When I got there I realised I still had the theatre lifters in my hand. I have them to this day."

Sister Elcock began changing her white uniform for brown overalls in the hope that they would be less conspicuous to the Japanese. Sister Alma Skerry had washed her hair and had it in butterfly clips, over which she now attempted to fit a steel helmet.

In the wards, patients who could do so were ordered to lie under their beds, leaving the mattresses on top for protection. Others ran for shelter beneath the cliffs of Kahlin Bay. Bedridden patients were lifted by wardsmen and nurses and placed under the beds. While this was being done the hospital was shaken by six heavy explosions. Rock, debris, glass and building materials were hurled up by the blast, damaging three wards and outbuildings. A naval ward was wrecked. Huge rocks crashed through the roof on to beds vacated only moments earlier but bounced off the mattresses without causing injury to any of the patients.

One patient in the aborigines' ward could not move, nor

"ALL PATIENTS UNDER BEDS!"

were enough staff present to lift him to comparative safety beneath his bed. He was Banya, a leading pagan member of the Gobaboingu tribe at Milingimbi on the Arnhem Land coast. He had been admitted with a rare form of paralysis believed to have been caused by eating a poisonous plant. Banya was terrified by the explosions and that was aggravated by the fear he could see around him. Several months later he recovered and was repatriated to Milingimbi. There he told a Fijian missionary, the Reverend Kolinio Saukuru, that he wished to renounce his pagan ways and become a Christian. He explained that when the raid began and other aborigines had run for the cliffs he had been left alone in the ward — alone, he said, except for one nurse who had stopped at his bed when she saw his distress and sat with him, comforting him, disregarding her personal danger while the bombs crashed down. "I understand Christianity now," Banya had said. "Show me how I can be a Christian."

Captain Aubrey Koch might have been pardoned for believing that the Japanese were following him and were determined to destroy him. As already related, Koch was captain of the Qantas flying boat *Corio* when it was shot down near Koepang on January 30, and had survived the crash and a long swim. He arrived in Darwin only a few days before the Japanese — in time to demonstrate the technique of sheltering under a bed. Knowing that he had been through it all in Koepang the nursing staff quickly followed his example.

Koch recalls: "Three of the bombs fell very close. The walls shook and pieces of the ceiling fell in. Nurses under the beds stayed there only a few minutes. When the first shock was over they returned to work and continued getting patients out. After the first wave of bombers passed I decided to make for the beach about two hundred yards away. I could just walk. A doctor and nurse helped me to a clump of bushes on the beach. Japanese planes were diving low and strafing the buildings. As I lay there I saw a Japanese fighter on the tail of one of our planes. When the first wave passed a nurse brought me a mattress and something to eat. Some patients wanted to return to the hospital but I warned them the Japanese would come back, and they did. During the second raid I kept low in the bushes in case the beach was machinegunned. I saw a sailor who had swum ashore from one of the ships. His lungs were injured by concussion and he'd haemorrhaged badly during his long swim. However, he arrived at the right place to get treatment."

Another patient was Charles Cudday, an employee of the Department of Civil Aviation who had been operated on for appendicitis less than twenty-four hours earlier. Cudday has given me the following account of his own reactions:

"I was lying in bed in a bit of a stupor as the anaesthetic had not quite worn off. I was chatting to the sister when the bombing started. I said to her, 'It sounds like an air raid.' She said, 'Don't be silly, if it was an air raid we'd have had an air raid warning.' Just then a chap came in, hobbling on crutches, then as the noise got louder and closer he went outside and a couple of seconds later came rushing back without the crutches shouting 'Bloody Japs! Bloody Japs!' Everyone raced out and got in trenches and among rocks and left me lying there in bed. Very soon the bombs fell closer and the plaster started falling off the ceiling so I put a pillow over my stomach as a shield. Well, after the raid was over everyone came back and, strange as it may seem, one is not afraid during a raid because you're wondering how your mates are. Well then the casualties started coming in and I had to have a look to see if I knew any of them. Then a priest came along and wanted me to make confession and be prepared in case there was another raid but after a lot of argument I got a bit hot under the collar and told him to go and look after the others as they were in more need of him than I was. Later the sirens went again and the Japs came back and I thought now this is where little Charlie will cop it because he didn't get prepared. Next morning the lot of us were taken to Berrimah hospital."

Sister Jaffer returned to the operating theatre when the raid ended. Surgeon-Commander James and Surgeon-Lieutenant James were already there and the postponed appendix operation was deferred indefinitely. More serious cases were on hand. The theatre was damaged but serviceable and surgery began at once. The first case was one requiring the amputation of a leg.

Anticipating such an emergency, Sister Jaffer had her cupboards packed full of sterile dressings and announced that if necessary she was ready to cope with a hundred theatre cases. Yet if all the patients had been sent to the theatre that would not have been enough. In the next few hours one hundred and forty-eight men were admitted to hospitals, most of them to the civil hospital. Sixty-eight had wounds caused by bomb fragments and bullets, and eighty had wounds caused by blast, flying debris and burns. Another seventy-eight were treated for lacerations, abrasions and contusions not requiring admission to hospital. Two had fractured arms not caused by bombs but by falls as they ran for shelter.

Casualties had begun arriving at the hospital within ten minutes of the first bombs falling. Thereafter the medical and nursing staff under Surgeon-Commander James and the Chief Medical Officer, Dr Bruce Kirkland, worked without pause throughout the day and far into the night. Matters were complicated by damage to the electric steriliser in the theatre and by the loss of blood, serum and saline stored in the ward that was demolished. Primus stoves had to be used to boil water. When emergency battery lighting failed after several hours' use the surgeons continued in the light of torches held by volunteers. Loss of the telephone exchange meant that communications had ceased between the hospital, A.R.P. headquarters, the Red Cross, the military services, and the hospitals at Bagot and Berrimah.

Sister Elizabeth Cousin had been Matron of the hospital from 1939 to 1941 but then resigned. In mid-December when the evacuation of women not in essential jobs was ordered she escaped going with them by resuming nursing. The new Matron, Sister Doris Knox, assigned her as sister-in-charge of the outpatients' department and there, on February 19, she had the busiest day of her life.

It did not start that way. By 9.30 she and Dr Rupert Catalano had treated only one patient. They stood together at the front door of the hospital, admiring the morning and waiting for business. Three quarters of an hour later the medical and nursing staffs[1] had on their hands a disaster involving more dead, dying and wounded than any previously on Australian soil.

Doctors rushed off to the theatres and wards. Apart from Kirkland, James and Catalano, they included Dr J. Taylor and Surgeon-Lieut. L. A. Hardy. Sister Cousin was left alone in the outpatients' department with instructions from Kirkland to give anti-tetanus injections where necessary, to suture the wounds she could, and to send on to him and other doctors in the wards only those cases she was unable to treat herself. The first casualties were escorted in by Constable Eric McNab and the Reverend C. T. F. Goy. Goy, with shaving soap on his face, had run to help a man shot in the shoulder near his church and drove him

[1] Several were decorated, including Dr. Kirkland, Sister Elcock and Sick Berth Petty Officer P. A. McKenzie. Dr. Catalano, Sister Cousin, Sister J. Morris and Nurse Edna Rawlings were commended for brave conduct.

to the hospital while the raid continued. McNab remained as a kind of casualty-ward receptionist, presenting cases in what he thought was the necessary priority to Sister Cousin. Between times he kept the floors clean and in his official capacity became the last custodian of dead bodies taken to the hospital. He also became a patient. Several days after the raid he was found to have four broken ribs, burst ear drums, amnesia and shock.

Events at the hospital were not without bitterness. Kirkland had arranged with the Army's senior medical officer, Lieut.-Colonel J. B. McElhone, that in an emergency the Army would contribute an operating team to the civil hospital. The team did not arrive, thereby throwing additional strain on the naval and civilian doctors and nurses, who were working as never before. In his official report Surgeon-Commander James had this to say: "In my opinion there was no adequate reason for the failure to adhere to this plan; even if there were a reason, there was no excuse for Dr Kirkland not being notified of the change."[2]

During the afternoon an urgent request was sent to the 119th Australian General Hospital for nurses to assist the civil hospital staff. Four arrived at once and, according to James, greatly relieved the strain that the civil nurses had been under since the raid began.

At five o'clock Sister Jaffer left the theatre for a hurried meal. She did not know it then, but the meal had been prepared by one of her own patients, Cook L. J. F. Hoffman of the Navy, who had assumed control of the hospital kitchen and worked unceasingly without electricity to prepare hot meals for the staff and patients. Sister Jaffer had been on her feet for seven hours and had not eaten since breakfast. On the way to the nurses' home she met Dr Kirkland and Matron Knox. Kirkland told her an evacuee train was leaving for the south (it had already gone) with all remaining women, as a Japanese landing was feared.

"We can't go and leave all these patients to look after themselves," Sister Jaffer said. Ten sisters, included Jaffer, volunteered to stay and were allowed to do so.

Sister Jaffer worked until eleven o'clock by which time she had been on duty for sixteen hours. An hour later she was relaxing in the nurses' dining room with her feet on the table. A distressed sister entered and said breathlessly, "Have you heard

[2] In the Medical History of the War, Volume II, there is this comment: "Relations between the Army Director of Medical Services and other senior medical officers were often not satisfactory."

"ALL PATIENTS UNDER BEDS!"

the dreadful news? They've released all the prisoners from Fannie Bay gaol!"

"I was most relieved," Sister Jaffer recalls. "I thought that perhaps the Japanese had landed."

"Will that matter?" she asked.

"Oh, yes, most of them are in for rape," she was told.

Sister Jaffer replied: "Good. If the Japanese are coming tomorrow then give me an Australian tonight."

Dr Kirkland, meanwhile, had been called to Larrakeyah Barracks for urgent consultations and returned at 1.30 a.m. on February 20 with Lieut.-Colonel McElhone. Surgeon-Commander James had just finished his last operation. His official report records that McElhone then demanded that all patients were to be evacuated at once to the 119th A.G.H. at Berrimah. McElhone said he had information that Larrakeyah Barracks were to be bombed during the following day. Why that should have warranted nocturnal evacuation of a hospital that had operated successfully under difficult conditions for many hours after having itself been bombed is not clear. Surgeon-Commander James said it was better to leave the patients where they were than shift them so soon after operations. He said that the A.G.H. at Berrimah, situated near the R.A.A.F. air base, was just as likely to be bombed as the civil hospital. James expressed his "strong opposition" to the move but was over-ruled. "A definite order was given by the army's medical director and I had no option but to comply with it under protest," he recorded.

Sister Jaffer was stopped on her way to bed and told to begin work again. Army trucks arrived before dawn and she helped supervise while three hundred civilian and service patients on stretchers, some still in a state of shock and others unconscious, were carried out to the vehicles. The walking wounded cared for themselves. While James argued his case for not disturbing them his last patient was left in the operating theatre. When he lost the argument the patient was taken directly from the theatre to a truck, the last in a convoy, in which Sister Jaffer also rode. "He was vomiting all over the place," she recalls.

Fifty rabbits and guinea pigs used by pathologists in testing for tuberculosis and other diseases were alive in the animal house at the hospital laboratory when the raid began. After his long day Dr Kirkland remembered them and decided that to avoid unnecessary cruelty they should be destroyed. He went to the laboratory prepared to give lethal injections — but the cages were empty. Kirkland assumed the animals had been

131

destroyed by someone else and was about to leave when he heard a voice from a house nearby.

"Looking for something, Doc?"

Kirkland crossed to the house, previously unoccupied, and found a group of twenty shipwrecked seamen and destitute wharflaborers who had taken possession. He explained that he had come to destroy the laboratory animals but couldn't find them.

"We found 'em first," a seaman said. "We ate the bastards."

Kirkland was horrified. "But they may have had active germs in their bodies," he said.

"We cooked 'em well," the seaman said.

Evacuation of the civil hospital meant that it was empty while the 119th A.G.H. became overcrowded.

The 119th arrived in Darwin in April, 1941, and occupied buildings at Bagot, four miles from town, originally intended to house sick aborigines. If Kahlin hospital was thought to be badly located militarily Bagot's position was worse, for it lay midway between the civil and R.A.A.F. aerodromes.

Accommodation for the staff was inadequate. Nursing sisters at first had to travel twelve miles a day in trucks between the hospital and their quarters at East Arm quarantine station. After a serious road accident in which a sister's arm was amputated the staff moved to tents and huts at Bagot. These were constantly swamped during the wet season. Laundry facilities were primitive but had to be tolerated.

Towards the end of 1941 a new 1,200-bed hospital at Berrimah, nine miles south of Darwin, was far enough advanced for the first three hundred patients to be accepted. A medical officer, Major J. H. Coles, the new Matron, Sister Edith McQuade White[3] and six other sisters began on December 30 to prepare the wards for occupation. It opened as an A.G.H. on January 1, 1942, with about eighty patients transferred from Bagot. As Kahlin also had a service wing this meant the A.G.H. was housed in three separate locations. Berrimah was as badly situated as Kahlin and Bagot; it was only one mile from the end of the main runway at the R.A.A.F. aerodrome and within half a mile of the flight path of planes taking off and coming in to land. One is not surprised that yet another branch of the

[3] Later Principal Matron in the Northern Territory.

"ALL PATIENTS UNDER BEDS!"

hospital had to be opened at Adelaide River, seventy-two miles away.[4]

On February 18 the first battle casualties were admitted to Bagot. They were eleven men who had been wounded in the attack on the *Houston* convoy. On February 19, Matron McQuade White was in her office at Berrimah when she heard the roar from an armada of aeroplanes.

"As soon as we were convinced they were enemy planes we got our patients under the beds," she recalls. "Some ran outside into the long grass. Other scrambled to a few slit trenches."

Low flying Japanese planes machinegunned four of the wards and one patient too ill to be moved outside was killed while sheltering under a bed. A machinegun bullet went through the roof, the mattress above him, and became embedded in the back of his neck.

Another tactical mistake seems to have been made with the location of an anti-aircraft detachment within a short distance of the hospital. Its machinegunners fired furiously and accurately and were credited with shooting down one Japanese plane. But they also received attention from the fighter pilots and so, by its proximity, did Berrimah hospital.

Soon every bed was occupied. Extra beds were erected on the verandahs and these, too, were filled. As at Kahlin, surgical teams led by Major Coles and Major J. M. Mack worked through the day and night. The nursing staff remained on duty for thirty-six hours. They were reinforced and assisted by physiotherapists.

Matron McQuade White was in the Admission Office when an ambulance drew up with a young American airman on a stretcher. His face was covered by blood-soaked bandages. The Matron directed stretcher bearers to a ward, placed the man on a bed, removed the bandages, and found a gaping wound down the centre of his face extending from the forehead through nose and chin. Haemorrhage was profuse. Matron McQuade White tried to arrest the bleeding and cleaned the wound as well as possible for inspection by a doctor. The patient had been restless and only semi-conscious but revived to ask where he was. When told he said, "I got one of those little yellow devils but one got me."

[4] By March 7 there was also a Casualty Clearing Station at Noonamah, 27 miles from Darwin, and a fifth branch hospital at Katherine, 220 miles away.

The airman was Lieutenant John G. Glover, U.S.A.F., who had parachuted to safety after his P.40 was riddled by enemy bullets. He was given an injection of morphia just as the Japanese began a second raid on the nearby aerodrome. Glover heard them and became anxious. Although in the comparative safety of a hospital, which had nevertheless been attacked, he felt exposed and defenceless without his own fighter plane. With the aid of an orderly the Matron lifted Glover, mattress and all, and put him under the bed. She stayed there with him, squatting, wearing a steel helmet that felt heavier every minute in such an awkward position.

Glover talked incoherently. He was shocked and had lost much blood. But the Matron soon became aware that in his more coherent moments he was agitated about the loss of two watches, one from each wrist. She remembers trying to console him by saying there was nothing to worry about, but his concern for the watches, rather than for himself, was apparent.

"There were two of them ... two of them ..." he repeated.

Morphia, meanwhile, had deadened his pain and as the raid ended he fell asleep. It was not until ten o'clock that night, almost twelve hours after he was shot down, that Major Coles and others of the Berrimah surgical staff were able to attend to his wounds.

Surgeons, sisters, nurses, physiotherapists and orderlies worked without pause until dawn. In the piccaninny daylight at six o'clock Matron McQuade White changed her uniform for the new day. She had not been to bed. As she did so she felt papers and other articles in her uniform pocket and remembered they had been given to her as Glover was passing through the Admission Office. They included a wristlet watch.

"I was pleased that at least one of the watches he had raved about was safe and I hurried back to the ward to deliver it, thinking how thrilled he would be," she recalls.

She was disappointed. "Thanks ... but where's the other?" Glover wanted to know. He repeated, "I had two, one on each wrist when I took off in that Kittyhawk."

The Matron was too busy to worry about a watch and hurried away. Shortly after leaving the ward she met a chaplain who showed her a watch he had picked up on the edge of the aerodrome beside a crashed aeroplane. It was still ticking.

"That will be Lieutenant Glover's second watch; he's been asking for it," she said, and returned it to him less than half an hour after walking away. Glover was overjoyed. He was well enough to be evacuated the same day on the hospital ship *Manunda*. Matron McQuade White met him again months later. The severe wound stitched by Major Coles had healed so that only a faint scar was visible down the centre of his face. He is now a Colonel in the U.S.A.F.

Two chaplains, the Reverend C. T. F. Goy (Presbyterian) and Father Jack Cosgrove (Catholic) visited the hospital. Goy remembers it well: "Every bed was occupied, some by merchant seamen who were groaning in pain, their bodies blackened by burning oil which had overtaken them in the harbour. Many were dying . . . in a strange place . . . some in a foreign land. Identification was difficult and often impossible. They carried no papers and we had no idea who they were or where they'd come from. Nor did we know to which faith they belonged. Jack Cosgrove and I were great friends. We said our prayers together for the dying so that whatever their faith, if indeed they were Christian, they had the benefit of their clergy's ministrations. In the same way we buried the dead by saying a joint funeral service over them."

This was a duty they also performed on the beaches where unidentified dead from the wrecked ships were washed ashore. As shore burial was impossible, and as piles of decomposing bodies made it urgently necessary, Surgeon-Commander Clive James had them placed on a barge on February 20 and taken out for burial at sea.

Matron McQuade White had just returned from giving Glover his second watch when a convoy of military trucks drew up at the entrance. Nursing and medical staff from Kahlin hospital with their patients had arrived and wanted to be taken in. They included Sister Audrey Jaffer, who was still caring for the man taken directly from the operating theatre to her truck.

"Sister Jaffer, I presume?" the Matron said. They were old friends.

Berrimah was full, but Edith McQuade White took in her stride the arrival of another three hundred patients and staff.

Sister Jaffer says: "She made us feel that we were welcome and wanted. There were no beds but she soon had mattresses spread on the floors of the wards and the messes and there we rested for a while. I was glad to stretch out fully dressed but the period of rest was short. Soon the sirens sounded. No bombers came but as I was on my feet I stayed on them and thereafter did not get my clothes off for three nights."

The load was lightened that day by the embarkation of one hundred and ninety sick and wounded in the hospital ship *Manunda*. Our old friend Charles Cudday, he who had failed to get spiritually prepared at Kahlin, was one of them. Let him write the valediction:

"When I arrived at Berrimah from Kahlin I was put in a bed and said to the Sister, 'What are all those holes in the roof?' It looked like a colander. She said they'd been machinegunned and one chap had been killed although they put him on the floor and piled mattresses on top. A bullet got him there. She had just left when the sirens went. She came running back blowing a whistle. A couple of nurses came in and lifted me and my mattress and put me on the floor and piled mattresses on top of me and went into the trenches telling me not to worry as I would be quite safe. After a few minutes I thought, Now that's what they told that other chap yesterday and he copped it, so I rolled out from under the bed and took a blanket and pillow and went bush. Whether I fell into a trench or what happened I don't know but I passed out or went to sleep. When I woke up everything was quiet so I stood up in the trench and then an orderly sang out, 'There he is!' and two of them came running over with a stretcher and put me on it and took me back to the hospital. Did I cop it from the Sister! But when I said she told the dead chap the same thing yesterday she up and left me. Well after an hour or so somebody brought in a lovely dinner of roast pork, roast potatoes, peas and cabbage and a plate of baked custard and put it on the table near my bed so I got it and ate the lot. I will never forget that meal. It was the first I had for two days since they took out my appendix. I had just finished when the Sister came in. She looked at the empty plates, looked at me with her hands on her hips and told me they would have to get the stomach pump and get all that food out of me or it would kill me. Fancy wasting good tucker like that! I told her I would sooner die with a full belly than an empty one and miserable. Anyhow she went off growling. After a while I wanted to go to the toilet and I sang out until I could wait no longer, so off I went and was just getting back into bed when along came my friend the Sister. After another tongue lashing she said she was getting rid of me that night as I was to be put on the hospital ship and sent south. I wrote a note asking for somebody to collect my two ports of clothes from my home. But the house was full of sailors from the bombed ships and they were wearing my clothes. So I had only a pair

The Administrator of the Northern Territory in 1942, Mr. C. L. A. Abbott

A seaward view of bombs bursting near the police barracks and Government House

The office occupied by the N.T. Administrator (Mr. C. L. A. Abbott) in the grounds of Government House (on left). The bomb crater was only a few feet from the building. Abbott, his wife and staff sheltered under the building. One half-caste maid was killed whilst there with them

The remains of the Post Office, where 10 people died

Crater of bomb which destroyed postmaster's residence in background. Nine people died in a trench nearby

The remains of the wharf, showing twisted rails and bogies

The severed wharf; the railway trucks are on the seaward side, cut off from land

Barbed wire entanglements were erected in the town as invasion appeared imminent. The premises of A. E. Jolly & Co. were in the main street

Surgeon Commander Clive James (centre, front) with staff at civil hospital after bombing. They worked night and day treating the injured

Oil storage tanks on fire during a subsequent raid

Mitsuo Fuchida — a photograph taken in 1961 when he explained his conversion to Christianity

"ALL PATIENTS UNDER BEDS!"

of pyjama pants belonging to Darwin hospital when I arrived at the jetty. There were bodies stacked on the shore like firewood. I was put in a bunk on the hospital ship and different patients were crying out for water. The medical staff was so short that I used to swing out of my bunk and give them a drink or light a smoke for them and I would spend most of my time tending the others. One day I was caught and got into hot water for walking around barefooted, they said I would catch my death of cold, so they got me a pair of sandshoes from the Red Cross, there was also a lot of gangrene around and they thought I might catch that too. When I got home my wife didn't know me, I'd changed so much since I last saw her two and a half months ago, I was just a walking skeleton."

CHAPTER 11

R.A.A.F.—Second Raid

> *'The R.A.A.F. station was practically deserted.'*—MR. JUSTICE LOWE.
>
> *'There is little excuse for the chaos that ensued.'*—The Chief of the Air Staff.

With the All-Clear at 10.40 a.m. Group Captain F. R. W. Scherger, the acting Officer Commanding Northwest Area, R.A.A.F., went to the operations room and tried to assemble the crews of Hudson bombers to make a seaward reconnaissance and, if possible, locate the Japanese carriers. In view of our present knowledge of the task force it is fortunate that the crews could not be quickly found. The communication system at the base had been shattered. All messages had to be carried by hand, either by runners or motorcycle despatch riders. When Scherger finally located a crew with a serviceable aircraft the time was 2.30 p.m. They took off but the Japanese were not seen.

Meanwhile Scherger set out to restore order. Although the base was yet to receive its heaviest attack, the first raid had been severe enough to seriously upset routine and threaten discipline.

Air Marshal Williams (whom Scherger had failed to reach when the first raid developed) arrived independently and was shown maps of the Timor Sea with prospective search areas for the Hudsons. Scherger says that because he had been off the base he was unaware at that stage of the message from Bathurst Island warning that a raid was imminent. In fact he did not hear about it until that evening.

By 11.55 a dense pall of black smoke from the shattered town and harbour shipping had drifted across Francis Bay to the

R.A.A.F. station. It brought with it the acrid smell of burning oil.

Those who thought about luncheon were about to go in search of it when the sirens sounded again. Lookouts aboard *H.M.A.S. Platypus* had seen twenty-seven aircraft in three triangular formation approaching the town from the south-west at an estimated height of eighteen thousand feet.

"Jesus, look at them!" a sailor said. "I wonder if they're going to drop paratroops this time?"

It was not then known but would soon be discovered that identical formations at a slightly different altitude were flying in a head-on direction, making fifty-four planes in all. They were twin-engined land-based Betty bombers from the Celebes and Ambon.

The time was 11.58 as men and women already shaken returned to the trenches and shelters. On *Platypus* and other ships in the harbour observers were sure they were about to be bombed again and braced themselves for a second ordeal. But the planes passed overhead to the R.A.A.F., ignoring the blossoming anti-aircraft bursts below them.

While Scherger and Williams were studying the maps and wondering what counter measures, if any, were possible against the Japanese, a staff officer came in quickly to tell them that hostile planes were approaching.

"We walked outside and went to a trench that I had dug myself. By the time we reached it the bombs were falling," Scherger told me. "We had just got in when the first pattern struck. Two bombs straddled us, landing fifteen yards on either side of the trench, which undoubtedly saved us."

If there had been time to think about it, Scherger might have had pangs of conscience about the kind of welcome being given his distinguished visitors. Not only did he have an Australian air marshal as a guest but General Patrick Hurley, of the U.S.A.F., was also present. The Liberator in which he had arrived was destroyed on the ground and another had to be sent for him.

In the few minutes that followed, the R.A.A.F. base was subjected to pattern bombing that was terrifying in its intensity and efficiency. Men on ships in the harbour had an uninterrupted view. Lieut. Owen Griffiths, on the bridge of *Platypus*, described it thus: "With one big crash they dropped their entire loads on the aerodrome and buildings. This was the first time I had seen a large number of bombs fall together on a target. It was a fearful sight. With a noise like the roll of heavy thunder, a thick cloud of smoke, dust and red and yellow flame shot into the air and left a long line of smoke to join up with the flame clouds already hanging over Darwin. Surely nothing could be left alive in that area!"

But in that respect Griffiths was wrong. Though the target was smothered with heavy bombs launched from two directions only six men among hundreds in the shelters were killed.[1] From the ground the twin formations appeared to cross each other. Bombardiers laid their patterns so accurately that almost nothing except the officers' mess and quarters, the operations building and the water tower were not badly damaged. The hospital, recreation huts, messes, two hangars, equipment stores, four airmen's dormitories and several houses were wrecked. Men and women (there were six nursing sisters on the base) emerged from shelters dazed by noise and concussion and shocked at the desolate ruin around them. Captain James Funk arrived at dusk from Daly Waters to fly General Hurley to Sydney and described the base as the most complete job of destruction he had ever seen. When I went to the station two hours after the raid most of the buildings were still burning furiously. Four of the men killed, Aircraftmen Barton, Latham, Neaylon and Smith, were in a trench that received a direct hit. They were members of a transport section led by Flying Officer Leslie G. Fenton[2] which subsequently distinguished itself by remaining on duty to a man while hundreds of others abandoned the base. Latham had driven to the aerodrome without authority between the first and second raids. He was driving a truck carrying a load of bombs intended for dispersal at Batchelor, seventy miles away, but had wanted to make sure that a younger brother also serving with the R.A.A.F. had survived the first raid. While he was there the second raid began. Latham jumped into a trench with Barton, Neaylon and Smith. The four were killed instantly by a direct hit and were the only men in the transport section not to answer a roll call next day.

Another bomb which landed two feet from the corner of a trench at transport section headquarters failed to explode. Fenton was sheltering in that trench. Latham's ammunition truck, an American G.M.C., was splintered by bomb fragments. All ten tyres were flat. The petrol tank was punctured and petrol dripped

[1] They were Leading Aircraftmen L. A. Barton, of Rainbow, Victoria, P. S. Latham, of Baan Baa, N.S.W., and A. V. L. Schulz, of South Hummocks, S.A.; Aircraftmen S. G. Smith, of South Perth, W.A., F. Neaylon, of Woolahra, N.S.W.; and Cpl. R. Simons, of Allenby Gardens, S.A.

[2] Later a director of Melford Motors, Melbourne.

a few feet from broken electric cables which were showering sparks. Fenton and his men tried to tow the truck away but it could not be steered. Three tons of bombs had to be manhandled to another truck.

Work in the aerodrome hospital had been mounting with the arrival of evacuees from the Netherlands East Indies. Overloaded Hudson bombers were flying in daily from Timor and Ambon with sick and wounded servicemen and civilians. Six planes had come in that morning and were shot at by anti-aircraft gunners. In some of the Hudsons passengers stood throughout the flight to make room for others. Among the last to arrive were Flight-Lieutenant Joseph Horan and Flight-Lieutenant Trevor Jenkins. Both were ill, Jenkins seriously so with malaria. But both were also R.A.A.F. doctors whose help was urgently needed. They went to work at once with the senior medical officer, Squadron Leader Donald Howle.[3] The staff also included six qualified nurses — Senior Sister Ila Smith, Sister Rose Charlton, Sister Helen Keogh, Sister Matilda McDowell, Sister Constance Watt and Sister Elizabeth Doherty.

As the Japanese advanced, Howle had directed the digging of enough slit trenches to accommodate all patients. Practice evacuations of the hospital were carried out by day and night. During one trial a pilot saw the white uniforms of nurses in the trenches; that same day the uniforms were treated with khaki dye.

On February 19 all hospital beds were occupied. Breakfast was over and sick parade and ward rounds were proceeding. Squadron Leader Howle was examining a patient from the N.E.I. who had experienced Japanese bombing. The patient lay on his side looking through an open window. Howle was startled when the patient jumped up and shouted, "Christ Almighty! They're Zeros!"

"I thought he was delirious until I heard the sirens and saw the bombs falling," Howle recalls.

Within five minutes all patients and staff were in the trenches, a process that had to be repeated two hours later during the second attack. Sister Constance Watt remembers it all in vivid detail: "The noise was terrible. The roar of scores of planes, the rattle of machineguns, the anti-aircraft fire, the explosion of bombs and petrol drums and the crackle of burning trees and buildings. The tropic sun blazed through us; our legs ached

[3] Now of Tamworth, N.S.W.

in the cramped trenches and our parched throats became almost unbearable. It seemed like fifty hours down there. Stones and rubble rattled in on top of our steel helmets. We bent our heads as low as possible. Racing thoughts insisted that the next bomb might be on our own backs. Long breaths were held and fingers clenched against what might come. The air was filled with dust and noise and the smell of burning, and the agony of this inferno was increased by the blistering noon-day sun. There were near-misses and the earth around us shuddered. Gaping cracks appeared in the sides of our trench and the dirt poured in. It seemed impossible that we could escape a direct hit. One Sister prayed aloud: 'Oh, God, let us get out of this.' We remembered a warning about fractured jaws and put pieces of anti-blast rubber tubing between our teeth. How one clutches on a straw in such extremity! Suddenly a man hurtled into our trench. It was our mess steward, Lobie Griegger. 'Come and help,' he cried. 'One of the boys was running for the scrub and he's been killed by a daisy-cutter.' He was told that if we got out we'd all be killed. We pulled him down to the bottom of the trench and gave him a phenobarb to swallow. Finally the bombs ceased. We were afraid to move, or couldn't move, until we heard a voice. 'Sister, are you there?' It was Squadron Leader Howle. He gave us the courage to emerge. We were dishevelled but unhurt. Through the smoke and dust we could see that the hospital was a blazing wreck."

It was indeed. A bomb had burst in the Administration section. Howle's office, twenty yards from where he sheltered, was destroyed. But there were wounded and dead men to attend to and the medical staff were soon at work. Flagging energies were whipped along. Casualties were treated in the open, by the roadside, in the midst of bomb craters and burning buildings, in the heat and the dirt. Howle had been left without a hospital but he had four ambulances equipped with emergency gear. These were used as surgeries, and to transfer badly wounded men to the A.G.H. at Berrimah. The dead were a problem. Howle inquired and found that the cemetery people had left town. The bodies of Wing-Commander Archibald Tindal and six other men were kept in an ambulance for the remainder of the day.

"I had no idea what was happening and I couldn't find out," Howle told me. "I had no information about where to go or what to do. We were left on our own. Everyone else seemed to be leaving the station. I saw the commanding officer, Griffith, driving around in a staff car and I asked him what we should do. He held up his hands and drove off. So we followed the rest of them down the road. We went for half a mile and established an aid post in the bush. Later we returned and set up a hospital in the sisters' quarters."

The front steps of the quarters were gone and the sisters had to swing up eight feet, hand over hand, on a broken rail. There were gaping holes in the walls and the roof hung precariously. No pane of glass remained intact, nor was there an electric light globe. Kitchen crockery was scattered in thousands of fragments. The refrigerator had burst open and its contents littered the floor. The iron stove was splintered. The water and electricity supply had been cut. The sisters' uniforms were riddled with bullet and shrapnel holes. But the kitchen clock ticked amid the debris on the floor. That night they were instructed to pack and transfer to the A.G.H.

What followed represents a bewildering episode in Australian military history. It was an unfortunate sequel that has led to criticism and controversy that survives to this day.

Air Chief Marshal Scherger does not mince words about it or spare his beloved service. He told me: "There was an awful panic and a lot of men simply went bush. I thought at one stage that they had disappeared to a man. Electricity and water had failed and communications ceased to exist. We were in a horrible mess."

Rumours, lack of training, lack of firm leadership and garbled verbal orders all appear to have contributed to deplorable but perhaps understandable behavior by those who had taken two severe drubbings in the space of two hours. Men unquestionably ran away, but they were not only airmen. The leaders in what later became known as The Adelaide River Stakes[4] included civilians who had not been under direct attack.

Following the second raid Wing-Commander Griffith summoned his senior administrative officer, Squadron Leader Swan, and gave a verbal order that all airmen were to move half a mile down the main road and then half a mile inland. At this vague rendezvous point (I have been unable to discover whether half a mile east or west of the road was intended) arrangements would be made to feed them.

The order led to utter chaos. In being passed by word of

[4] Adelaide River, seventy-two miles south of Darwin, was the nearest town and the road ended there.

mouth from one section to another, sometimes with officers present and sometimes not, it became garbled to the extent that it was unrecognisable against the original. In its ultimate form it was interpreted, especially by those desiring such an interpretation, as an order for immediate and general evacuation of the area. Highly exaggerated rumours of an impending Japanese invasion had already reached the base from the town and spread quickly among those wanting to believe them. In the circumstances existing, little credulity was needed to accept such stories. Indeed, they may well have been true.

In the absence of restraint, men gathered their belongings and began streaming off the station. A few officers succeeded in checking groups at points outside and inside the gates. But the gates were not necessarily used. Dozens crawled through or over the fences and the situation quickly became out of hand. Though the Northwest Area staff could see what was happening and issued countermanding orders, the damage was done and hundreds of men were already beyond recall.

Two military chaplains, the Rev. C. T. F. Goy and Father Jack Cosgrove, drove along the road in the early afternoon on their way to the Berrimah hospital. Goy recalls passing hundreds of airmen carrying blanket rolls and packs. They were walking aimlessly southwards, unaware of a destination or how they would reach it. He questioned several men who told him bluntly that they were "going south."

One said the station command intended to evacuate and they had been ordered to disperse.[5] "We've been told to go bush," another said, in what was evidently a wishful interpretation of Griffith's order to rendezvous in the bush to be fed.

Goy had seen the appalling damage at the R.A.A.F. and knew the service had been badly hurt. But as a man with some military experience he also knew that such an order was wrong and in all probability had never been given.

"I discussed it with large groups of them," he told me. "It wasn't long before many agreed that there must have been a mistake and, to my great joy, I saw dozens of officers and men pick up their swags and packs and begin walking back to the station."

When I spoke to him, Griffith did not mind discussing the order and was convinced that it had been necessary. He said: "The station sirens were put out of action. We were thus deprived of the means of giving warning of subsequent attacks.

[5] Bad as the situation was, the station was never abandoned.

I did not think it proper to leave the men on the station without a warning system. I discussed this with Scherger and then ordered that the men should move to a dispersal area about half a mile away. I have been criticised because the order was given verbally but there was neither time nor means to give it any other way. Mr Justice Lowe has said it was an unfortunate order. It would have been more unfortunate if another raid had developed and the men had been caught in the mess halls. This was a proper precaution for any commander to have taken. The warning system was rebuilt as a matter or urgency and was operating again by next day. Unfortunately, and this cannot be denied, the low state of morale caused many airmen to run away. They did not come back as I expected. Some went on but others just stayed in the bush; I found some sun-baking in the scrub and others simply idling. These stragglers should have been brought in by subordinate commanders."

Air Chief Marshal Scherger, later the nation's highest ranking officer, told me that in the grave circumstances of the moment Griffith's order for dispersal was "correct in concept." He added: "If there had been another raid while the base was crowded with disorganised men there might have been catastrophic losses. In retrospect, the order would have been better had it been properly policed and the men kept under control. They should have been fed by units and subordinate commanders instructed to ensure that discipline was maintained."

Scherger remembered that there were excellent non-commissioned officers and airmen who showed not the least sign of panic and who, anticipating Japanese landings, emphatically expressed their intention of fighting with infantry units. Scherger[6] had a special word for men in the Hudson squadrons and in the transport and equipment sections. These men left the station with others but did not walk further south than was necessary to realise that no plan existed. They then returned to the base. Several merely went into Darwin to see what had happened to the town and from there to the civil airfield where R.A.A.F. units were operating normally. All who reported there were fed and told to sleep in the open. At parades of the forward echelons of the two Hudson squadrons next morning there was one hundred per cent attendance. They were trained men who had been together for a long time. Strong friendships had developed among them and that helped morale. Flying Officer Leslie

[6] The Royal Commissioner commended Scherger for conspicuous bravery and the capacity he showed for restoring order.

Fenton was one of few who had taken the initiative in making his own plans. The men in his transport section knew exactly what to do in a raid. Vehicles and equipment were taken to selected dispersal areas. Later he reported proudly that from the moment of the All-Clear they worked unceasingly in driving, towing, dismantling, salvaging and camouflaging vehicles.

But hundreds of men at the R.A.A.F. station that day were strangers in a strange land, lacking purpose and the co-operative spirit needed to sustain them. By late afternoon only one hundred remained and by nightfall the base was almost deserted. While some were only half a mile away under the discipline of officers and N.C.O.s., others got as far afield at Batchelor (65 miles), Adelaide River (72 miles), Daly Waters (390 miles) and one reached Melbourne (2,500 miles) in thirteen days.

On February 23, four days later, 278 men were still missing.

The bombing produced several tragically ironic twists of fate.

None could fit more completely into this category than the fact that the first operational radar set in Australia was being installed on a cliff at Dripstone Caves, a few miles north of Darwin, on February 19. It faced the Timor Sea and was capable of picking up enemy aircraft one hundred miles away. But the antenna had not yet been erected.

In 1941 the C.S.I.R. (as it then was) through its radio physics laboratory at Sydney University, went about producing a radar set that could detect ships. It was intended to direct coastal guns for the protection of Australian ports and was to be Army equipment. Research experts found that the set could "see" the Tasman flying boat from New Zealand when it was thirty miles from Sydney. Dr F. W. G. White, chairman of the Radiophysics Advisory Board[7] and Dr J. H. Piddington improved the reception until aeroplanes could be detected one hundred miles away. This was reported to the Chief of the Air Staff, Air Chief Marshal Sir Charles Burnett, who asked that the scientists go ahead with a crash programme to develop three of the sets for the R.A.A.F. They were to be installed at Rabaul, Darwin and Kiama, N.S.W.

On January 28, 1942, Wing Commander (now Group Captain) A. G. Pither, Director of Radar (then R.D.F.) at R.A.A.F. headquarters, went to Darwin to select a site and acquire a building to house the equipment. He remembers that the Area Commandant, Air Commodore D. E. L. Wilson, was sceptical both as to

[7] Later Sir Frederick White, Chairman of C.S.I.R.O.

the efficiency of radar and Pither's ability to get a building.

"Get one if you can but the Public Works chief is uncooperative," he warned Pither.

On the contrary, Pither found that the officer-in-charge, E. W. Stoddart, was most helpful; he promised that a building of the type and size specified would be erected at Dripstone Caves by early February, when Pither expected to return with his magic boxes and his men. Stoddart was as good as his word.

The R.A.A.F. had established its own radar school at Richmond, N.S.W., and the first students were about to graduate. Pither selected three young pilot officers, Harry Hannam, Bruce Glassop and Frederick Hull. On February 5 the first flight arrived in Darwin with Glassop, Hannam and the set.

Pither recalls with surprise and perhaps a little bitterness that the new "boffin boys" were greeted by Darwin base officers with a lack of interest that amounted to apathy. "Nobody would believe it was possible to see an enemy aircraft on a screen from one hundred miles away," he told me. "Radar, or Radio Location as it was then known, was in the realm of fantasy to most of them."

When the equipment had been installed there was further trouble. "We could not get any signals or pick up our own planes within half a mile," Pither says.

After the bombing one of the designers, Dr Piddington, was sent from Sydney to help. The fault was found and a few days later the set came alive with symbols that represented aeroplanes. The Japanese could be seen more than one hundred miles away and Darwin had thirty minutes warning of impending attack.

Pither believes, however, that if the radar had been working on February 19, the bombs would still have fallen simultaneously with the sound of the sirens. When it located its first enemy planes a warning was passed to the R.A.A.F. The message was not believed, or at least was not acted upon, and again falling bombs constituted part of the warning system. Thereafter, not surprisingly, the radar commander's word that enemy planes were approaching was never questioned.

CHAPTER 12

"Kill Twenty Japs Each!"

> *'Darwin is an important operational area but not a vital area in the same sense as Sydney, Newcastle and Port Kembla.'*—
> The Secretary of the Department of the Army on April 22, 1942.

> *'Army headquarters' staff retired to the bush on February 20 . . . The majority of the troops were not bombed but some soldiers left their units.'*—OFFICIAL WAR HISTORY.

On February 17, when the Australian Prime Minister, Mr Curtin, sent a controversial request to Mr Winston Churchill for the diversion to Australia of certain A.I.F. units he said that Darwin was one of the first places that should be reinforced. On February 18, War Cabinet decided to ask General Wavell that part of six squadrons of American fighters being assembled in Australia should be retained for the defence of Darwin. The events of February 19 were to give sharp point to the requests, though both were too late.

The Official War History[1] mentions the unsatisfactory military situation then existing and says it had been clear for some time that all was not well with the Army in the 7th Military District, as the Northern Territory command was known.

The general officer commanding was Major-General D. V. J. Blake. His troops were restless and discontented with long periods of tropical service. Some units had been there for up to two years. There was a belief among many, including officers, that Darwin was being used as a kind of military Siberia.

---

[1] *Australia in the War of 1939-45.* Volume V: 'The Southwest Pacific Area, First Year' by Dudley McCarthy.

Factors existed over which Blake had no control and for which he was not to blame. These included the inadequate lines of communication to southern supply bases and the policy of placing two classes of soldiers — A.I.F. and militia — in the same area. The A.I.F. men complained of their retention under monotonous conditions in a military backwater when they might have been overseas; militia units regarded service in the Northern Territory as banishment and even as punishment. Darwin itself offered little scope for off-duty recreation. These factors, combined, led to a higher-than-average incidence of psychiatric cases among men reporting ill who were colloquially diagnosed as "going troppo." The ailment was marked by lassitude, dejection and audible monologues. Men talked to themselves, or to lamp-posts, or to non-existent dogs. They went so far as to take imaginary walks with imaginary dogs on imaginary leads. Subsequently this led to a form of burlesque among troops who were not mentally ill, but it began as a malady caused by ennui. This did not apply only to the army. A number of shore-based sailors whose morale was described by the Naval-Officer-in-Charge as "regrettably low" were sent south with anxiety neuroses.

But those with any kind of military awareness realised the existence of certain irregular factors for which they could and did hold Blake responsible. More than twenty units[2] were deployed on the coast in the immediate vicinity of Darwin — a fortress area with fixed defences of ten guns. The deployment positions were tactically unsound and offered a chance of successful counter action only in the unlikely event of an enemy landing in the particular areas.[3] If the Japanese had made two assault landings in the Adelaide River and Daly River districts and had linked these forces by north-easterly and south-westerly thrusts of about fifty miles, the entire Allied strength in the Darwin area would have been irretrievably cut off — with all its installations, aerodromes, naval base and reserve supplies of food. That might have been achieved in less than a week by marines who

[2] Fighting units present on February 19 were: Coastal defence — East Battery, West Battery, Emery Battery, Darwin Fortress Company, 2/4th Pioneer Battalion, A.I.F., 148th U.S. Field Regiment Battery ("Y" troop), 2nd Heavy Anti-Aircraft Battery, 14th Heavy Anti-Aircraft Battery, 1/54th A.A. Searchlight Company. 3rd Brigade — 27th Battalion, 43rd Battalion, 2/14th Field Regiment A.I.F., 14th Anti-Tank Battery, 23rd Field Company. 23rd Brigade — 19th Machinegun Regiment, 8th Battalion, 147th U.S. Field Artillery Regt., 11th Anti-Tank Regiment ("M" Battery), 2/11th Field Coy., A.I.F.

[3] Official War History.

could well have been landed from the cruisers and destroyers which escorted Admiral Nagumo's carrier task force. That it wasn't done appears to be just another of the inexplicable errors — perhaps the very first — the previously invincible Japanese then began making.

The essential factor over which the Army had most direct control but did little about was the supply position, and this alone might have lost the land war in the north if one had begun. A depot had been established at Adelaide River but the bulk of the supplies for North Australia were held in Vestey's meatworks, a prominent target on Bullocky Point in the city area. This major supply depot was ahead of the fighting units. After Blake's withdrawal of 7th Military District headquarters on February 20 to camps in the bush[4] supply trucks were required to go in advance of the forward echelons each day to draw rations, thus committing an elementary tactical error.

The most that can be said is that the Army had two fighting brigades and its fortress artillery, a considerably greater force, though the troops were untried, than the almost bereft R.A.A.F. The three militia infantry battalions and the machinegun regiment, recently arrived, were constantly watchful, almost hourly expecting word that an invasion fleet had been sighted. When the bombs fell they went to action stations believing it was a pre-invasion softening-up and that any one of them might fire the first shot against an enemy attempting to make the first hostile landing on Australian soil since Captain Cook.

Larrakeyah Barracks, on a point of land overlooking the entrance to the harbour, was assumed to be an obvious target for the Japanese. One of the most incomprehensible facts of the raids is that it was left alone.

The barracks, begun in 1933, had taken five years to build. They were by far the biggest establishment anywhere in a bomb aimer's vision — seven 2-storey blocks each about one hundred yards long, officers' and sergeants' messes almost as big (but incomplete), and a central headquarters office block. The entire area covered about fifty acres. Moreover, coast artillery and anti-aircraft guns on Emery and Elliott Points were adjacent to it and must have been clearly visible.

Why was it ignored? That question has never been satisfactorily answered. One theory is that the Japanese wanted to preserve the barracks intact for their own use after Darwin had

[4] Blake's advanced headquarters was established beside the road 22 miles from Darwin. Rear headquarters was at Coomalie Creek, 56 miles.

been occupied. But that seems to be discounted by the fact that although invasion appeared imminent to us, the idea had been specifically rejected by both the Japanese army and navy staffs. That was known to the air attack planner, Commander Genda, and the air attack leader, Commander Fuchida. Both told me of the rejection and admitted they had been disappointed. Their statements are supported by Japanese historical records.

Another theory, the charitable one, is that the pilots mistook the new civil hospital for the barracks. The hospital, as we have seen, was situated on the opposite side of Kahlin Bay only a few hundred yards away. Its five long wards and an administration block could conceivably have been mistaken for Larrakeyah if one is prepared to overlook the red crosses on the roof. In any event, six heavy bombs landed there and caused severe damage.

The Japanese might have recognised Larrakeyah for what it was by the sandbagged wall, thirteen bags high, that surrounded the headquarters, giving the unmistakable appearance of a fortified area. But they were completely negligent of the barracks and this seemed to be deliberate. They remained so far distant that several officers, instead of sheltering in trenches, sought vantage points from which to get a better view of the proceedings.

Major George Plant, the education officer, says that he sat on the edge of a trench for a few minutes with Lieut.-Col. J. B. McElhone, the Assistant Director of Medical Services, who then said, "This is no bloody good to me, George; I can't see what's going on." They walked to the edge of a cliff and from there had an elevated view of action in the harbour.

Although thus comparatively remote from danger, the bombing nevertheless shook some of the headquarter's staff. An account of the events written for the Official War History recorded that some soldiers left their units. Luncheon in the Larrakeyah officers' mess was marked by moroseness. Few wanted to talk about the largely unopposed hammerblows the Japanese had inflicted on the town while leaving them alone. They were pre-occupied and perplexed by this reversal of what might have been expected. They were agitated and tense, waiting for direction but also for what now seemed to be the inevitability of invasion. Matters were not helped by the failure of the power supply, which meant a meal of bully-beef and bread for the sixty officers. One who remained cheerful was Lieut.-Colonel Cliff Peters, Blake's adjutant, a veteran of World War I who had flown with Ross Smith and Lawrence of Arabia. Another who could not be shaken in any imaginable circumstances was a sergeant clerk who had been a major with the British Army in World War I. He wore the Military Cross.

During the afternoon when a little of the tenseness had eased the sergeant asked Major Plant for a leave pass until midnight on the pretext of wanting to see the damage in the town. That would not have been remarkable except that the sergeant had previously taken leave when he wanted it without asking for a pass. But now, with Darwin almost under siege and in ruins, he insisted on having one.

Later he told Plant he had gone into town with two other sergeants and the knowledge, gained through his official duties, that the Administrator was intending to spend the night at Flagstaff House with Major-General Blake. Mrs Abbott and the domestic staff had been evacuated. To the three sergeants it seemed a pity that the contents of the Government House refrigerators and pantries should remain unappreciated even for one night. They set about ensuring that that should not happen, and leave passes were necessary if their plan were to succeed.

The three men, immaculately uniformed, approached the officer of the town picket, a young lieutenant. The following is Plant's story (and he provided names):

"Sir," the ring-leader said to the lieutenant, "we have an engagement tonight to dine with the Administrator and we would like to keep it. However, we know what the situation is and we are afraid we may be shot at as we go through the gates; we wondered if you would give us an escort and safe conduct?"

If the lieutenant wondered why three sergeants would be dining with the Administrator in such troubled circumstances, even though the invitation had been issued some time earlier, he must have been reassured by the ribbon of the Military Cross on the chest of one of them, and the knowledge that he had indeed been a British major.

They were given an escort who saw them past the guard without explanation and then returned to his duties. Government House was in darkness but they entered and found light. The water pipes had been burst by bombs (this was the reason Abbott had moved out) but these men were not seeking water. In that respect they were dismayed to find the refrigerators were not working and all the diplomatic liquor had been undiplomatically removed. Nevertheless, they set the long mahogany dining table with places for three in silver and crystal, including glasses for sherry, white wine, red wine and port.

"KILL TWENTY JAPS EACH!"

There was no power for cooking so they settled for a cold collation — His Honour's chicken and salad. Regrettably, one feels, it was necessary that they wait upon themselves; one coloured waitress was dead and the other had gone with Mrs Abbott. That may have detracted a little from the propriety of the occasion; but if it did, one sergeant helped matters by asking his colleagues to rise while they drank the Loyal Toast.

"Gentlemen, The King," he said, and deferentially raised his glass of water. (It had been taken from a tank.)

"His Majesty!"

"God bless him!"

Each felt a little guilty at not doing the washing up, but compromised by taking their dishes from the dining room to the kitchen and putting them in a sink. Then they left by the front door, greeting the guard at the gate.

When I told Abbott this story some years later and went so far as to identify one of the sergeants he discounted it and added: "The overhead tanks had been pierced. I do not think there was either light or power. At my request a constable had been placed on guard at Government House. The lack of light and water were the reasons why General Blake urged me to stay with him."

Then there follows this significant paragraph in a letter he wrote to me: "The constable may not have stayed there all night as next morning when I went to Government House with General Blake the drawing room was covered with charred newspapers that had been rolled up and used as torches. On the floor there was a brooch of ribbons *including the Military Cross*[5] which was identified as belonging to a sergeant who was too old for a commission in the second war."

Major-General Blake was plagued by the absence of information about Japanese intentions.

One can sympathise with the turbulence of his thoughts while awaiting the expected invasion.

He now knew that a carrier task force had come into the Timor Sea without observation. Unquestionably, it would be the same force reported from Portuguese Timor by the Australian consul, David Ross.

However, its strength and the direction it had taken after the air raids were matters for conjecture.

For all Blake knew it might have continued steaming south.

[5] My italics.

It might have passed Cape Fourcroy on the south-western tip of Bathurst Island and be now sailing south-eastward, unmolested, towards Darwin.

The day passed and the night wore on and Blake must have worried that the sound of enemy shellfire might announce invasion as the sound of bombs had announced the air attack. This was a fearful situation for any commander.

In the early hours of the morning on February 20 a dispatch rider arrived at Flagstaff House with the information that a strong Japanese force, under naval escort, had been sighted sailing towards Koepang, four hundred miles to the north-west, with the obvious intention of occupying it and possibly Darwin.

Abbott says the military appreciation at that time was that landings would take place at the mouth of the Adelaide River and at the mouth of the Roper River in the Gulf of Carpentaria. The latter force was expected to move westwards to cut off the escape of all forces north of Mataranka — in other words, the entire military strength in the north. The troops landing at Adelaide River were expected to reduce the Darwin garrison.

Nothing of the kind happened. The reliability of Army intelligence can be gauged from the knowledge we now have that such an operation was never seriously intended by the Japanese, and certainly never worked out in tactical detail. After the carrier task force struck it withdrew at once. The carriers, in fact, were heading north-west when their aeroplanes returned. But, of course, we had no reconnaissance planes to tell us that. It is not so surprising, therefore, that during the night Blake prepared to move his line of defence beyond The Narrows, a restricted neck of land on the Darwin promontory through which the road, the railway and the water supply all reached the town. What is surprising is that this decision should have been taken after the first shots had been fired.

The Army prudently prepared for the worst. Anti-tank guns took up positions along the main roads. Barbed wire entanglements had already been erected on the beaches and would soon criss-cross the town itself. Machinegun posts overlooking the possible landing places were manned. Two American officers, Captain Wayne C. Bailey and Captain Thomas Millford that night attended a briefing by an Australian they later described as a "blood and guts lecturer" who assured them: "If what we expect really happens everyone in Darwin will have to kill twenty Japs each to stay alive."

CHAPTER 13

The Adelaide River Stakes

> *'To most of the people of Darwin the rapidity with which the second raid followed the first meant only one thing — it was a pre-invasion bombardment. Therefore it is not too surprising that many left as fast as they could. The siren was the starting signal for civilians to enter The Adelaide River Stakes. The exodus, though disgraceful in many ways, was in the best interest of the Armed Services.'*
> —OFFICIAL WAR HISTORY.

> *'The four bank managers left town the same night, going ahead of their staffs and in some cases without notifying their clients. This was annoying but they had been ordered by the Administrator to leave, complete with their funds and accounts.'*—OFFICIAL WAR HISTORY.

War time rationing of essential supplies was supposed not to discriminate between persons on a personal basis, but often it did.

When Oswald ("Ossie") Jensen, a lanky bachelor, crawled from beneath his mosquito net at six o'clock on February 19, he sat on the edge of his bed and contemplated his most urgent problem — how to get enough petrol to keep his four utility trucks running.

Although Jensen was Darwin's biggest electrical contractor to the defence services and government departments, with thousands of pounds worth of vital installations to complete, he was little better off than other people when it came to keeping his trucks on the road. Men twiddled their thumbs while others supplying them with wire and conduit sat in vehicles which were out of fuel. Jensen begged and would gladly have stolen petrol to keep his gangs working. But his begging fell on unreceptive ears and there was no opportunity to steal. Many other businessmen had the same problem but it irked Jensen when he saw that bookmakers, cafe proprietors, and gambling den operators were not similarly affected. He was upset by the sight of senior service officers escorting nurses to the Star Theatre and elsewhere in chauffeur-driven staff cars.

It did not help him that Jensen was one of the town's senior citizens. Although only forty-three years old he had been in Darwin for twenty-seven years, having come there when his father, Christian Jensen, a Dane, arrived to take a job with Vestey's meatworks. In those days Darwin was a town of red-blooded citizens who resisted oppression by rioting. Ossie Jensen had taken part in a 1919 march on Government House when one thousand angry people demonstrated against what they alleged was the maladministration of the Administrator, Dr J. A. Gilruth. They had stormed over the fence and been restrained by armed police and soldiers. The Administrator and several of his assistants, as well as the Judge of N.T. Supreme Court, were subsequently recalled by the government. Jensen, nevertheless, was a kindly man who was known to almost everyone in town. But they could not help him get petrol.

Now, after pondering his problem, he showered and dressed and walked briefly through the garden his father had established. It was lush with autumn-leaf crotons, red and pink hibiscus, and the air was heavily laden with the sickly-sweet smell of henna. Papaws hung in pendulous groups from trees which Christian Jensen had nurtured before his evacuation to Katherine a week earlier. Ossie thought he might eat one for breakfast but decided against it when he found the fruit beyond easy reach. Instead, he went to Gee Fong Ming's cafe, a few doors along from his own electrical goods shop in Chinatown, and ate steak and eggs. That was just as well because a long time was to elapse before he got another good meal.

Jensen opened his shop for business. The employees straggled in — Ernest ("Snowy") Bryant, Jack Anderson, and Roy Bliss. They collected wire, conduit and tools and, with Bryant as foreman, went off to their jobs, using a single vehicle to conserve petrol. Jensen served a few customers and was then visited by a friend, Jack Ferguson, who knew of his fuel problem.

THE ADELAIDE RIVER STAKES

"Hey, Ossie," Ferguson said, "there's two cases of kerosene lying on Vestey's beach near my shack. You'd better nip out and get 'em quick and lively before someone else knocks 'em off."

Jensen thanked him, closed the shop immediately, and drove to the beach. "I was desperate for fuel. I intended adulterating the petrol with kero and hoped that it would take us twice as far," he recalls. On his way he met E. W. Stoddart, the engineer-in-charge of the Public Works Department, and stopped him to complain that electrical contracts were being held up because his trucks couldn't move. "I'm desperate and I'll steal it if I can," he warned Stoddart.

"So will I," Stoddart said.

"But you're a public servant . . ." Jensen began.

"Yes, a government servant, but I can't get enough either," Stoddart said.

After retrieving the two cases of kerosene — sixteen precious gallons — Jensen drove to his home in Smith Street, opposite the Catholic Church, and began to unload it. Though streaming with perspiration and dirty from his labour he smiled as he passed his father's last 'gardening' project. This consisted of three 44-gallon drums with the tops cut off which he had sunk in the ground among the crotons at an angle of forty-five degrees. He believed war would soon come to Darwin and had built drum-shelters as a farewell gesture.

As Jensen finished stacking the kerosene beneath his house, which sat on eight-foot concrete piers, he saw that the town's motor sanitary truck had arrived. There was no sewerage and only the newest homes had septic systems. Jensen was a little impatient with the driver, Ludo Dalby, who was walking towards the outhouse next door with a pan on his shoulder. The truck was parked directly across his driveway.

"How long are you going to be, mate?" he asked.

"Only a minute," Dalby said. "Just as long as it takes me to make this transfer."

Simultaneously both men became aware of the drone of aeroplane engines. They looked up but took little notice and Dalby resumed his walk down the driveway. Then they heard a whistle followed by a bomb explosion . . . and another.

"They're Japs!" Dalby said. He dropped the pan and began running.

Within moments both men had disappeared. Dalby found a trench in the yard of the home he was visiting. Jensen crawled inside one of the drum-shelters, bending his six-feet four-inches

157

frame in such a way that he was completely protected.

When he emerged at the end of the raid the sanitary truck was already on the move. "That bloke was really in a hurry to go somewhere else," he recalls.

The "somewhere else" was Adelaide River, seventy-two miles away. With a junior government clerk in charge, and with eight well-known citizens perched on the roof, the truck left town with its load shortly after the raid ended. An Official War History report records that it was the first vehicle to reach Adelaide River. That seems to discount a widely known story that the truck, top heavy with its load of pans and passengers, overturned at a bend in the gravel road. It was said that while the passengers and crew were man-handling it back on to its wheels a party of provosts arrived. One asked, "What seems to be the matter here?" A wag among the passengers replied, "We're just having a stocktaking, mate."

Meanwhile Jensen's employees began arriving at his home. Like him, they were shaken. Jensen remembered a single bottle of whisky he had kept for an emergency and now gave each man a stiff drink. While sipping it, grateful for the steadying effect on their nerves, the town was rocked by a blast that sounded like the sudden eruption of a volcano. *Neptuna* had blown up at the wharf and been split in halves. Jensen dropped his glass and lost the whisky. The bottle was empty.

After the second raid Jensen returned to his shop and found it undamaged . . . except for the door which had been broken open by soldiers who were carrying batteries to an army truck. He thought of looters.

"What do you think you're doing with my batteries?" he demanded.

"You'll get paid," a soldier said. He produced a slip of paper authorising him to impress everything and anything the army might need. Months later he was surprised to receive a cheque covering payment in full.

Jensen realised that business in Darwin, though brisk the day before, was now a thing of the past. Streams of evacuees were already leaving town. Many were shocked and had but a single thought — to get as far away from Darwin as possible. Tomorrow there would be no customers for electrical gadgets or anything else. With one or two exceptions, notably Koolpinyah butchery and iceworks which remained open throughout the war, the entire commercial life of the town was soon in voluntary liquidation. Jensen closed his shop, containing several thousand pounds worth of equipment, and also his career as a businessman.

The question uppermost in Jensen's mind, as with so many others, was what to do next. Darwin was his permanent home and he had no desire to leave for one of the big cities of the south. With several employees he decided to drive ten miles from town and establish a camp in the bush near Knuckey's Lagoon. They loaded one of the trucks with food and gear and began the journey. Before leaving town they were stopped by a military policeman who said menacingly, "Keep going! Don't come back here. We don't want bloody civvies in this town." For that and other reasons to appear later it is not surprising that an Official War History summary included this observation: "The poor quality of the Provost Corps stationed in the area was noticeable. This unit did not operate in a praiseworthy manner." Two who made a similar discovery were Judge Wells and the chief warden, Arthur Miller. At dusk that night they were at Parap police station with Constable Lionel McFarland, having farewelled the evacuee train. All three ran outside when they heard pistol shots. There they saw two provosts shooting out the headlights of vehicles, an apparently belated precaution against observation from the air. As an American army truck approached a provost shot at it from a distance of fifty yards. He was drunk. Judge Wells remonstrated with the man and disarmed him and his colleague.

The provost's instruction to "get going" held special significance for Jensen later when he discovered that some of the looting which followed was done by military policemen. Nevertheless, he took the advice. Jensen, Bryant, Anderson, and Bliss drove seventy-two miles to Adelaide River. The road was crammed with vehicles, all of them moving south past infantry and anti-tank positions hastily set up beside the track. Soldiers cursed the motley disorganised convoys of civilians and deserting servicemen whose vehicles raised clouds of dust from the gravelled road.

Among the first to leave were some of the officials of North Australia Workers' Union in the union truck. For several weeks they had been advocating a scorched earth policy in the north in the event of invasion. An Official War History investigator was told: "The only scorching done by these chaps was along the road to Adelaide River."

Chinese and Greek cafe proprietors left their premises at once, some without bothering to close the doors. When Captain

A. C. Gregory was deputed by the Administrator to find all the food he could for stews to feed shipwrecked sailors he had little difficulty entering the buildings.

An ice-cream vendor rode away on a bicycle equipped in front with a box containing ice and icecream. As he rode he shouted, "No more icecream! No more icecream!"

One businessman rushed from his shop in Smith Street, jumped on his bicycle and began pedalling. But the chain was broken and he was getting nowhere. He dropped the machine and ran across the street to a bicycle leaning against a wall. He jumped on that and rode away with the owner chasing him, shouting for him to stop. There is an apocryphal story that when this cyclist reached Adelaide River he discovered there, for the first time, that both tyres were flat.

A Chinese set out with a three-ton load on a fifteen-hundredweight utility truck. Six miles south of the town the vehicle gave up the unequal struggle. The driver began walking, abandoning food and household goods to which other evacuees and servicemen helped themselves.

One man chased a moving truck in Cavenagh Street while carrying a heavy parcel containing his belongings. As the vehicle gained speed it became obvious that he would have to decide whether to wait for another means of transport or discard the parcel hampering his progress. Finally he dropped it and, overtaking the truck, was helped aboard by men sitting on top of the load.

The hotels were vacated with food and vegetables still on the tables and in refrigerators that were unserviceable as soon as electric power failed. There it rotted. The ornate Hotel Darwin, opened only a year or so earlier as the chief wonder of the north, was abandoned. Later it became a naval officers' mess.

Bruce Acland, a Department of Civil Aviation radio operator, wrote reproachfully in his diary: "The great stampede was on. People of all colours and creeds were fleeing in and on all sorts of vehicles. Soldiers, sailors, airmen and civilians were simply 'going through.' They were walking, running, riding bikes, driving cars and some were even on horseback."

Gangs of men under Matthew Luke[1] were put to work repairing street damage. Luke, a road foreman employed by the Public Works Department, had watched the raid with his repair gang from a secluded spot on The Esplanade. None of them

[1] He remained in Darwin throughout the war, and was later a member of N.T. Legislative Council.

bothered to take shelter. Luke recalls that when it ended some of his men picked up their tools and resumed work as though nothing had happened. They stopped for lunch at noon and returned at one o'clock complaining that they had been unable to get a meal because the cafes were either closed or abandoned. Next day Luke and his gang began cleaning up the streets. Several of the additional men he employed were wharflaborers who no longer had a wharf and seamen who had no ships. To assist in the work Luke went to the R.A.A.F. to recover a mechanical grader that belonged to the Public Works Department. There he discovered that it had been used as an evacuation vehicle and was known to have arrived at Adelaide River with nine passengers after a journey of twenty-two hours. Several men who joined Luke's gang stayed with him for the next three years. One rationalised his decision by saying, "There's no chance of the Japs invading a rotten joint like this so I'm staying."[1]

On February 20 it was estimated that not more than five hundred civilians remained in the town. Few were former permanent residents. The majority were ship-wrecked seamen. They camped in the old hospital in Packard Street and in abandoned homes. They were authorised to find beds wherever they could. Most of these men had only the clothes in which they swam or were rowed ashore. Many were without footwear and all were hungry. Emergency clothing and food were distributed, and Captain Gregory kept a stew bubbling for those who wanted it.

That day the Administrator told Arthur Miller he was held personally responsible for the survey records which were still

[1] On March 25, 1955, the then Minister for Territories, the Hon. Paul Hasluck, spoke at the unveiling of a plaque in memory of the men and women who died at the Post Office. The plaque had been erected on part of a wall of the old Post Office that was incorporated in the new Legislative Council building. Hasluck referred to the "panic evacuation" of the people after the bombing and to February 19 as "the anniversary of a day of national shame."

He had many critics. The Darwin paper, *N.T. News*, said in an editorial that "this was not the occasion for the political butchering of a piece of dead history." Mr. F. W. Drysdale, M.L.C., said he had been present during the bombing and saw no evidence of panic that could not have been avoided if the civil and military authorities had done anything about directing activities. Mr. J. A. McDonald wrote to the Editor and accused Hasluck of "eating our salt, drinking our beer, and insulting his hosts by declaring that this was our day of shame." McDonald agreed that there had been an exodus but said it was led "by departmental heads and their satellites." Another correspondent, Tony Torey, wrote that "in a similar emergency the Alice Springs Derby would be on again, with a bigger field and a better track."

where he had left them on the office verandah. He had not thought of them for twenty-four hours. Simultaneously Barney Lyons, a cartage contractor, drove by in a garbage truck.

"I want you to take a load of records to Adelaide River," Miller told him.

"What in?"

"What's wrong with the garbage truck?"

Lyons did not demur. He helped load vast quantities of records. Miller, Cecil Goodman, Billy Byers, Laurie Rorke, Ted Warton and Jim Pott left in a convoy next day. Lyons returned with a piece of paper acknowledging his services and was eventually paid.

The Darwin area came under military control on February 21. Major-General Blake was in sole charge from that date but, contrary to common belief, martial law was never proclaimed. Indeed, the civil law remained paramount. Judge Wells stayed and assumed magisterial as well as his judicial powers. With him was Constable Lionel McFarland, who was the only civil policeman in the town between April, 1942, and November, 1943. He retained the right of arrest for any misdemeanour and frequently took servicemen into custody and brought them before Judge Wells. McFarland not only made arrests; he gave evidence, wrote the court depositions, and prosecuted. On a few occasions he prosecuted in the Supreme Court, which is probably unique for a constable. In his spare time he acted as the judge's chauffeur.

The Administrator did not leave Darwin with his wife, in spite of a recurrent story that he did. He established a temporary office in the police headquarters and from there directed rescue operations and the evacuation. That night we know he spent with General Blake at Flagstaff House, having ordered the closure of hotels and banks and accepted responsibility for the release of gaol prisoners. Not until February 21 did Abbott go to Adelaide River. His visit was then necessary, and requested by Blake, to help clear the area of about five hundred civilian refugees. Every one was medically examined and three hundred were called up for military service. The remainder were sent south by rail and road. Abbott arranged for rations to be issued to these men, and for the collection and return to Darwin of municipal vehicles needed to resume the town's sanitary and garbage services. He returned to Darwin on February 23 and opened headquarters in the Lands and Survey Office notwithstanding that the town was already under military control and that Blake himself had shifted his *advanced* headquarters to a camp in the bush twenty-two miles to the south. Abbott and his staff were ahead of the most forward troops. He established a Mess in the abandoned Catholic Convent; this was run by a volunteer cook and steward who had survived the sinking of *Zealandia*. Abbott then had no authority in the town and might have left at once. However, considerable looting of private premises had begun and he remained to see that stocks in abandoned stores were taken over by the Army on a proper basis. Check-lists were prepared, requisitions issued and receipts given in the absence of the owners, most of whom eventually received payment.

Abbott's chief problem was to get the town cleaned up. He has described this an an 'Augean task.'[3] In addition to the civilians who had vacated their homes, units of the American Army which had been camped in tents on The Esplanade had been withdrawn to camps along the highway from ten to thirty miles from town. All left behind a considerable mess. Decaying food had become a serious problem. Homeless cats and dogs were everywhere; they had to be destroyed or found homes in military camps. Caged birds, many starving and thirsting, were liberated. The Reverend C. T. F. Goy, describing this in a letter, wrote: "I will always remember walking around Darwin on the following nights. They were streets of darkness and empty houses, with doors swinging in the breeze and abandoned cats and dogs howling mournfully. It was all very eerie and depressing."

Not until March 2 when all these matters were under control did Abbott go to Alice Springs. From there he conducted the administration of the Northern Territory until the civilian population was able to return to Darwin in 1945.

Darwin's newspaper, the weekly *Northern Standard* owned by the North Australia Workers' Union, was due to be published on Friday, February 20. Some of the pages were already in type on Thursday and the editor, Jock Hector, had wondered what story he might use as the front page lead next day. A few minutes later he was to have on his hands the story of the worst tragedy ever to have happened on Australian soil. But he could not print it because by publication day he had no electric power or staff and few subscribers. The paper was not published that

[3] Augean—Filthy, like the stables of Augeas, which Hercules cleaned by turning the River Alpheus through them. (Oxford English Dictionary.)

week and did not resume until 1946. The manager, John Coleman, then returned to his old job after several years in the navy and was dismayed to find that a roomful of irreplaceable files containing copies of every paper printed in Darwin, and dating back to 1873, had been deliberately destroyed. The old newspaper office was left standing and is there today, but the files were taken away for destruction, apparently because they were thought to be a fire hazard. It was from these files that some of the earliest writers on the outback researched their material.

One other newspaper was published in Darwin at that time. This was *Army News,* a weekly managed by Captain Bill Sellen and edited by Lieut. Alex Baz.[4] Its first issue after the raid appeared on February 21. It was a duplicated sheet containing an apology that lack of power had prevented earlier publication. But the Japanese attack, the subject of this book, was dismissed in four paragraphs. These included an official statement by the Minister for Air, the Hon. A. S. Drakeford, that the known service casualties numbered eight. Nothing was said about destruction in the town or the sinking of ships in the harbour. In its following issue *Army News* quoted the Australian Broadcasting Commission, the British Broadcasting Corporation and Tokyo Radio reports of the raid but gave no first hand account of its own. In this issue the "known" casualties, according to Drakeford, were said to be thirty-nine — fifteen killed and twenty-four wounded. Alex Baz recalls that strict censorship was imposed and he was prevented by senior officers from publishing in his own town his eye-witness story of what had really happened.

A story has persisted to this day that when *U.S.S. Peary* sank she carried to the bottom a fortune in gold bullion. That has been denied by the U.S. Navy. A Darwin salvage diver, Carl Atkinson, who bought the wreck, found documents and personal trinkets which he returned to relatives of the men killed, but there was no trace of bullion. *Peary,* as we have seen, was in the Philippines before coming to Darwin and was supposed to have taken the gold aboard before sailing. Whether true or not, that had the ingredients of an adventure story containing the magic words "gold" and "treasure"; not surprisingly the legend survived and was embellished.

I regret my inability to substantiate it but as compensation

[4] Later a Sydney television executive.

offer an account of what happened to more than three hundred thousand pounds in the tills and strongrooms of the four trading banks, and to various household effects.

Few people in Darwin on February 19 resisted the impulse to run for shelter when the sirens sounded and bombs exploded on the wharf. Nevertheless, about twenty men knew that duty to their banks and customers made it necessary for tills to be cleared and strongrooms locked.

In the minutes immediately following the first bombs, money was handled in the banks at a speed seldom equalled; but unlike the sausages in the butchers' shops and clothing in the drapers', it was treated with due regard to its value, if a little less reverently than usual.

The largest amount of cash was held in the modern premises of the Commonwealth Bank at the corner of Bennett and Smith Streets. Two other corner sites on that intersection were occupied by the Commercial Bank of Australia Ltd. and the Bank of New South Wales. The English, Scottish and Australian, the Territory's oldest established bank, was on its original site in Smith Street nearer The Esplanade and about one hundred yards from The Commonwealth. Because of its construction it was known at The Tin Bank.

The Commonwealth's manager, Clarrie Read, says that not less than two hundred thousand pounds was in his custody. If that seems a large amount for a small town it should be remembered that Darwin had become the centre for thousands of Australian and American servicemen. They all had to be paid and the Commonwealth Bank supplied the cash.

The staff of twelve worked seven days a week and almost every night to cope with the work. In addition, task forces leaving Darwin were paid in the currency of the territory in which they were to operate. Hundreds of thousands of U.S. dollars, Dutch guilders, Filipino pesos, Malayan dollars and Portuguese petakas were issued to units embarking for various destinations. Large amounts of foreign currency were negotiated for servicemen arriving from overseas. The Bank frequently received remittances of up to half a million pounds.[5]

Clarrie Read arrived in Darwin in November, 1941. Only three months later, acting on the Administrator's instructions, he nailed to the door of each of the banks an unprecedented government notice ordering them to close.

[5] Not long after the raid £100,000 on its way to the Bank, then at Alice Springs, was lost in a plane crash.

AUSTRALIA'S PEARL HARBOUR

As the bombs fell on the wharf Read instinctively ran from his office to the strongroom door and was met there by the accountant, David Owens. He called to the tellers to bring their tills and cash boxes. These were put on the strongroom floor without being checked.

"There was cash lying all over the floor," Read says.

The strongroom had two combination locks, the numbers of which were known only to Read and Owens. Each locked his own combination and only then did they go to the trenches behind the Bank. These had been dug by two Territory wanderers for a few pounds and a bonus of liquor every hour they stayed on the job. The trenches were designed to accommodate twenty, but forty or fifty men of all nationalities found shelter there.

At the Bank of New South Wales and the Commercial Bank the managers, Dick Harding and Sid Iles, also supervised storage of cash and securities in the strongrooms before leading their staffs to cover. Of the four, the Tin Bank was nearest to the firing line. Only one other building separated it from The Esplanade overlooking the wharf; and it was just one block from the Post Office, with open ground between.

The manager, Keith Crooks, arrived from the Post Office as the first bombs fell. Jack Murphy was in the teller's cage and a Chinese cook, Jimmy Que Noy, was preparing smoke-oh in the Bank's own mess. Crooks told Murphy to bring his tills and cashbox to the strongroom. They were joined inside by Que Noy, five other members of the staff and a customer, Dennis Connors. A ledger was jammed in the door to prevent it locking. There they stayed until the raid ended.

None of the banks were damaged, although in a raid some weeks later the Bank of New South Wales was gutted and the Commonwealth and Commercial Banks scarred by fragments.

On the afternoon of February 19, Read, Crooks, Harding and Iles waited on Judge Wells — they had been unable to see the Administrator — to seek advice on whether or not they should re-open on the following day. Wells could not tell them what to do nor could Army officers they saw at Larrakeyah Barracks. The District Finance Officer, Colonel A. Ross, said he was remaining in Darwin with his records (a decision soon to be changed) and that decided the bankers to open for business as usual on February 20. However, at 9.30 p.m. the four managers were summoned by the Administrator to Flagstaff House.

"I'm ordering you out of Darwin with all your cash, your

securities and your records and I want you to move before midnight," Abbott told them.

A 3-ton truck belonging to a hardware company was commandeered by police and put at the disposal of the bankers to take them to Adelaide River. They were handed an order signed by Major-General Blake giving them "freedom of the road", though it had no legality. Martial law had not been declared and the roads were not then under military control but the signature of a major-general had a miraculous effect upon officers of lesser rank who challenged their right to be leaving.

Read, Crooks, Harding and Iles[6] had two hours in a blackout in which to pack. Ledgers had already been balanced. There was not enough space on the truck to take all the records, so the last page of each customer's account was torn out. Notes and silver were taken but two of the banks had to abandon copper which amounted, in all, to more than two hundred pounds.

Keith Crooks recalls: "I had ten thousand pounds in cash and hundreds of thousands in securities, Treasury bonds and scrip." Iles and Harding had similar amounts but Read had more than two hundred thousand pounds in cash alone. Between them there was three hundred thousand pounds in immediately negotiable coin and paper. In the next few days they sat on it, sat beside it and slept beside it on a journey of one thousand miles by road and rail to Alice Springs.

The managers left Darwin at 12.30 a.m. on February 20 without their staffs, having been assured by Abbott that they too would be evacuated within forty-eight hours. At Alice Springs on February 28, Harding wired the Administrator and reminded him of this promise. He did not receive a reply. Three weeks later the staffs were still in Darwin, filling in time by helping to clean rubble from the streets. The Commonwealth Bank staff received a coded telegram a week later but the code book had gone with Read and they could not decipher it. Next day the message was repeated in clear; it contained best wishes from head office but no instructions. Finally one of the clerks, Bill Emmerson, hitch-hiked by air to Alice Springs and returned with movement orders.

Iles, Crooks, Read and Harding rode on flat-top rail trucks and then in open Army trucks to Alice Springs, always with one of their number guarding the boxes containing their precious

---

[6] Read, Crooks and Iles have retired. Harding is still serving his bank. When this was written he was manager of the Woolloongabba, Queensland, branch.

cargo. At overnight stops they took turns to sleep in the truck. All carried revolvers.

Crooks recalls: "We were a sorry-looking lot when we reached Alice Springs after five days. We were burnt red and black by the sun and our lips were cracked. We treated these ills with cold beer prescribed to be taken internally by the publican at the Stuart Arms. Quick cures were effected."

Premises to re-establish branches in Alice Springs were unavailable. The E. S. and A. alone was represented there. Read beat this problem for the Commonwealth Bank by taking over a large cell in a disused gaol and was soon back in business in the Northern Territory. Though the door had a heavy locking bar he took the additional precaution of paying aboriginal trackers two shillings a night to camp outside the cell. The cell walls were covered with chalk and charcoal records of the sentences served by previous occupants. When Read left for better premises the Bank's term was also recorded on the wall.

Crooks went on to Adelaide and set up a Darwin branch there. Customers used Darwin cheque books as though nothing had happened. On re-opening his branch in Adelaide he had tellers check pay-in books and cash that had been dropped into a steel trunk in Darwin a fortnight earlier. "It balanced to the exact penny," he told me. "Most of the money belonged to Chinese storekeepers who could easily have cheated us. They were scrupulously honest."

Harding returned to Darwin later in the year to find that his bank had been destroyed by bombs. He also found that the Tin Bank had been burgled. The book and voucher rooms were littered with stationery and records were scattered throughout the building. Robbers searching for the bank's cash, however, were disappointed; that was circulating in the normal way in the Darwin office two thousand miles from Darwin.

It seems scarcely credible that in the dire circumstances then existing, with invasion apparently imminent, the military force was so disorganised that men wanting to enlist in the Army were turned away. Some who went to Larrakeyah Barracks that day to be enlisted were rejected. Others asked provosts how they could join the Army but were told to get out of town and then were stopped by other provosts.

There seemed, indeed, to be a breakdown of the military control within its own establishment. The result was a period of chaos leading to attempted dictatorship by military policemen whose only authority was a uniform and an armband. Civilians were given orders in a manner that inferred trouble for anyone who disobeyed. A number of men were threatened with revolvers.

The Army's inability to control its troops culminated in a serious outbreak of looting. In the days and weeks that followed few Darwin homes evacuated by their owners escaped the attention of thieves masquerading under the pleasanter title of souvenir hunters. The few civilians in essential occupations who remained in the town armed themselves to protect their homes. Unoccupied houses were raided by packs of servicemen and stripped of all they contained. Matthew Luke kept an aboriginal nulla-nulla to deter them from breaking into his house. Soldiers who tried told him frankly they were looking for anything they could pick up. Looters took furniture, refrigerators, stoves, pianos, clothing, even children's toys.

The Administrator recalls: "It is difficult to explain why it went on unchecked for so long. The onus must lie with the commanding officers of units camped close to the town who apparently did not attempt to control their men. It was not uncommon for soldiers to be arrested in private homes while in the act of ransacking. There weren't enough guards to protect the houses; they were busy looking after the stores. An instance of the prevalence of looting is that while the Royal Commission was sitting in Darwin from March 5 to 10, soldiers were at that very time taking refrigerators, radios, sewing machines and clothing in Army lorries to the wharf and selling them to sailors on the motor vessel *Yoochow* for cigarettes and tobacco. Captain L. E. Tozer, R.A.N., saw what was going on and the police at Brisbane, the ship's destination, were informed. They were able to stop most of the property being thrown into the Brisbane River when the crew discovered the vessel was to be searched. Twenty members of the crew were convicted but it was not possible to do anything at the Darwin end."

The looting was by no means confined to men in the ranks. A Major holding a position of trust that gave him access to private property was sentenced by Judge Wells to twelve months imprisonment on each of two counts of larceny. He was confined in the Alice Springs gaol.

An Official War History paper dealing with the raids has this to say: "Much of the [looted] property found its way into the camps of Americans and Australians which sprang up as the services deployed at battle stations. Refrigerators, crockery and cutlery lying around in unguarded premises were taken away as the troops would not bother to get an impressment order. A sinister type of looting developed later with individuals selling stolen goods for gain."

Lieutenant Graham Robertson, who commanded the anti-aircraft guns on the Oval during the first engagement with the Japanese, is engagingly frank about the part taken by his unit in the looting. He said that by February 20 a serious supply problem began to be felt, and added: "The entire Army system had been shot to pieces. We had little food and the anti-aircraft crews doing heavy work in the tropical heat weren't getting enough to eat. We were also short of a few other home comforts and I saw no reason why we shouldn't borrow what we could find in the abandoned Hotel Darwin opposite the Oval. I organised a raiding party. We found beds unmade, cigarette butts in the ashtrays, half-consumed drinks on tables, and other evidence that the place had been evacuated in a hurry. The electricity had failed. Refrigerators were not working and food was beginning to rot, so we helped ourselves to chickens and vegetables and anything else we could use. While we were doing that a provost officer arrived. He wanted to know who we were and what we were doing. I walked him out the front and talked to him there while the boys got the stuff out the back door. Thereafter we had the best equipped gun sites in the north — cane furniture, smokers' stands, inner spring mattresses. We were also very lonely in the next few days while we waited there on that promontory for the invasion we all believed was imminent. The ack-ack boys were there . . . and a few provosts . . . but a lot of other troops had gone and so had the civvies."

The looting, ironically perhaps, is defended in an attitude of extreme Christian charity by the United Church chaplain, the Reverend C. T. F. Goy. He told me: "There has been much talk of looting. I can vouch for the fact that many of the troops were under orders from their officers to take furniture, refrigerators and other useful articles from abandoned private homes. I had one such order addressed to me, so I should know. Houses were being destroyed every day and their contents with them. In these circumstances I think they were justified in acquiring a few comforts for their camps. Officers' and N.C.O.s messes were soon equipped with carpets, chairs and radios. The furnishings of the ornate Hotel Darwin made splendid equipment for our messes. And why not? I know that steps were later taken to prevent looting and that some servicemen were punished with gaol sentences but the very atmosphere in Darwin after the first raids suggested that anything useful should be used. I often walked through the streets at night past houses that had been abandoned in a hurry. I'm sure very few of the owners begrudged the use of furnishings by servicemen who came to defend Darwin. In any case, those who lost anything were reimbursed by the War Damage Commission."

Astonishingly, there was a kind of looting-in-reverse — the acquisition by people of goods they didn't want from others who couldn't use them. Dozens of motor cars were literally given away but were of little value in a town where petrol quickly became unobtainable except for military and essential services. The result was that most of the vehicles were taken over by the Army on impressment orders and the owners eventually paid. Roy Edwards, escorting his wife to the south, gave his sedan to Vincent J. White, the Assistant Director of Native Affairs, at Adelaide River. White could not use it but the Army could. Yam Yan, a Chinese merchant, managed to reach Adelaide River with a truckload of goods. There he discovered that the evacuee train, at a pinch, might have room for him but certainly not for the truck and merchandise. He presented it all to an unknown bystander.

Question: Do you want a motor car, Bill?
Answer: No thanks.
Such conversations were commonplace.

Louis Harmanis, an amiable Greek still living in Darwin, is a witness who qualifies within the limits of the foregoing: he volunteered for service, was rejected and later accepted, and saw his own home being looted.

In February, 1942, Harmanis had been in Darwin for twenty-five years, having arrived as a boy of seven in 1917. He had established himself as a builder and prospector. His wife, Helene, and daughter, Jasmine, had been evacuated on the *President Grant*.

At 9.30 on the morning of the raid Harmanis was in the Public Works Department yard waiting for an order for copper nails to be filled by the storeman. He had expected to be gone only ten minutes from the wharf, where he was repairing a launch used by the Department of Civil Aviation. To get the nails he had to submit requisition forms which took longer than expected. His watch showed 9.55 before he was ready to return to the job and by that time Paddy Hickey, the departmental plumber, had prevailed upon him to wait for a cup of tea. Both men looked up when they heard aeroplanes and Hickey said, "Why would planes be dropping leaflets?"

"Leaflets be damned!" Harmanis shouted. "Go for your life!"

Later Harmanis hurried into town to search for his brothers, George and Steve. Like hundreds of others, he was stunned by the severity of the raid. Like others, too, he forgot his job to seek relatives and establish whether or not they had survived.

He found George and Steve and his sixty-years-old father-in-law, Jack Kailis, who reluctantly agreed to leave town on the first evacuee train.

But now, in the small town where they had been brought up from childhood, the three Harmanis brothers were lost. For an hour or so they walked around aimlessly, trying to solve the predicament of how they would live in a town that had died. Louis Harmanis foresaw a battle for existence — unless the Army would have him.

With his brothers he visited an Army camp on The Esplanade and spoke to a provost officer. "What's going to happen to us civvies?" he asked. "What about giving us a uniform? We might be able to help."

"I can't help you," the officer said. He seemed sorry. "Get out of town the best way you can."

They had no better luck at Larrakeyah Barracks, where the headquarters staff was preparing to evacuate. Others who went there were also rejected. They included Keith Jarvis and Billy Bryson from the Don Hotel who were told: "Come back tomorrow; maybe someone will be able to fix you up then."

The Harmanis brothers then rode bicycles two and a half miles to Parap and planned, if necessary, to go on to Adelaide River. But at Parap a road block was in place and armed provosts barred their way.

"You can't pass this point," they were told. Louis Harmanis asked if they could join the evacuee train but was told it was reserved for women and old people.

"Well what'll we do?" he asked.

"Why don't you join the Army?" a provost said.

Late in the afternoon they returned to town and decided to outflank the blockade. That involved crossing Darwin harbour in George Harmanis' launch, *Sea Dog*. Two other men, Paddy and Leo Hickey, also brothers, went with them. At Delissaville the launch was abandoned and the five men began walking seventy miles south-east to the railway at Darwin River. They set out the same night, each carrying about sixty pounds of food and camping gear in a sugarbag. Two and a half days later they reached the railway. At one o'clock next morning a train pulled in to the siding. Harmanis and his friends tried to get on board but the guard, Robert Pender, said they could not. It was a freight train, he explained, and not licensed to carry passengers. Louis Harmanis saw other men sitting on flat top trucks beneath machinery being taken from Darwin. "A scorched earth policy," Pender said.

"What are those men doing there if you can't carry passengers?" Harmanis asked.

"They're riding illegally," Pender said.

"That'll do us," Harmanis said. "We'll ride illegally too." Pender did not prevent them joining the train.

Harmanis recognised faces he knew. Some were Greeks, some Australians, some Malays, and among them was one old Chinese opium smoker who had been reduced to a bag of salty plums, a Chinese preserve.

"What about the quid you owe me, Louis?" the Chinese said. "You pay me now, eh? I might not see you again."

"I haven't got a quid," Harmanis said truthfully. "Anyway, don't you know there's a war on? We've got a moratorium or something . . ."

The Chinese knew all about the moratorium on soldiers' debts. "You're not in the Army . . ."

"I soon will be," Harmanis said.

At Adelaide River the train was met by six provosts led by an officer. All were armed with revolvers. It was here that the road became an impassable track to Katherine. The provosts had been stationed at Adelaide River to ensure that only men they passed as unfit for military service were allowed to remain on the train. The officer pointed his revolver at Louis Harmanis. "Hey you! Come over here . . . and you! . . . and you!"

"Don't point that gun at me!" Harmanis said. "I'm not a Japanese."

The provost officer flared. "Never mind your insolence!" he shouted, continuing to point the revolver at Harmanis' chest. "Get down from that train and come over here; don't you know martial law has been proclaimed?"

Harmanis did not know it, and it had not been proclaimed, but he had to obey. With others of military age he was taken to a nearby paddock where twenty or thirty men were being held like cattle. They included Oswald Jensen and Snowy Bryant, who gave each of the new arrivals a plateful of stew. Jensen greeted his old friends and then began to revile the provosts.

"What've you got against them?" Harmanis asked.

"Nothing . . . except that they're a bunch of military copper bastards! I got to Katherine . . ."

From Adelaide River, which he had reached by road on February 19, Jensen had been able to go on next day by train to see his aged father in Katherine. He was one of more than one hundred people crammed into cattle trucks and clinging to flat top vehicle trucks. In common with most of the others, he had neither food nor water. At Ferguson River and Pine Creek, after the locomotive had drunk its fill from the overhead tank, the passengers slaked their raging thirsts from the standpipe. A few, fully clad, took quick showers.

At Katherine late that night Jensen's first thought was for food. Fortunately it seemed to be provided — an open bag of unshelled peanuts was standing on the platform. Jensen, still in the white overalls he had worn to work the previous morning, scooped up a handful and began eating; then the hand of self-appointed law fell upon him in the shape of a burly provost.

"In there!" he said curtly, threatening Jensen with his pistol and indicating the ladies' rest room. It was already occupied but this wasn't the moment to demand single rooms. A few minutes later they were joined by a third evil-doer — another hungry man who had also forgotten himself and stolen a few peanuts. He was inclined to be cheeky.

"Drop your gun you copper bastard and see how good you are then," he invited.

"Get in and shut up or I'll drill you," the provost said.

While these three men were locked in the rest room the train drew out for Mataranka and Larrimah. When it had gone the provost released his prisoners.

"Get out, get going, and keep going!" he said.

"But the train's gone!" Jensen protested.

"That's your funeral. Teach you to steal. Get going, I said."

Jensen didn't know it then but soon discovered that during his incarceration his father had been brought back to the train and was now on the way to Mataranka.

Back at Adelaide River two days later DX902 Sapper Oswald Jensen was inducted in 9th Australian Army Troop of Engineers. "It was a sheer case of survival," he recalls. "I was happy to be getting fed and to have someone responsible for me. I didn't care whether they paid me or not . . . just as long as I was kept away from provosts."

He was on hand when Harmanis and his friends were inducted, and all returned to Darwin. On the vehicle strength of Jensen's unit were three of his own utility trucks. He had not been paid and he was not allowed to drive them. They were officers' staff cars.

"One of them gave me a ride once," he recalls. "I told him it was my truck and he said, 'It might've been; it's the Army's now.'"

Jensen was put to work as an electrician installing floodlights on the wharf, a dangerous spot during recurrent Japanese raids. After one such raid he returned to his unit and was told: "Your house has gone, Ossie. The Japs got it today."

"What does it look like?" he asked.

"Like builders' left-overs," they told him.

He was taken to see it. Most of it was next door. A bomb had penetrated the roof and exploded inside. Even the concrete piers were uprooted. His father's drum-shelters were still there but nothing else worth salvaging. The cane lounge furniture looked like a pile of unravelled rope.

"But there were worse tragedies," he told me. "That night our illicit still blew up without any help from the Japanese. We were making raw spirit from dried prunes. Next moment hot prune juice was falling on naked bodies everywhere and men were squealing like children."

One other tragedy affected him. One night the Army decided that Darwin's colourful old Chinatown was not a fit place for human habitation and burnt it down. Only the concrete floors and a baker's oven remained. Jensen's shop disappeared with the rest in a pillar of military smoke.

Harmanis had little better luck. On his first day back in Darwin he went to his former home in McMinn Street. An Army truck was standing at the gate. Two soldiers were carrying radios and furniture from the house.

Harmanis cocked his rifle and said, "Drop that and get!"

"If we don't take it someone else will," they told him . . . but then took his advice.

Harmanis read a notice tacked on the door. "The unfortunate owner of these premises was forced to evacuate. Trespassers will be dealt with. Town Major."

Harmanis went to the Town Major's office to complain that

he had seen his house being looted. But he might have saved himself the trouble. A few days later it was hit by a bomb and blown to pieces.

"At last I was happy . . . happy that it had gone," Harmanis recalls. "I could see that while it was there I would worry; now I had nothing to worry about."

CHAPTER 14

The Forsaken Aborigines

> *'The Aborigines were most loyal and faithful.'*—The Administrator, MR. C. L. A. ABBOTT.
>
> *'Evidence was given before me that the natives of Melville Island were in all probability more favourably disposed towards the Japanese than towards us.'*
> —MR. JUSTICE LOWE.

The departure of the European and Asiatic population between December and February caused considerable unemployment among aboriginal men. Those so affected were repatriated to their tribal country. Wargite and Larakia tribesmen from the Darwin area went to Delissaville settlement west of the harbour. Nevertheless, on February 19 about one hundred were still working in the town.

For some weeks the belief had been widespread that in the event of an air raid the aborigines would panic and run, but so far as I've been able to discover not one left Darwin except by direction.

When the bombs fell they prudently took cover, then emerged smiling though visibly shaken and assuming a nonchalance they obviously did not feel. But they retained a sense of humour. One man named Bismarck who I imagined from his name would be made of stern stuff frankly confessed: "Got plenty fright, all right. Me go walkabout now, quick-time I reckon. Flesh belong me, him got pimple all-the-same-goose."

Within a month Bismarck was back in his country, dancing around campfires at night with tribesmen who burlesqued the air raids, the great explosions, the upheaval of earth, the fear of men, the stampede from town and the closing of the shops.

Soldiers were killed in mime, ships sunk and aeroplanes shot down as they had seen on that first day. A didgeredoo was made to sound like a siren, like the drone of a bomber and the express of falling bombs.

And the Songmen chanted:
Ah-me, Ah-me, Nay-be, Nay-be!
Ah-me, Ah-me, Nay-be, Nay-be!
AIR PORCH! AIR PORCH!

Twelve men employed by the Army at Larrakeyah Barracks remained after the headquarters had moved to camps in the bush. A few days later they were found there by Patrol Officer Bill Harney. They had no corporals, sergeants or officers to instruct them in their duties so they played cards. Harney explained that other raids were likely and an invasion probable. He said he could arrange their repatriation.

"We wait till next Friday, Bill," one of them said. "Soldier come back then for pay day."

Nym Clark, an old retainer employed by a building contractor, Charlie Clark, was with his employer in a house near the police barracks when it was demolished by a near-miss. Covered with dust and bleeding from superficial wounds, Nym ran from the building to get help for Clark, believed to be buried in the wreckage. He was unconcerned about himself and lamented loudly, "My long-time boss bin finish."

But Clark had crawled under a table. When the roof collapsed the table prevented it falling on him, though he was temporarily buried. He was extricated and walked out of the room across the top of his roof, which was on the floor around him.

Air Force officers have testified that when airmen fled after the heavy raid on the aerodrome the aboriginal employees remained on duty until dismissed and told to go.

A group employed on sanitary duties had been near the wharf when it was hit. They sheltered in a gutter and emerged unscathed, but so dirty that one shed his shirt and trousers. He walked through the town wearing only a military cap, sox and boots. He was found thus by the Assistant Director of Native Affairs, Vincent White, who asked if he were all right.

"Yes, Vin, our mob okay," he said. "That's because we speak English. But them myall Liverpool River fellers, they're frightened, they can't understand, they don't speak English."[1]

No aborigines were killed in Darwin that day, although Leo

[1] They were primitive bushmen who had walked 250 miles to "see the lights" in Darwin.

Goodman, as we have seen, had a narrow escape at Government House when the Administrator's office was demolished. Leo's foot was pinned by a slab of concrete and had to be extricated by the Administrator.

"It was just a little-bit accident," he says now. "When that half-caste girl, Daisy Martin, was killed I thought I would die, too, but I pulled through all right."

George Mungalo of the Larakia tribe recalls: "I was working in the pearl shed for my boss, Roy Edwards. I was packing shell. Japanese divers got it for us. I heard this whistle and I looked up topside and I said, 'Hello, Japan-man, he come.' He come all right. I run into the house to my missus, Ash Edwards, and I say, 'Look out missus, bombs coming now.' Roy's not there, see; he's up the town. I grabbed Ash and I took her to the trench and we got in it together. Bombs come close all right. I can see that Japan-man in aeroplane, he looked down and he's laughing. Oh yes, I'm frightened all right, but I'm not frightened for myself, only for my missus. I been with the Edwards family since me little-bit-kid. I born there on Lameroo Beach, right in front of our house, and I don't want that house to be finish or my missus to be finish. I properly frightened for her. After Japan-man fly away I run up town and find my boss, Roy, and I tell him Japan-man bin come. He knows all right. I filled up car with petrol and they going away. I'm sending them away. 'Don't worry about me, missus, boss,' I say. 'Me stop here and look out for house.' That night all Larakia people come together. Tommy Imabul there. Peter Edwards there. Billy Shepherd there, Chook-Chook too. Bob Secretary there, Bob Secretary he owns Darwin, he the big boss of all this land, it belong to his father before, and that one's father before, before the white man come. We go down to Lameroo Beach, that where I born, for council meeting. 'Don't move. We stay here,' I say. We got plenty sugar, plenty tea, plenty bread, plenty flour. I take them from my house. We sleep there on beach. Two nights we sleep there. Then Bill Harney, that old feller belonga Native Affairs, he come. He talk: 'More better you go along Delissaville.' We got no boat. We got no truck. But we got foot all right. We like that old feller, old Billarni, so we do like he says, we walk to Delissaville. Oh yeah, plenty long way all right. Three days, three nights we walk. But we got flour, tea, sugar, we make damper, we all right, we get there bye-'m-bye."

Within a fortnight all male aborigines had been cleared from Darwin and headquarters of the Native Affairs Branch was shifted to Mataranka, two hundred and eighty miles to the south. It was the only branch of Northern Territory Administration remaining in the northern area; all others, apart from isolated policemen, had moved to Alice Springs.

White, Harney, Gordon Sweeney and Fred Morris established five control camps at Koolpinyah, Adelaide River, Pine Creek, Katherine and Mataranka. The Mataranka camp alone had a population of six hundred and fifty people from dozens of tribes.

The camps were created specifically to control aborigines removed from their tribal country and hundreds of others who wandered into areas of military occupation seeking food and tobacco. With the closing down of all business premises north of Newcastle Waters tobacco became unavailable to thousands of men and women addicted to it. A small but significant number of derelicts were also deprived of alcohol and opium dross. Opium had been obtainable by subterfuge from some of the dingy dens of Darwin's Chinatown. As he walked past, an aboriginal known as an addict threw a two-shillings piece through a window or door and continued walking. On his way back he retrieved, often between his toes, a small packet of dross then lying on the footpath. In that way it was difficult for police to apprehend suppliers. These derelicts were habitual prisoners in Fannie Bay gaol, but deprivation which came with the evacuation led to their eventual rehabilitation. The opium trade in Darwin has never been resumed.

Soon after the bombing heavy reinforcements began pouring into the Darwin area for the Army, the R.A.A.F. and U.S. establishments. Bomber and fighter strips were built in dispersed localities and supply installations grew along the road to Mataranka. Within a few months more than one hundred thousand men were in camps on this northern perimeter of two hundred and eighty miles. In addition the Main Roads authorities from three states moved in with men and equipment to construct the all-weather lifelines that became the Stuart and Barkly Highways to Alice Springs and Mt. Isa.

Inevitably, as in all such situations, the question of sex and fraternisation with aboriginal women was raised. Experience in Europe and the Middle East in two wars would have been enough to convince the Army medical authorities of the need for precautions to prevent infection and the resulting dissipation of its fighting strength. But the medical history of the aborigines contained supplementary physical elements which were not only potentially dangerous to servicemen but could

THE FORSAKEN ABORIGINES

easily have precipitated a national scandal. While the incidence of venereal disease among the aborigines was low, it was notorious that leprosy and tuberculosis had spread alarmingly throughout the tribes.

Any doubt of that was dispelled when word was circulated that Gordon Sweeney had recovered a group of escapees from Channel Island leprosarium and had them shipped back to Darwin in the railway department's specially reserved "leper van". Nor were the doctors comforted by the knowledge that among the worst leprosy areas in the Northern Territory was the Pine Creek-Katherine-Mataranka-Roper River line where the majority of base troops would be stationed. To have soldiers infected by venereal disease was bad enough, both for the service and the victim. But to have them exposed to the danger of leprosy with its history of banishment from society was unthinkable.

The Army acted quickly and strenuously, unimpressed by the medical theory that for leprosy to spread from one human being to another required long and intimate association in conditions under which it could flourish. It decreed that no aboriginal might camp within five miles of any military establishment. If an Army camp was required within five miles of an existing aborigines' camp it was the latter which had to be moved. This made necessary the series of control camps, and in each case they were remote from Army camps. Any aboriginal found wandering in forbidden areas, no matter that it might have been sacred ground in his tribal country, was removed at once to a control camp.

Within a few weeks nearly two thousand aborigines were under control. The men were needed and welcomed as laborers. They were given work as timber cutters, sawmillers, camp scavengers, storemen, drivers, sanitary workers and, surprisingly, even as slaughtermen and kitchen hands. They were paid five shillings *a week*. But the Army saw to it that they were transported to and from the control camps each day in its own vehicles.

Moreover, no aboriginal female was allowed to leave the vicinity of the control camp in which she resided. Vincent White now says: "The consequence of this edict was that most aboriginal women and girls spent more than three years of enforced exile in these camps."

"Exile" might be regarded as a poor description of their circumstances. Some would prefer to say that they were prisoners in their own country. While wondering what other class of people anywhere in the world would have submitted unprotestingly to such treatment, one can appreciate that it achieved its objective so well that a senior medical officer at Adelaide River was able to say: "The Army in the Northern Territory is the cleanest in the world."

For three years the aboriginal population remained the responsibility of the Native Affairs Branch, which had a staff of four. The Army provided two soldiers to each camp, one to supervise hygiene and the other to issue rations. The rations included food, clothing and tobacco for males but only food and tobacco for women. When the war ended they were understandably ragged. Their behavior remained exemplary. People from remote tribes, foreigners to one another, fraternised readily and exchanged their cultures in song and dance. The basic pay rate of five shillings a day for a private soldier seemed a princely sum against the five shillings a week that aborigines were paid. They were often advised by soldiers to agitate or strike for better conditions but did not do so. They would not have known how to do so, or why they should. Their cheerfulness was not only sincere but infectious. In a situation of utter boredom, with few amenities, no female company, and not even a war to fight, some white soldiers acknowledged the beneficial influence of aboriginal friendship on their morale.

In a number of respects the aborigines were helped by their contact with the Army. They were well fed. A few were trained as mechanics and in semi-skilled trades. Military hospitals treated aboriginal patients as though they were white soldiers. Illness knew no colour bar. And at this level of mercy which seemed insensible to segregation the Army made history by creating the first confinement facilities in the Northern Territory for expectant aboriginal mothers.

The modest maternity ward at Katherine hospital may well have been the point at which the door began to close on their primitive lives and the first steps taken towards sophistication and assimilation.

It should not be forgotten that aborigines arrested the first Japanese prisoners of war on Australian soil, an event that impressed them so deeply that several mission-educated women did something they had never done before — they wrote descriptive letters to friends who missed the fun. Two of these letters, disclosing flashes of unconscious humor, have survived and are in my possession. One pilot, Hajime Toyashima, came upon a party of aboriginal women after being forced down on Melville Island. According to one of them, "Missus Aloysius", they were terrified.

"I was the first one to see the Japanee man," she wrote. "My friends were out looking for honey nest. I was minding all the babies. The babies were all playing and when one boy saw the Japanee he yelled. Then that Japanee came to me and he salute me. I got properly big fright, all right. I ran away from that Japanee man. He picked up a baby and went into the bush with him. I found my friends and we went looking for that Japanee man and we found him with that baby in his arms. One of my friends went to him and took her baby away from him. He asked if the baby belongest to her, and he put his hand in his pocket and took out a watch and gave it to a boy. We asked him where are all his friends but he didn't answer. That night we hide in the bush and that Japanee man he sleepest alone. Next day our men come back and Matthias and Louis find that Japanee man and take him to the mission station."

Beatrice Piampireiu of the Tikalaru tribe graphically described her fright: "We never give our legs a chance to stop running."

Matthias Ngapiatilawai of the Mandiupi tribe, then aged twenty-one, has said of his part in the affair: "I was returning to the camp but found the women had left the place. That's funny, I think. Then suddenly I heard a noise and I saw this strange man. He had a big overall on (flying suit) and inside these I could see a big lump that told me it was a revolver. 'Japanee', I said to my friends, so we moved out into the thick bush around the camp and waited for him to come up. I crept up behind a tree and when he passed I put the handle of a tomahawk in his back and I say 'Hands up!' That Japanee man was amazed when he saw so many native people. He put his hands up. We took off his clothing, everything except his underpants, and I've got his revolver, also a map."

On the walk to the mission station the Japanese wanted the map burnt or returned to him but Matthias refused and saw that it was handed to Air Force intelligence officers.

During the evacuation between December and February the Administration did not discriminate between European and Asiatic women and children, and concerned itself to a lesser extent with those of part-aboriginal blood. These half-castes, although then legally aborigines, were frequently the wives and children of white men who demanded and were given equality of treatment for them.

Unfortunately there were no white husbands to press the claims of fullblood aboriginal women and children for the right to be sent away in ships and aeroplanes. Notwithstanding the efforts of a few dedicated men these people were simply sent back to the bush whence they had come.

Non-aboriginal women who submitted to evacuation were told they were being sent away from a danger area for their own protection. If danger existed for them it was surely no less for women whose skins were totally black — but in many cases only a shade blacker than some of the half-castes. Such discrimination seemed even less defensible when other factors were taken into account. A number of female half-castes at that time were in truth light-skinned aborigines who had been born in the bush or in town humpies. They were distinguishable from their fullblood sisters only by the faint sophistication that a little mission or institutional education had given them. Both groups were equally without civil rights. For the part-aborigines, male and female, equality with Europeans was not granted until 1952, by which time some of the men were wearing war ribbons and decorations.

The aborigines in Darwin were chiefly old retainers of families they had served faithfully for years, sometimes through more than one generation. A few had taken, and keep today, the surnames of the European and Asiatic people with whom their lives had become identified. The Administrator has described them as faithful and loyal and points to the case of a man named Sam who worked for him. Sam had a dual personality; he was a civilised cook and valet, but could also spear fish and track game as well as the most primitive Arnhemlander. Sam and his wife, Silver, were one hundred miles from Darwin during the air raid. After some weeks Abbott, then in Alice Springs, received a message that Sam and Silver were on their way to him and had reached Mataranka, six hundred miles from Alice Springs and three hundred miles from their starting point. They had trudged through swamps and swum flooded rivers, camping at night in trees to avoid crocodiles. Sam's eyes failed and Silver led him over the last stages of the trek to Mataranka at the end of a stick. Abbott recovered them there and they went with him to Alice Springs, grateful simply to have been taken in again by their "boss". Subsequently Lord Gowrie heard Sam's story and was moved by it. He asked Sam why he had done it. "I had to go back to Boss," he explained.

There were many, however, whose long association with civilised settlement had effectively weaned them from bushcraft and the skills essential to the nomadic life they were now being asked to resume. Nor was it appreciated that some aboriginal women lived in Darwin to be near their own half-caste children. In many cases these coloured children had been forcibly taken from rural areas and placed in Darwin's Half-Caste Home, whence they graduated to marriage with Europeans, Asiatics or other half-castes or to a sordid life of prostitution, drunkenness and crime. The cruelty of these enforced separations was now compounded by the evacuation of one and the "bushing" of the other.

Vincent White recalls: "The separation of half-caste children from aboriginal mothers in these circumstances, with neither knowing whether they'd ever see the other again, was poignant in the extreme."

One is not surprised that the mothers wailed piteously and frequently inflicted "sorry cuts" on their heads with stones and knives until blood poured down their faces and bodies.

Official gallantry had decreed Women and Children First. But not black women and children.

The boats sailed, the aeroplanes took off with their cargoes of women, but the aboriginal women, apparently regarded as neuter gender, were left behind.

> My kid, Ruby, leave along boat;
> Missus, she fly in aeroplane;
> Me can't stay Darwin, me go bush,
> May-be I die. All-a-same.

Those who did not go to control camps were returned to their tribal country by the Native Affairs Department. Throughout the war hundreds remained on Bathurst and Melville Islands and at mission stations along the Arnhem Land coast, and were thus nearer the advancing Japanese than the defenders of Darwin.[2]

---

[2] That can also be said of one white woman, Mrs Harold Shepherdson, wife of the superintendent of the Methodist Mission at Elcho Island in north-eastern Arnhem Land. When the wives and children of other missionaries serving on the coast were evacuated by lugger, Mrs Shepherdson refused to leave her husband. She was the only white woman on the coast during the war years, and spent a great part of her time in bush camps on the mainland with the aborigines. She nursed them when they were ill, she helped to feed them, and she kept in touch with her base by radio. The Shepherdsons had already been fifteen years on the coast

Forsaken and segregated as these people were, there were others in worse circumstances.

At a lazaret on Channel Island in Darwin harbour seventy men, women and children suffering from leprosy became untouchables indeed. The patients included Europeans, Asiatics, aborigines and part-aborigines among whom discrimination did not exist. Like the people of Molokai they had been reduced, or raised, to a common social level by a socially unacceptable disease.

All were the responsibility of the Federal Department of Health which controlled the leprosarium. From their barren eyrie in the harbour they had a front-stall's view of the death of a city in a civilisation that had banished them. The European superintendent and his wife were evacuated and the patients left to fend for themselves. As though they, too, were repelled, the Japanese pilots ignored them.

A few days later when invasion threatened, these unfortunate abandoned people were led from the island by Gregory Howard, a coloured man who was himself a patient. Howard ferried them across a narrow strait in a launch, and reached the mainland. There, on the fringes of mangrove swamps, he built bush shelters with assistants who often had only one hand or one leg or one eye.

The halt aided the halt. The blind led the blind. Limping men and women supported themselves with sticks. Some had hands so withered that they had to be spoon-fed. There were times, as they struggled through the mangrove slime, when they had to crawl.

At night they fell exhausted and slept where they lay, huddling around campfires with which they attempted to repel sandflies and mosquitoes. These added intolerably even to the burden of lepers whose sense of feeling was deadened by the attrition of nerves.

They carried food from the supplies left on the island. Those who were able hunted lizards, snakes, crabs and grubs. When they could no longer support themselves Gregory Howard returned alone to replenish their stocks. Three months later several of the patients went back to their island home. Crude as it was, Channel Island offered permanent shelter. Buildings were intact and the rainwater tanks full. They were visited regularly by doctors from the services and food was brought to

when war began; they are still there today, completely devoted to each other and their life work of caring for dependent people.

them. Surprisingly, the patients who returned were those least disabled by the disease. The worst sufferers wandered far afield in scarcely credible attempts to reach their tribal country. The majority were still missing in May when a search was organised by Patrol Officer Gordon Sweeney, of the Native Affairs Department. With aboriginal guides he patrolled the area east of the harbour, anticipating little difficulty in overtaking men and women who were cripples. None were found.

Late in August, six months after the escape, Sweeney was approached by an aboriginal messenger who walked into Katherine. He carried a letter written by a leprous hand on a scrap of newspaper. It read:

> Dear Mr Sweeney. — All the lepers are here except three who have died. Billy will show you where to find us. We need medicine and food. — Gregory Howard.

Sweeney walked into an area ten miles west of the railway at Pine Creek, about one hundred and sixty miles from Darwin. He recalls: "We located the camp and found the lepers from Channel Island. They included seven of the worst cases — men and women who had lost limbs. They were being cared for by relatives and friends who were able to hunt and by others, not lepers, who took food to them at weekends from cattle stations where they were employed. In the six months since the bombing and their dispersal, in spite of serious physical disabilities and without medical attention or adequate food, they had travelled one hundred and sixty miles on foot. They were heading towards their tribal country. Several tribes were represented in the camp, among them two Mudbras whose country was yet more than one hundred miles to the south. Kinship ties had not failed them; sick natives were able to travel through foreign tribal territory because of the system of skin-grouping which ensures 'brothers' and 'sisters' for all aborigines wherever they are living. After I spoke to them they agreed to return to Channel Island. I arranged with the railway authorities for the 'leper' van to be left at the nearest siding. The patients were loaded into the van and it was hooked on to the next northbound train. I travelled with them to Darwin and handed them over to the chief medical officer, Dr Bruce Kirkland."

In December, 1941, the Native Affairs Department recommended to mission authorities that establishments for part-aborigines on Melville Island and Croker Island should be evacuated. The Garden Point mission on Melville Island was controlled by the Catholic Church and Croker Island by the Methodist Church.

Neither responded until, in February, 1942, Bishop F. X. Gsell agreed that the nuns and children at Garden Point should go. They were brought to Darwin in the auxiliary naval vessel *Southern Cross* and were at the convent when the town was bombed.

At that time none of the five Methodist missions on the Arnhem Land coast or Anglican Missions in the Gulf of Carpentaria and on the Roper River had been evacuated. Vincent White was officially critical of what he called "the cavalier fashion in which the missions regarded the survival of their charges."

"The danger had been pointed out to them. They had adequate warning. The children should have been taken away much earlier when it could have been done without risk," he says. The mission authorities say they had been promised a Navy ship to evacuate their people but it did not arrive.

The missions could not expect immunity from attack by the Japanese. Indeed, they were legitimate military targets and highly vulnerable. All had two-way radios used to transmit the reports of coastwatchers, who were sometimes the missionaries themselves. Every mission had an aerodrome which was or could be used by the Air Force. Milingimbi, in the Crocodile Islands, was later used as a R.A.A.F. base as was Gove, near the mission at Yirrkala. Emergency landing fields were built at Cape Fourcroy, not far from Bathurst Island mission, and on Melville Island. Groote Eylandt was a refuelling base for Qantas flying boats and R.A.A.F. Catalinas. Whether as bases then existing or as locations for future bases, all these places were tactically important to Australia; it is surprising not that the Japanese attacked them at all but that they did not attack sooner and more frequently.

The air attack against Darwin electrified the Methodist mission authorities. Arrangements were made at once to send away from all stations everyone except the male staff, the male part-aborigines and the fullblood aborigines, male and female. The mission lugger *Larrpan* with the Fijian missionary Kolinio Saukuru at the helm took the staffs east and southward into the Gulf of Carpentaria to the Roper River. From there they were sent overland to the highway at Mataranka.

But in early April, 1942, there were still more than ninety

part-aboriginal children at Croker Island. A voyage to Darwin in *Larrpan* was considered too risky. Japanese submarines were active in Clarence Strait, which separates Melville Island from the mainland, and in Van Diemen Gulf. On April 7 ninety-six children aged from four days to eighteen years were landed from dinghies at Barclay Point on the Arnhem Land coast. With them were the mission superintendent Keith Wale; a teacher, Miss J. March; a nurse, Sister Olive Peake; a cottage mother, Miss Margaret Somerville; and Mrs Phil Adams, wife of a mission worker and her baby. The party was escorted for part of the distance by the Reverend Leonard Kentish, a Methodist, and the Reverend G. R. ("Dick") Harris, an Anglican. Their trip is remembered as an epic of courage in the story of the war in North Australia.

More than one hundred people had to be fed in the bush three times a day. Before leaving Croker Island women working at fire stoves baked seventy loaves of bread, one hundred buns, three hundred biscuits and five fruit cakes. The sixty miles' journey from Barclay Point to the first refuge at Oenpeli mission was expected to take one day in motor vehicles. It took four days and had to be completed in relays. This must have been one of the strangest convoys of the war. In the first truck to leave Barclay Point were nineteen girls and Miss Somerville. The younger girls, Mrs Adams and Sister Peake were in a second truck. Dozens of creeks had to be crossed. The route was through trackless bush. Several tyres were punctured in the rough going and had to be repaired. Young children strayed from camps and became lost but were found again. The party bathed in and drank from the same waterholes. When food was short they ate goannas.

One of Miss Somerville's most precious possessions on this stage of the trek was a bottle of yeast with which she made bread in camp ovens. Before reaching Oenpeli the two trucks were separated and had not regrouped before darkness fell. One party camped all night in the bed of a creek without food, which was on the truck ahead. At Oenpeli late at night Mrs Adams was near collapse. For twelve hours she had been bumped through the bush with a young baby in her arms. Sister Peake put her to bed and took charge of the infant, whose curly hair was matted with grass seeds and its body a mass of prickly heat. In the next three weeks that baby crossed Australia in half a suitcase with a pillow on the bottom.

When the first party reached Oenpeli they found the store

locked. The key was in Dick Harris's pocket — and he was somewhere in the bush with a broken down truck. Every scrap of food at the mission was in the store. Therefore the Methodist missionary, Len Kentish, committed burglary on Anglican property by climbing over a wall and through a wire barricade that had been built especially to keep people out. By midnight he had rice and sugar for the children.

After some days the entire party was together again. From morning till night the women baked bread in wood-burning stoves. They left Croker Island with food for a fortnight, but as the Oenpeli wireless transceiver had broken down, communication with the outside world was impossible and they remained there for four weeks. Bullocks from Harris's herd were killed to provide the fifty pounds of meat needed for every meal.

Miss Somerville was responsible for feeding the multitude. "We must have driven Dick Harris mad but he never complained," she recalls.

While at Oenpeli one of the small boys died. He was Charlie Hayes, a four-year-old Croker Islander, but he was the only casualty in what became an epic journey. For the first sixty miles between Oenpeli and Pine Creek only one truck was available, and that was needed to carry supplies. So most of them walked and a few rode mission horses. They had seventy loaves of bread, one thousand biscuits, and limited quantities of salt beef, rice and syrup. They slept under the stars on the bare ground.

Bob Randall, then aged eight, remembers every day of the arduous trek. "We were walking . . . and walking . . . and walking . . . and then we fell down and ate our rice and syrup and slept without stirring."

Thus began the second leg of a journey across the continent by one hundred people who, when a check was made, were found to have exactly fourpence halfpenny between them.

"Talk about mad missionaries!" Miss Somerville recorded.

The West Alligator River was crossed in dugout canoes. The mission trucks were taken across on a raft made of petrol drums and bush timber. Still there was no track and members of the party again became separated. The children's feet were cut and sore and some were badly sunburnt.

At Nourlangie, one hundred and fifty miles from Pine Creek, they were met by government lorries in the charge of Constable Alfred Johnson. It was here they said goobye to Len Kentish who had been so helpful. None were then to know that it would be a final goodbye. A few months later Kentish was abducted by the Japanese in extraordinary circumstances[3] and executed.

But now they had five lorries and in two days reached Pine Creek, a military town already full of Australian and American troops who stood goggle-eyed at the sight of these strange women and children emerging from the Arnhem Land bush. For the women Pine Creek represented just another kitchen on the route; they cooked thirty dampers, hundreds of scones, and kerosene tins full of rice for a train trip to Birdum. The train was fully in keeping with their earlier means of travel. The party was allotted three cattle trucks. But such was the improvement that Miss Somerville recorded: "They were large airy trucks about twenty feet long and eight feet wide. We could spread blankets and move around. We had never had such spacious means of travel and to us it was luxurious . . ." Next day, for the first time since leaving Croker Island, the women shared a meal they didn't have to cook. All were invited into an Army mess for ladles of steaming stew and slices of bread, and they dipped their mugs in coppers of scalding tea. Then there were stewed apricots. Luxury, indeed.

From Birdum there followed three days of riding in a convoy of military trucks to Alice Springs through heat and red dust that were unimaginable. One young girl, a brunette, rubbed olive oil into her hair and arrived as a dusty redhead. For six hundred miles on gravelled roads the corrugations were severe, but small children were now so travel weary that they curled up on the trays of trucks and slept with their heads on the floor within inches of the wheels.

At Alice Springs the women had their first hot bath in a month. A baker brought bread. There was a telephone and electric light and real beds to sleep in. The only children on sick parade were several with stomach pains and distended abdomens; later they were discovered to have been chewing pituri, a wild tobacco used by the aborigines as a narcotic.

Another train took them to Adelaide. They were jammed into small carriages, feeding themselves from issued rations that included one hundred loaves and tins of fishes, tins of jam, tins of fruit, tins of milk. These were stacked under seats and in luggage racks. And so the multitude came to Adelaide . . . and to Melbourne . . . and to Sydney, two months after they had left Croker Island.

[3] See Appendix 2.

CHAPTER 15
Aftermath

1. *The Military Inquest*
'The result at the R.A.A.F. station was deplorable.'—MR. JUSTICE LOWE.

On March 3, 1942, the Federal government appointed Mr Justice Lowe[1] of the Victorian Supreme Court as a Royal Commissioner to inquire into the circumstances of the February 19 raids.

The terms of reference included the preparedness of the naval, military, air and civil authorities; the damage and casualties; the degree of co-operation between the services; the steps taken to meet the attack or minimise its effects; whether any military commander or civil authority failed to discharge his responsibilities; and to recommend what changes might be necessary to meet a recurrence of an attack of this nature. The Commissioner was assisted by Mr J. V. Barry, K.C.,[2] of Melbourne, and Mr H. G. Alderman, of Adelaide. Hearings were conducted at Darwin from March 5 to 10 and in Melbourne from March 19 to 25. Approximately one hundred witnesses were examined.

It was obviously going to be of considerable assistance to me in researching this book if I could have access to the transcript of evidence taken on oath before the Commission. Accordingly, on March 10, 1964, I wrote to the then Minister for Defence, the Honourable Paul Hasluck, asking to be permitted to view the transcript.

The Minister replied on April 2, 1964, denying permission. He said the hearings had been held *in camera* and many service witnesses who gave evidence had been assured of secrecy. The Minister regretted he could not release the document for public scrutiny but softened the blow by telling me it was one of

[1] Later Sir Charles Lowe, Chancellor of the University of Melbourne.
[2] Later Sir John Barry, a Judge of the Victorian Supreme Court.

very few sets of documents not made available to the Official War Historians, of whom he was one.[3]

Two days later I wrote again asking simply that the names of the witnesses might be released so that I could write to them personally. Senator Shane Paltridge, who had succeeded Hasluck as Minister for Defence, replied on May 6 refusing this request for the reason that it would be an invasion of privacy.

I understood the first refusal but not the second. If a witness did not wish to speak to me he had only to say so. All I asked for was a list of names. These decisions did not stop me seeing most of the people vitally concerned, including high-ranking officers who are still serving. But I was prevented comparing statements made in the heat of the moment with what may have been more considered judgments twenty years later. And I was not able to assess the reliability or otherwise of evidence on which the Royal Commissioner based some rather remarkable conclusions that led him to a number of inaccuracies.

Mr Justice Lowe made two reports to the government, one on March 27 and the other on April 9, 1942. In them he directed rebukes at a number of people, notably the Administrator and serving R.A.A.F. officers and men. He seemed less anxious to castigate the Chief of the Air Staff, the Air Board, and the Federal Government and its predecessors for failing to equip the Darwin base with modern weapons manned by experienced airmen, which might well have come within his terms of reference.

Although Australia had then been at war for two years and five months, and with the Japanese for ten weeks, the R.A.A.F.'s total front-line aircraft in North-western Area consisted of seventeen Hudson bombers and fourteen Wirraways.

This modest force was not all at Darwin. Eight of the Hudsons, *without crews*, were at Daly Waters, more than three hundred air miles to the south. Six of the remaining nine at Darwin had arrived on the morning of February 19 from Timor with base staffs being evacuated. Nine of the fourteen Wirraways were at Batchelor. The five in Darwin, based on the civil aerodrome, were unserviceable.

The only other aircraft present were American. If the Wirraways are discounted, as they must be, it will be seen that the R.A.A.F. did not have a single fighter under its control to help repulse the first attack on Australia in conditions of war that

[3] *Australia in The War of 1939-45.* Volume I: 'The Government and The People' by Paul Hasluck.

made it inevitable. Even if the Wirraways had been serviceable they could not have been used as fighters. There had been a fiasco at Rabaul when Wirraways attempted to compete with Zeros, culminating in a notorious signal to the Air Board by their commanding officer, Wing-Commander J. M. Lerew. This message had read *"Nos morituri te Salutamus"* — "We who are about to die salute you." Lerew was abruptly transferred in the fit of high-level pique thus created; but presently a directive was issued that Wirraways were to be reserved for dive-bombing. On home territory, of course, there were no targets to bomb and Wirraways did not have the range to reach foreign territory and return. Thereafter they were used for seaward reconnaissance or stayed on the ground.

But it was not solely in fighting aircraft that the Air Board and governments had failed the defenders of Darwin. Communications at the vital tactical and operational levels were primitive. The Department of Civil Aviation had a voice-link but the R.A.A.F.'s ground-to-air messages had to be sent by telegraphy. R.A.A.F. planes that did have radio-telephony used equipment that by 1942 was obsolete.

The R.A.A.F. had been in Darwin since 1939 and the new station four miles from town was occupied in January, 1940. In 1941 Batchelor was established as a satellite airfield and the main centre for bombs, ammunition and fuel. Yet independent communication between the two bases was so poor that following the destruction of the civil telephone exchange the Batchelor detachment first heard of the bombing by railway telephone.

Flying Officer (now Wing-Commander) Colin G. Harvey, then aged twenty-two, remembers that the Wirraway unit at Batchelor, of which he was a member, had constant difficulty in clearing messages to and from Darwin because of frequency and distance considerations. The distance was less than seventy miles.

Harvey and other officers were deeply troubled and began to improvise. One of twenty-four American Flying Fortresses brought from the Philippines had crashed on the railway line near Batchelor. They salvaged its up-to-date radios. Though having to work without circuit diagrams they re-assembled the gear and soon had it operating effectively with power supplied by car batteries. Harvey's intention was to use the Flying Fortress equipment, with its outstanding radio-telephone capabilities, to set up a base control station at Batchelor that would give a reliable voice link with Darwin. This intention had not been completed on February 19 but when Harvey heard of the attack he was able to inform southern aeradio stations as far as Townsville, one thousand miles away, with a length of wire from his office window used as an aerial. Later in the day he intercepted high priority coded messages for North-west Area from the Air Board; because the Darwin base was then still off the air these "intercepts" were flown there by the commanding officer of the Wirraway squadron, Squadron-Leader Brian ("Black Jack") Walker, in a yellow Moth Minor training plane. Harvey's improvisation was later supplemented by other salvaged equipment. First from a farm shed and then from a bulldozed hole in the ground it provided effective communications to the P.40 fighter group soon to be built up at Darwin, Batchelor and Adelaide River, and continued to do so for several months until an adequately equipped Fighter Sector was formed.

The short-sighted policy which made necessary the use of such makeshift equipment was not criticised by the Royal Commissioner. The policy, or the lack of it, could be translated to other spheres and was irrefutably the responsibility of governments, political parties and higher commands that were soon searching for scapegoats elsewhere than within their own ranks.

A vital matter on which Mr Justice Lowe was critical was that affecting the failure of the R.A.A.F. and Area Combined Headquarters to sound a general alarm following receipt of the signal from Bathurst Island that a large formation of planes was approaching Darwin.

"The A.W.A. station received the message at 9.35 and passed it to R.A.A.F. operations at 9.37. No general alarm was given in the town until just before ten o'clock," he said.

The report added: "Evidence was given before me that according to the routine usually observed R.A.A.F. operations would communicate a message to Area Combined Headquarters and that A.C.H. would communicate to Navy and Army headquarters. R.A.A.F. operations, in the normal routine, would also communicate a message to A.R.P. headquarters.

"On full consideration of the evidence I find that the failure of R.A.A.F. operations to communicate with A.R.P. headquarters is inexplicable. The excuse given for the delay was based upon the fact that earlier in the morning a number of U.S. P.40s had set out for Koepang and, meeting with adverse weather, had returned. Some discussion, it is said, ensued as to whether the planes referred to in the above message were the American planes returning or enemy planes, and that this discussion accounted for the greater part of the delay.

"I find it difficult to accept this explanation. The evidence shows almost conclusively that most of the American P.40s had actually landed on the R.A.A.F. station when this message was received and that the remaining two or three machines stayed on patrol at some height.[4] Moreover, the direction from which the planes were reported was not that in which the P.40s would normally be returning. In any event, the R.A.A.F. station commander, Wing-Commander Griffith, stated expressly that he did not consider the planes flying southward over Bathurst Island might be returning American planes. Another significant fact was the jamming by the enemy of the radio-telephone from Bathurst Island after the message had been sent.

"The delay in giving the general warning was fraught with disaster. It is impossible to say with certainty what would have happened if the warning had been promptly given at 9.37 a.m. but it is at least probable that a number of men who lost their lives while working on ships at the pier might have escaped to safety.

"There is much in the evidence, too, which suggests that a warning of twenty or even fifteen minutes might have enabled vessels in the harbour to get under way, and to have had a far better opportunity of avoiding attack. A twenty-minutes warning might also have enabled officials at the Post Office who were killed to have gone to a place of safety.

"Much evidence was given in an attempt to fix the precise responsibility for the delay in giving the general alarm and in tracing the actual communications which passed from R.A.A.F. operations to other quarters. I have felt that time cannot usefully be spent in the circumstances in determining this matter but it is plain that the station commander must take some responsibility for the failure of the action on the part of R.A.A.F. operations."

Mr Justice Lowe did not mention earlier warnings given by John Gribble, the coastwatcher on Melville Island, and by David Ross, the Australian consul in Timor. He may not have been aware of them.

When his report was printed various comments were made on it by the service departments and incorporated in later editions. The view of the Department of Air was written by Air Vice

[4] These figures are incorrect. Five planes landed and five stayed on patrol. Also incorrect is the Commissioner's conclusion that some had actually landed when the Bathurst Island message was received. Flying Officer Saxton, of R.A.A.F. operations, told the Official War History that Lowe "misunderstood his evidence."

Marshal W. D. Bostock on April 24, 1942, for the Chief of the Air Staff. In discussing the failure to give warning of the raid he had this to say:

"The delay . . . was explained to some extent by the fact that it was known that a number of P.40s were returning on account of bad weather, and also the fact that some were on patrol in the neighborhood. These factors suggested in the mind of the operations room controller that the planes could only be the P.40s. This was a mistake which cannot entirely be excused, especially in view of the report that a large number of aircraft had been observed at a great height, and the knowledge that bombing aircraft could be used by the enemy from Ambon, which they already held. The responsibility for the delay was shared by the Area Combined Headquarters. The failure that occurred is not to be attributed to the system itself but rather to the inexperience of those who were operating it at that time . . . and to the fact that this was the first enemy action against the Australian mainland. The facts are such as to warrant the withdrawal and replacement of certain officers and other ranks. That has already been done."

Mr Justice Lowe was critical, as he had a duty to be. Australia's situation in March, 1942, was desperate. Those who failed their service could not expect to be whitewashed. Much of the criticism was valid. However, there are some aspects of the report that I do not agree with. I thought it was unfortunate that he included a paragraph critical of Melville Island aborigines. The Commissioner said he had been given evidence, but did not name the source, that the Melville Islanders were in all probability more favourably disposed towards the Japanese than towards the Australians. He said a contrary opinion had been expressed by a Catholic missionary, Brother McCarthy, and that the allegations had not been fully investigated. Judge Lowe said he drew the government's attention to the opinions in order that there might be fuller investigation if it was thought necessary. Even in this context, it seems unfortunate that the comments were made in such a widely circulated document as the report of a Royal Commissioner. The Melville Islanders were devotedly loyal and at the end of the war were rewarded for their services. It would be interesting to know the identity of the witnesses who made these statements, but here again I have been at a disadvantage in being refused access to the Minutes of Evidence.

Nor does His Honour appear to have been adequately generous in his attitude to the valiant efforts made by the ten American pilots, four of whom were killed in circumstances of high courage while attempting to fight a numerically superior enemy. The Royal Commissioner may have been poorly informed; indeed, that would seem to be the only reasonable explanation of why he should perfunctorily dismiss the Americans with these few words: "At the R.A.A.F. station the American P.40s which were grounded attempted to take off and to attack the Japanese planes. They were, without exception, shot down." There is no mention of the fact that they *engaged* the enemy and may have shot down one or two planes. And he does not refer to the five other P.40 pilots led by Lieut. Oestreicher who were already in the air except to list them among the casualties.

One of the survivors, Lieut. Max Wiecks, told me in an interview: "It should be said that those of us who were flying were not any more nor less gallant than the people caught on the ground or in the convoy at anchor in the bay during that incredible bombing." The need for such modesty, and Wiecks' own accuracy in this regard, can be judged on the facts related in Chapter 4.

As already shown, some the the Royal Commissioner's statements are clearly erroneous. His conclusion that the P.40s had landed at the R.A.A.F. before the warning message was received from Bathurst Island is a case in point. I have seen Lieut. Oestreicher's combat report and spoken with other American survivors. All agree that the P.40s left Darwin at 9.15 and did not turn back until 9.35. Major Pell's flight could not have landed before 9.50 and it probably was not until a minute or so later. Yet the Bathurst Island report was passed at 9.37. This was by no means the only inconsistency in the report but such an obvious mistake caused hostility among R.A.A.F. officers better acquainted with the facts. His criticism of Wing-Commander Griffith, in this respect at least, was based on false information or on evidence that was misunderstood. Several officers later complained to their superiors of what they said was "the injustice of a civil judge reporting on professional efficiency in an armed service." While that may be a rather fragile argument it does seem that Mr Justice Lowe was critical of mistakes while being himself mistaken.

Nevertheless, his report accurately reveals an unhappy state of affairs in other respects. He made these comments about conditions at the R.A.A.F. after the raids: "The base was practically deserted. For several days thereafter men were struggling back but at a parade on February 23 the muster showed two hundred and seventy eight still missing. As the casualties were very small the result can only be regarded as deplorable. I saw some of these men before me and am satisfied that their quality was not unsatisfactory but that failure arose owing to lack of training and leadership at the relevant time. Competent officers told me that most of those concerned were non-flying men who had been chosen for technical skill and promoted for technical efficiency. There was no guarantee that such men were capable of leadership; in time of crisis it might be shown — as it was — that the quality of leadership was missing."

The Royal Commissioner described Wing-Commander Griffith's verbal order that the men should go into the bush half a mile away to be fed as "extremely unfortunate", and added: "The men were not paraded in sections when the order was given nor were they brought together at all. The order was passed to Squadron-Leader Swan and was to be passed by him to the subordinate officers and by them to the men. What happened in the result was that the order was completely distorted and by distortion reached the men in various forms. Some stated they had to go three miles, others seven miles and others eleven miles. Many of them simply took to the bush. Some were found as far afield as Batchelor, some at Adelaide River, one at Daly Waters and another, by an extreme feat, reached Melbourne in thirteen days."

Mr Justice Lowe commended Group-Captain Scherger for his "great courage and energy . . . which is deserving of the highest praise." He also commended Squadron Leader Swan for his conduct during and after the raids, and said it would be unfair to attribute blame for lack of organisation and dispersal to Griffith, who had been less than three weeks in Darwin.

The opinion which Air Vice Marshal Bostock wrote for the Department of Air also included these statements: "The second main failure in which the Air Force was gravely at fault was the lack of effective aerodrome defence measures, i.e., training relating to action in case of a bombing attack, the definition of duties for individuals in charge, and lectures to officers and men — especially in regard to panic. There is no doubt that a good deal of difficulty resulted from the impossibility to provide adequate equipment and labour. In an attempt to meet difficulties in providing dispersal and camouflage close to the aerodrome, over-dispersal had taken place. Aircraft and personnel were deployed to aerodromes as far distant at Daly Waters [390 miles] and Batchelor without adequate arrangements and communications. Officers commanding squadrons had been forced not only to be responsible for the operations of their squadrons but for the administrative work connected with transfers to isolated aerodromes in country where facilities were entirely absent. Given a little more time there is no doubt that communications, training and aerodrome defence would have been strengthened, and with officers who had had war experience *improvisation*[5] would have been adopted to a greater extent. Dispersal can be carried to a dangerous degree unless it is realised that aircraft must be available at short notice. Improvisation must take the place of equipment to a great extent. This severe lesson has had the effect of making responsible officers realise what is required with regard to better training of officers and men in leadership and aerodrome defence, and that the improvisation of effective communications is an absolute necessity of the highest priority."

Air Vice Marshal Bostock did not spare his own service in referring to the stampede from the R.A.A.F. station and the absence for days of large numbers of men. After attributing what happened to a lack of training and equipment he wrote: ". . . In spite of this and the fact that the majority of men were experiencing enemy air attack on a heavy scale for the first time there is little excuse for the chaos that followed."

From this distance and with a knowledge of all the facts further criticism would be easy but pointless.

Moreover, the administrative problems existing in all services in early 1942, especially in the R.A.A.F., were such that some allowance must be made for them. From a force of three thousand men at the outbreak of war it had expanded in two and a half years to sixty-seven thousand. They had all to be fed, clothed, equipped and trained. If faults there were — and that is admitted — they originated with governments elected by the people.

It seems to have been a regrettable decision, apparently deliberately taken, that airmen who distinguished themselves while others were doing the opposite were neither commended nor decorated by their service. The names of several were sent to

---

[5] My italics.

the Air Board with appropriate recommendations. Air Chief Marshal Scherger has remembered what he describes as the "superlative behavior" of a number of officers and N.C.O.s. "They were magnificent and it seems odd indeed that they were not recognised," he told me. From an entirely different source it has been learnt that the Air Board reaction, expressed in colloquial terms, was broadly, "You don't give gongs for a schemozzle."

The Royal Australian Air Force had already distinguished itself elsewhere and, Darwin aside, lived to fight valiantly on other days.

Darwin was one battle in which it was beaten, as the British and French armies were before Dunkirk, as British and Australian armies were in Malaya, as the Americans were in the Philippines; and as the Germans and Japanese were in the final analysis, with resolute and heroic help from the R.A.A.F.

2. *The Civil Inquest*

'Witnesses committed perjury. I refuse to accept the findings of a Royal Commissioner when they were based on such evidence.'
—The Administrator, C. L. A. ABBOTT.

One of the strangest conclusions drawn by the Royal Commissioner is his statement that the morale of the townspeople was not noticeably affected by the raids and that nothing in the nature of immediate panic developed.

The contrary is true. Morale flagged even before the damage was seen and the casualties counted. A mass exodus of the population followed within an hour of the All-Clear and by mid-afternoon the road to Adelaide River was crowded with cars, trucks, bicycles and men on foot. As we have seen, even a sanitary cart and a road grader were used. The pile-up of abandoned vehicles at Adelaide River reached such proportions that a separate park had to be established for them. The Assistant Director of Native Affairs, Vincent White, remembers what he has called "the milling, frightened crowd at Adelaide River on the evening of the raid." He says that had the Japanese bombed Adelaide River early on the morning of February 20, half the population of Darwin would have been casualties. "The arrival of the sanitary cart as a passenger bus was the only touch of comedy in a grim situation."

Having said that panic did not immediately ensue, Mr Justice Lowe then shows that it did: "Rumours quickly spread and were readily believed. Houses were abandoned in haste. I myself observed in the Hotel Darwin tables upon which drinks remained half-consumed, letters started but not finished, papers strewn about, beds unmade in bedrooms, and other signs of a very hasty exit. In other places I saw similar conditions. In one there were indications of a mail but partly opened. By the middle of the afternoon people were seeking to leave town by every available means. There is some evidence that policemen told civilians the town was being evacuated. There is other evidence that at least one police officer said martial law had been proclaimed and that the police must act under military authority. A long string of vehicles drew up at a petrol station. The Administrator, learning this, forbade them to be supplied. Actually, by some means, many vehicles did proceed towards the south. Many people went on foot and others on bicycles. The foreign element in the population was prominent in the attempt to escape. Business houses were closed and the civil life in the town practically ceased."

The report goes on: "On the night of the 19th looting broke out in some of the business premises and sporadic looting occurred thereafter even to the time when the Commission was sitting. This looting was indulged in both by civilians and members of the military forces. It is hard to believe that if proper supervision had been exercised this could have occurred. The Administrator arranged for a provost company to assist the police in keeping order but I am satisfied he was not fully acquainted with the conditions which were developing. Telegrams he sent to the Minister for Interior failed to give an adequate idea of the conditions. In my opinion this state of affairs was largely due to the fact that there had not been enough foresight of what might result from an enemy raid; consequently no plans were made for the resumption of normal conditions when it ceased. There had been an unfortunate difference between the Administrator and the A.R.P. organisation in January. I am not in a position to conclude whether the charges of apathy urged against the Administrator in relation to A.R.P. had any foundation, but at least I am clear that this difference prevented the police being aided by A.R.P. officers in preserving law and order after the raids . . . The absence of planning was largely responsible for the subsequent disorganisation. It is not an easy thing to improvise successfully measures to meet such a situation and the attempt to do so in this case was inadequate and a failure. Co-operation between the civil and military authorities was called for. This was afforded at too late a stage. In spite of the differences which had occurred between the Administrator and the A.R.P. a number of A.R.P. workers, on the occurrence of the raid, immediately went to the positions planned for them to act . . . and gave excellent service in attending to wounded, extricating the bodies of the killed, and aiding the police and military authorities."

On April 11, 1942, only two days after the Royal Commissioner's report was signed, the Administrator sent a letter of five thousand words to the Minister for Interior, Senator J. S. Collings, defending his actions and complaining bitterly about certain aspects of the inquiry, at which he had been refused the right of legal representation. The reasons for this refusal appear in the secret transcript but have not been made public.

Abbott regarded the Commissioner's strictures as being tantamount to neglect of duty. He had little knowledge of the evidence given and, like everyone else, was unable to see the transcript. It appears, indeed, that the pledge of secrecy given to witnesses encouraged wild exaggerations and defamation. My independent researches have shown that statements were made which can only be described as coming from the realm of fantasy and the desire to besmirch.

Abbott wrote to Senator Collings: "The evidence of certain witnesses was read to me. It was quite sufficient for me to see that deliberate and wilful perjury had been committed. One witness was asked whether he realised the seriousness of the statements he made upon oath. He said he did and continued to commit perjury. Yet this deliberate and malicious lying is privileged! One constable said he objected to loading glass and china from Government House on to a truck on February 19 when a half-caste girl was probably still alive and buried under the wreckage of my office. Pressed for confirmation, he repeated that it was the 19th and was supported by another constable. But that had been done by Police Sergeant Littlejohn on February 21. I drew attention to the extraordinary fact that Littlejohn was in Darwin when the Commission sat but was not called to give evidence although he could most definitely have fixed the date and the circumstances of the removal of the property from Government House."

Abbott was cross-examined for hours on this point, apparently in an attempt to discover whether or not police services had been misused by him on the 19th. As we have seen[1] the half-caste girl under his office was Daisy Martin, who was killed instantly. Abbott himself had extricated her with the help of his chauffeur and personal secretary, and they had also freed an aboriginal who was trapped by the leg.

Abbott complained, not surprisingly, that much other evidence against him was equally inaccurate and had been expressed by a particular section of the townspeople. The Commissioner reported that in view of this it was "at least dangerous to draw an inference against the Administrator when an examination of all the relevant evidence . . . might lead to a different conclusion."

Notwithstanding that comment, he was indeed critical and said that leadership was conspicuously lacking. And, in spite of it all, he refused Abbott the right to legal aid, though he asked for it.

Abbott referred to other instances in which he said the Commissioner's statements were not in accordance with fact. He repeated that evidence had been given which was "false and wicked." He then added: "It is most difficult to deal with charges of this kind when the evidence is not available for perusal and the witness has spoken in complete security without being subjected to cross examination. The Commissioner has made so many comments which are obviously based upon incorrect or untruthful evidence that I feel further action must be taken. I am too proud of my record to allow it to be besmirched by perjurers without availing myself of every possible avenue of vindication. It is unthinkable that a most important inquiry as this should have been conducted in such a manner. Instead of helpful information being elicited it seems that various witnesses used the Commission as a means to ventilate their spleen upon me for doing my job as Administrator. It also seems to me that no effort was made by Counsel assisting the Commissioner to rebut or check this evidence and that the functions of Mr Barry K.C., so far as I was concerned, became those of a Public Prosecutor. There appears to have been little attempt to cross-examine witnesses who made damaging and malicious statements about me. Hardly any senior officers of the

[1] Chapter 9.

Administration were called . . . comparatively junior officers have been preferred. I do not admit that I failed in the performance of my duties, I do not admit that I failed to show any qualities of leadership, and I refuse to accept the findings of the Commissioner so far as I am concerned."

On April 13 the Secretary of the Department of Interior, Mr J. A. Carrodus, addressed a memorandum to his Minister commenting on the report and expressing the view that there was no justification whatever for disciplinary action against the Administrator. He said: "He is entitled to be given access to the transcript so that he may know what evidence was given against him and the persons who gave such evidence. If, as alleged, some persons, including junior members of the police force, have committed perjury, they should not be protected at the expense of the reputation of the Administrator."

On April 20 the Minister himself wrote to the Prime Minister, Mr Curtin. He had also not been able to see the transcript of evidence though he had asked for it more than once. He told the Prime Minister: "I have a strong impression that Mr Justice Lowe bases some of his findings which reflect upon the Administrator on the evidence of one section of the community. His Honour himself speaks of the difficulty of evaluating this evidence correctly. While I would not desire to champion the Administrator if anything concrete could be proved against him I do feel, out of ordinary justice to him, that I should tell you of a steady flow of complaints from one section of the community that I have received since becoming Minister. Although sweeping accusations were made against the Administrator none of the accusers ever made an effort to substantiate his charges with sworn statements although repeatedly asked to do so, and on a promise of immediate action. I am of the opinion that the complaints were biassed and made with little sense of responsibility. I feel that the Administrator effectively disposes of the allegations against him in the report of the Commissioner. The Administrator asks that the matter be not left where it is at present. His reputation has been attacked but he is not given an opportunity of knowing the basis of the Judge's criticism or the persons who have given evidence against him. The position, as it stands, is most unsatisfactory to the government, the Administrator, and myself. I see no justification in recommending that any action be taken against the Administrator. Rather do I feel that he did a very good job of work in most trying and difficult circumstances."

This spirited defence of Abbott was certainly not dictated by party politics in a desire to protect a colleague. Abbott was a conservative appointed to the job by a conservative government. Senator Collings was a socialist and a member of the Labour government then in power.

Nothing further eventuated, but it can readily be seen that the worth of the Royal Commission to the war effort was negligible. And it ceases to be surprising, in all the circumstances, that I was refused access to the transcript.

3. *Reckoning for the Japanese.*
'I belong to Jesus.'—COMMANDER FUCHIDA.

The most optimistic Australian and the most despondent Japanese (if there were such people early in 1942) could scarcely have imagined the dramatic change the war would take within four months nor believe that the seemingly invincible armada which had struck Pearl Harbour, Rabaul, Darwin and Ceylon would be at the bottom of the Pacific Ocean. Yet on June 4, 1942, Admiral Nagumo's task force perished with fearful loss of life in a bitter reckoning at the Battle of Midway.

The carriers *Akagi, Kaga, Hiryu* and *Soryu* were all sunk. *Akagi*, in which Nagumo flew his admiral's flag as commander of them all and from which Fuchida had led so many successful attacks, suffered the ultimate disgrace in Japanese eyes of having to be scuttled. The fact that the Navy had never before scuttled one of its own ships made the decision an exceedingly distressing one.

Fuchida and Nagumo barely escaped with their lives. Fuchida suffered the further frustration of being unable to fly against the Americans in this decisive battle. While Nagumo's Force was steaming towards its last rendezvous Fuchida sat up in bed one night with sharp abdominal pains. As *Akagi* sped eastwards Fuchida pleaded with the ship's surgeons to allow him a few days before operating. But they were adamant and removed his appendix the same night.

"This was a hard blow for it meant I would be a helpless spectator of the exciting events about to begin," he recalls.

On the morning of June 4 he was wakened at three o'clock by aeroplane engines being warmed up in *Akagi's* hangars. An attack on Midway Island similar to the Pearl Harbour and Darwin operations was about to begin. Fuchida was unable to resist watching the launching of the strike forces he had led so successfully elsewhere. He climbed out of bed and stood shakily for a long time while his unsteady legs gained strength. If he was to get from the sick bay in the centre of the ship to the flight deck he had a long way to go. "I knew the surgeons would be angry but I had to do it," he recorded. "I began walking. The water-tight doors of every bulkhead had been closed for combat readiness, leaving only a small manhole in each door. It was an arduous task to squeeze through each of these in my weakened and painful condition and cold sweat soon ran down my forehead. I frequently felt exhausted and dizzy and had to squat on the floor to rest. The passageways were empty, otherwise I may have been detained and put back to bed. All hands were at their stations. The lights had been dimmed and I could see only a few feet. With a great effort I finally climbed the ladders up to my cabin just below the flight deck, clutching the handrails every inch of the way. There I paused long enough to catch my breath and put on a uniform before going on to the flight control post. The first wave of attack planes were lined up. My colleagues expressed concern that I had left my bed but understood when I explained that I could not bear to hear the sound of engines and remain below in the sick bay."

In retrospect it seems almost that Fuchida might have known this was to be the last time he would see many of his friends or the bustle of preparations on *Akagi's* flight deck. For not only did the four carriers sink; fifty-two aeroplanes and their crews, most of whom had been at Pearl Harbour and Darwin, were lost in combat that day. Another two hundred and eighty planes went down with the ships. This was a fearful loss to the Japanese in ships, aircraft, men and face, and one from which they did not fully recover. It was on this day that Nagumo and Fuchida and their compatriots knew what it was to be on the receiving end of the mass attacks they had repeatedly delivered since December 7, 1941.

Fuchida, weak from his exertions, collapsed on *Akagi's* flight deck, helpless and giddy. A parachute pack was placed under his head as a pillow and from there he watched the preparations and the launching. But at ten thirty Fuchida experienced for the first time the terrifying scream of dive-bombers and the crashing explosions of direct hits around him. He crawled along the flight deck to the protection of a command post and was appalled by the destruction in his beloved ship. There was a huge hole in the flight deck itself. The elevator, twisted like molten glass, was drooping into the hangars below. Deck plates reeled upwards. Planes stood tail up, belching flame and smoke. "Reluctant tears streamed down my cheeks as I watched," he recalls.

Fuchida staggered down a ladder to a room which was packed with badly burnt victims from the hangar deck. Neither of the two direct hits by American Dauntlesses would normally have been fatal to the giant carrier but they set fire to fuel and ammunition and induced explosions which devastated entire sections of the ship. As planes caught fire their torpedoes exploded, soon causing an inferno which made it obvious that the ship was doomed. Fuchida was horrified on returning to the deck to see that *Kaga* and *Soryu* had also been hit and were on fire. Very soon the situation in *Akagi* was such that Nagumo was forced to shift his flag to a cruiser, the *Nagara*, where Fuchida presently joined him in exceedingly painful circumstances. When *Akagi's* bridge and flight deck became uninhabitable Fuchida attempted to reach the anchor deck. Sailors helped him out the bridge window and from there he slid down a smouldering rope to the gun deck below. He could not use a connecting ladder to the anchor deck because it was red hot, as was the iron plate on which he now stood. Remember that this man had had his appendix removed only three days earlier. The only way to reach the anchor deck, however, was to jump, which he did. While he was in the air another explosion occurred in the hangar and the blast sent him sprawling. The force of the fall and the pain in his side were such that he was knocked out. On regaining consciousness he tried to stand but cried with pain and fell. Both of his ankles were broken.

Crewmen assisted him to the anchor deck. There he was strapped into a bamboo stretcher and lowered to a boat which took him to join Nagumo in *Nagara*. They were among the fortunate. Two hundred and sixty of *Akagi's* crew perished. Men caught below decks were prevented from reaching safety by fires and smoke. Not one man escaped from the enginerooms. Shortly before dawn on June 5 *Akagi* was scuttled by torpedoes fired from four escorting destroyers. For Commander Magotaro Koga, captain of the destroyer *Nowaki*, the pride of his own fleet was his first target of the war.

The carriers *Kaga*, *Hiryu* and *Soryu* also sank that day. The total loss of life was three thousand five hundred men. When it became inevitable that the ships would sink Admiral Yamaguchi, the commander of Carrier Division 2, summoned all hands to the flight deck of *Hiryu*, where he then had his flag, and publicly accepted responsibility for the disaster. He commanded them all to abandon the ship after announcing that he would remain aboard. The staff drank a silent farewell toast in water and Yamaguchi lashed himself to the bridge structure so that he might go down with the ship. Admiral Nagumo committed suicide on Saipan island towards the end of the war.

For Mitsuo Fuchida, one of the most brilliant air tacticians of the age, the war was almost over. He reached Japan in the hospital ship *Hikawa Maru* and then experienced extraordinary security measures in the government's efforts to keep news of the Midway disaster from the people. Fuchida was not moved ashore until after dark when the streets of Yokosuka naval base were deserted. Then he was taken to a hospital on a covered stretcher and carried in through a rear entrance, a reception far different from one he had earlier enjoyed as a conquering hero. His room was placed in complete isolation. Nurses and medical corpsmen were denied entry to him and he could not communicate with anyone outside the hospital.

"In such manner were those wounded at Midway cut off from the outside world," he recorded. "It was really confinement in the guise of medical treatment and I sometimes had the feeling of being a prisoner of war in my own country."

Finally he was discharged and went to the Naval War College as an instructor. One of his assignments there was to write a detailed report on the Battle of Midway. Later he became air operations officer at Combined Fleet headquarters under Admiral Yamamoto. He was still a dedicated militarist for whom defeat was bitter; so bitter, indeed, that he believed his effective life to be ended when the nation capitulated on August 15, 1945.

Yet, as he now sees it, it was just beginning and in a manner so dissimilar that the change is scarcely credible. How that came about is a fascinating demonstration of the malleability of human nature.

Fuchida's career began at the Japanese Naval Academy at Etajima on the Inland Sea in 1921. The Navy was already indoctrinating its future officers with the idea that America was a potential enemy and he grew up in that tradition. The Navy stood for southward advance through Asia and the Pacific which meant an inevitable clash with the United States. The Army preferred a policy of northward expansion which would involve friction with Russia.

Towards the end of 1936 Fuchida was sent to the Naval War College as a student. It was a critical time, for presently Japan renounced the Washington Treaty under which naval arms were limited. At the War College, that was followed by frank discussions among the officers of the problems of naval armament and the possibility of war, which many of them already considered inevitable.

In the light of subsequent events, Fuchida's attitude at the time is interesting. He believed the naval armament policy was hopelessly out of step with the radical changes that had taken place in aviation. He advocated abandonment of the idea that Japan might attain victory and become the supreme Pacific power merely by outbuilding her rivals in warships. He was convinced that conventional naval armament based on the surface strength of bigger and yet bigger battleships had become largely ornamental.

"In future," he wrote, "aircraft will be the deciding factor. Moreover, air warfare will be total warfare, requiring the complete mobilisation of all national resources and activities."

Thus spoke profoundly the eventual destroyer of Pearl Harbour and Darwin and a man who, unlikely as it seems, was finally to become a Christian evangelist — an advocate of goodwill, peace and brotherly love.

But that was still far in the future. Fuchida began the war as a warrior intent upon the annihilation of his country's enemies. In the months between the success at Pearl Harbour and the humiliating defeat at Midway he grew increasingly fretful and dissatisfied with the role of the Carrier Task Force, complaining openly that its strength was being vitiated by assignment to secondary missions in the south-west Pacific when it should have been concentrating upon the destruction of its main and ultimate adversary, the United States Fleet. Darwin, Rabaul and Ceylon, in Fuchida's view, were targets that might have been attended to by a single carrier while the remainder hunted the Americans. In this respect he became uncharacteristically critical of his own admiral, charging Nagumo with vacillation and pliancy and believing that he was not adequately presenting to Admiral Yamamoto at Combined Fleet headquarters a sufficiently forceful view that the United States Fleet must be sought out and destroyed. The validity of his contentions was demonstrated beyond question in the reversals soon to follow.

Fuchida's militarism did not die with the burial of the task force at Midway and the personal ordeal he survived, nor was it quenched by the horrors that fell on Hiroshima and Nagasaki and forced his country's capitulation.

At that time he was forty-two years old and had been promoted to captain in recognition of his brilliance. His parents were Buddhists and Mitsuo was taught the precepts of Buddha as a child. But from the day he entered the Naval Academy in 1921 he did not visit the temple or practise his religion again.

He told me: "My God was the Emperor. My religion was the Navy and the glory of Japan. That did not change when the war ended. I still belonged to the Emperor and believed only in him. My career was shattered but I managed to survive like thousands of others, living from day to day with our misery, wondering whether we should ever be able to build and fight again."

But Fuchida's private day of reckoning was close at hand, much closer than he could have imagined, and came upon him in exceptional circumstances.

In 1950 General Douglas MacArthur expressed a wish to meet the leader of the air attack force which had started the Pacific War at Pearl Harbour. Fuchida was summoned from his home in the Nara prefecture in southern Honshu and travelled by train to Tokyo. On emerging from Tokyo Central Station he was approached by an American missionary and handed a pamphlet. Fuchida's first thought was to discard it but Oriental politeness intervened; instead, he put it in his briefcase and remembered it in his room that night. What he found was a religious tract in the Japanese language written by Jacob de Shazer. Even then Fuchida might not have read on except for noticing the remarkable coincidence in relation to his own background that de Shazer had been a bombardier in the U.S.A.F. raids on Tokyo led by Colonel James Doolittle. Here was common ground and Fuchida became absorbed.

When Pearl Harbour was attacked de Shazer had been in camp in the United States. The news had made him angry and he had asked for a dangerous assignment that would help him take revenge against the Japanese as quickly as possible. He had been offered and had accepted an assignment in Doolittle's force. On April 18, 1942, Corporal de Shazer had parachuted from his bomber when its fuel supply was exhausted. He had landed near Nanking in Japanese-occupied China and had there been captured and interned. Subsequently he spent thirty-four of his forty months in prison in solitary confinement.

With others, de Shazer had been cruelly beaten and starved by his captors and his hatred of the Japanese had grown. A year later, by pleading with his guards, he had managed to get a copy of the Bible. He had been allowed to keep it for only three weeks but in that time he had read and re-read it avidly.

Fuchida told me: "His cell became a cathedral and he was saved. His hatred turned to love. When the war ended he returned to America and studied in Seattle to be a missionary. He learnt the Japanese language. He graduated and went back to Japan to teach my people to know Jesus."

The tract Fuchida had been given was entitled "I See the Need of the Japanese People. The Lord Showed Me the Way in Prison."

Fuchida was influenced by the story. "I obtained a Bible in the Japanese language and while reading it I too was saved," he said.

I saw him in California where he was living with his daughter, Miyako, now an American citizen married to James Overturf. His son, Yoshiya, is married to an American girl and recently graduated as an architect from the University of Oregon. There is a possibility that Fuchida himself, the man who inflicted such grievous wounds on America, may be granted American citizenship. A film about his life was being made in Hollywood. When I spoke to him he seemed less interested in the making of the film than in the fact that the money it earned could be devoted to extending his work for Christianity.

Fuchida supports himself by writing books and magazine articles about both facets of his life. He is equally frank in discussing Japanese treachery, his own part in it, and his present mission in life. He had recently returned from a preaching tour in Japan but preaching does not contribute to his income.

He says he is a layman belonging to what is known as The Layman's Church, which has no ministers and is non-denominational.

"I belong to nobody but Jesus Christ," he said.

BIBLIOGRAPHY

Australia in the War of 1939-45, Australian War Memorial

They Fought With What They Had, Walter D. Edmonds
(Atlantic-Little Brown and Co., Boston, 1951)

Front Line Airline, E. Bennett-Bremner
(Angus & Robertson, Sydney, 1944)

Australia's Frontier Province, C. L. A. Abbott
(Angus & Robertson, Sydney, 1950)

Midway, Mitsuo Fuchida and Masatake Okumiya
(Hutchinson, London, 1957)

Reminiscences of an Australian Army Nurse, E. McQuade White

Darwin Drama, Owen Griffiths
(Bloxham & Chambers, Sydney, 1946)

Tides and Eddies, Maie Casey
(Michael Joseph, London, 1966).

The extract from *They Fought With What They Had* by Walter Edmonds is reprinted with the permission of Atlantic-Little, Brown and Company, Boston. Ref. p. 31

APPENDIX I

NATIONAL EMERGENCY SERVICES
Civil Defence — Darwin, N.T.

SPECIAL — Notice to all householders, and occupiers of dwelling houses or any other habitation.

In the event of Enemy Raid or other form of Attack upon or in the vicinity of Darwin, it may become necessary for the Authorities to Issue an Order for the Evacuation of the Civil Population to some other place or places of safety.

Such Order to Evacuate will not be issued until after the Proper Authority or Authorities has or have issued a Proclamation declaring a State of Emergency.

The Civil Population will, after such State of Emergency has been declared, receive from the Senior Air Raid Wardens a Notice to prepare for Evacuation.

Such Notice will be issued by one or all of the following methods:
1. Written Notice issued to every Householder or Occupier of a Dwelling House or other habitation.
2. Verbal Notice issued to every householder or Occupier of a Dwelling House or other habitation.
3. A GENERAL ASSEMBLY of the Civil Population at their respective Zone Headquarters.
4. Special Notice in the Northern Standard Newspaper, and/or Notices posted in prominent places throughout the Areas.

Immediately such Notice of Intention to Evacuate has been issued, each and every person warned to Evacuate, will make all necessary preparations so to do.

Each and every Evacuee will be entitled to take the following articles, as personal belongings.
   (a) One small Calico Bag containing Hair and Tooth Brushes, Toilet Soap, Towel, etc. (personal only).
   (b) One Suit Case or Bag containing Clothing, and such shall not exceed 35 lbs. gross weight.
   (c) A Maximum of two Blankets per person.
   (d) Eating and Drinking Utensils.
   (e) One 2 gal. Water Bag filled for each family.

NOTE: Officers in charge of Evacuation have the power to examine luggage and determine what constitutes legitimate personal luggage.

The Senior Warden of the Group will communicate, through his Wardens, full instructions to every Evacuee as to method of Evacuation and time and place of Assembly.

Every Evacuee will be provided with IDENTIFICATION CARDS in duplicate, one of which will be handed to the Evacuation Officer on DEMAND, and the other KEPT ON THE PERSON.

EVACUEES WILL BE DIVIDED INTO SECTIONS OF FOURTEEN (14) PERSONS, ONE OF WHOM WILL BE DETAILED AS SECTION LEADER and RESPONSIBLE FOR THE CONDUCT OF THE GROUP OR SECTION.

RATIONS WILL BE PROVIDED BY THE AUTHORITIES AND ISSUED TO THE SECTION LEADERS FOR DISTRIBUTION.

PERSONS OTHER THAN THOSE TO BE EVACUATED WILL REMAIN IN DARWIN, AND OBEY THE INSTRUCTIONS ISSUED BY THE CHIEF AIR RAID WARDEN.

No Evacuee, shall take or attempt to take, with him or her, any domestic pet, either animal or bird, and any such pets owned by Evacuees should be destroyed prior to the Evacuation.

No facilities will exist for feeding of these pets after Evacuation.

Domestic Poultry would be an Auxiliary Food Supply for those remaining in Darwin, and as such will not be destroyed under any circumstances.

No person or persons will be entitled or allowed to use any privately owned vehicle, or vehicle plying for Public Hire, for the purpose of Evacuation from Darwin, and no method other than that ordered by The Commandant 7th Military District, and effected by the A.R.P. Authorities under such jurisdiction will be permitted in any circumstance.

N.B.—Any Person or Persons acting contrary to these Instructions or additional instructions issued by the A.R.P. Authorities may cause serious upset to the Evacuation Scheme, thereby endangering the lives of themselves and others.

Any Breach of the said Instructions will therefore be dealt with under the National Security Act, and the Offender or Offenders severely punished.

                A. R. MILLER,
                    Chief Warden, A.R.P.
                EDGAR T. HARRISON,
                    Permanent Officer
                    Civil Defence.

DARWIN, N.T.
  December, 1941.

APPENDIX II

Fate of the Reverend Leonard Kentish

In Chapter 14 the story was told of the help given by the Reverend Leonard Kentish in evacuating the last of the part-aboriginal children from Croker Island mission station.

It may be that his own tragic death in an extraordinary episode of the war is not directly related to the foregoing. Nevertheless, as a brave man who has already figured in these pages and a naval ship based at Darwin were involved, it seems fitting that their end should be recorded here, especially as Kentish became the first prisoner-of-war of the Japanese taken in Australian waters.

The small supply vessel *Pat Cam* was one of the busiest ships in Darwin waters during the latter half of 1942. In January, 1943, she called at Milingimbi mission and there embarked Kentish and five aborigines for a voyage to Yirrkala mission at the north-eastern tip of Arnhem Land. One of the natives was Paddy Babawun, a Marangu tribesman enlisted as pilot because of his knowledge of local waters.

On January 22, near Lower Wessell Island, a Japanese float-plane dived out of the sun without warning. The pilot had shut off the engine before beginning the dive. The aircraft was neither heard nor seen until it dropped a bomb which went through an empty hatch and blew the bottom out of the ship. A seaman was killed, the ship's two lifeboats were destroyed, and she sank in less than a minute. The commanding officer, Lieut. A. C. Meldrum, R.A.N.R. (S), and twenty others including Kentish and the aborigines found themselves swimming in shark infested waters almost before they realised what had happened. They were six miles from land. The float-plane returned and dropped another bomb in their midst. This had a similar effect on the men as dynamiting has on fish. Their bodies felt as though they were being crushed. One man's face was puffed up and his eyes blackened by the concussion. Three white sailors and three aborigines were killed. Kentish, Meldrum and Paddy were far enough away from the explosion to escape with a severe shaking.

Having survived such close attention the men in the water hoped the Japanese pilot would fly away, and such appeared to be his intention. However, he turned and landed the float-plane near the survivors in a perfectly calm sea. There were three men on board. Each drew a pistol and brandished it as though preparing to do a little close-range sharp-shooting at the men in the water. But they had other plans. Two of the Japanese stood in the cabin with pistols drawn while the third climbed out along a float and beckoned to the nearest survivor with his pistol. He was Leonard Kentish, B.A., B.D., chairman of North Australia District of Methodist Overseas Missions. In face of the threat, which he already had good reason to believe was seriously intended, Kentish swam to the plane and, unresisting, was hauled aboard. The Japanese immediately took off with their prisoner.

Kentish was not seen alive again by anyone who knew him. Not until July, 1947, almost two years after the end of the war, did his wife learn that he had not survived his imprisonment. He was taken to Dobo in the Aroe Islands and beheaded within a fortnight by Lieut. Sagejima Mangan. In August, 1948, this officer was hung at Stanley gaol, Hong Kong, for the crime. Asked if he had anything to say before the sentence was carried out he replied, "Yes. I thank you. Long live the British Empire."

Meldrum, Paddy and the other survivors managed to make a raft from oil drums and pieces of floating timber. Sixteen hours later they reached an uninhabited island. They lived on oysters and watched helplessly while two more of their colleagues, one black and one white, died. Two days later aborigines in a canoe answered smoke signals made by Paddy and came to their rescue. At that time Kentish's son, Noel, was aged six. He is now the Reverend Noel Kentish, B.A., a missionary in Tonga.

APPENDIX III
Attack on Florence D *and* Catalina

At 8 a.m. on February 19, as the Japanese were preparing to launch their attack force, Lieut. T. H. Moorer and Ensign W. H. Mosley left Darwin in a Catalina flying boat of the U.S. Navy for a routine patrol in the vicinity of Ambon, six hundred miles to the north. With them were six other men: J. J. Ruzak, A. P. Fairchild, J. C. Shuler, R. C. Thomas, F. E. Follmer and T. R. LeBaron.

Little more than an hour later, off the north-west cape of Melville Island, the Catalina was attacked by nine fighters. These were later seen to be part of the formation flying towards Darwin. Moorer subsequently reported:

"They set us on fire, destroyed the port engine, and put large holes in fuel tanks and fuselage. We were flying downwind at 600 ft. I tried to turn into the wind but all fabric except starboard aileron was destroyed. A speed of 110 knots plus full right aileron was necessary to keep the plane straight and level. There was no alternative but to land downwind. This was made more hazardous because the flap mechanism had been destroyed. Streams of fuel were pouring from both tanks and fire extended along the port side almost to the tail. Small balls of fire were bounding around inside the plane, and the noise caused by bullets striking us was terrific. We struck the water with great force but after bouncing three times managed to complete the landing. The action was so fast and radio equipment so damaged that it was impossible for me to contact our base ship, *William B. Preston*. One of our rubber boats was full of holes but we managed to launch another. By that time the entire plane aft of the wings was melting and was surrounded by large areas of burning gasoline. The performance of the entire crew was outstanding.

"After rowing for about thirty minutes we were picked up by *Florence D*, flying an American flag but with a Filipino crew. Shortly afterwards Japanese planes were sighted returning from Darwin. An S O S was intercepted from *Don Isidro*, about twenty miles to our north, stating that she was under continuous attack and afire, with many wounded. At noon, while we were going to her aid, a twin-float seaplane approached and dropped two bombs near us. We were then strafed by machinegun fire. The plane disappeared to the west, but it indicated the presence of surface forces. *Florence D* was entirely unarmed. While under attack the captain anchored and retired with all hands to the protected area of the main deck.

"At 2.30 p.m. 27 carrier-type dive-bombers were seen going towards *Don Isidro*. At 3 o'clock I heard the whine of a dive-bomber and was knocked down by a terrific explosion in the bow, followed by the explosion of ammunition. A second bomb hit us amidships, extinguishing all lights. I groped my way aft amid the burnt and wounded and ordered my crew over the side. As soon as I cleared the propeller I swam as far as possible from the ship. *Florence D* was well down by the bow and the churning propeller was almost clear of the water. The attack continued. Three bombs missed the ship and burst near us. We suffered terrible pain in the testicles, stomach, back and chest, and coughed and spat blood.

"I fear Shuler was killed in this way, for a bomb was seen to explode very close to him. I grasped some driftwood, but was pleased to see the ship's crew had managed to launch two life-boats. I was picked up after an hour in the water and took charge of the boat. Ensign Mosley was in charge of the other. We had 23 men and Mosley 17. Fortunately we were going with the sea, wind and tide, and by rigging a sail we were in sight of land before dark. At midnight we landed on a high tide on the west coast of Bathurst Island.

"Thomas was unable to walk because of a sprained ankle. We all had injuries of some kind. We began walking to Bathurst Island mission but had to abandon the attempt. On February 21 a R.A.A.F. aircraft spotted our boats and by writing in the sand we identified ourselves and asked for food, water and medicine. We had been without food for 48 hours. The plane returned later and dropped supplies. We were picked up on February 22 by *H.M.A.S. Warrnambool*, in command of Lieut. E. J. Barron, R.A.N.R. We were attacked by a Japanese flying boat while going aboard but *Warrnambool* laid a smoke screen and cleverly manoeuvred to avoid being hit."

APPENDIX IV

Japanese Aircraft Used and Lost

The official Japanese figures of aircraft used at Darwin were given to me by the Deputy Director of Naval War History, Mr Hitoshi Tsunoda. They are widely at variance with the estimates of all Australian observers. Nevertheless, one must accept — or at least record — the official Japanese statement.

Tsunoda produced written documents to show that 36 Zero fighters (Type 2600), 71 dive-bombers (Type 2599) and 81 level bombers (Type 2597), making 188 in all, flew off the four aircraft carriers. There were, in addition, 27 twin-engined land-based bombers (Type 2596) from Ambon and another 27 (Type 2601) from Kendari in the Celebes. Approximately 150 tons of bombs were dropped, consisting of at least 300 separate bombs.

The air attack leader, Commander Fuchida, confirmed these figures and went so far as to detail for my information which types had taken off from each of the carriers.

Estimates by Australian observers vary between 77 aircraft (Air Marshal Richard Williams) in the first raid only, and 186 (two short of actual) by Squadron Leader F. X. McMahon, who was at the R.A.A.F. station. One American historian has said that 320 planes took part. I am convinced that 188 in the first raid and 54 in the second are the correct figures.

Tsunoda claimed that only two Japanese planes failed to return. They were a dive-bomber from the carrier *Kaga* and a fighter from the carrier *Hiryu*. The fighter pilot was First Class Pilot Hajime Toyoshima, who crash landed on Melville Island and was later taken prisoner by aborigines.

At first I was told that the two men in the dive-bomber were Petty Officer Katsuyoshi Tsuru and Petty Officer Yukio Togo. Later I was told, in writing, that their names were Petty Officer Musashi Uchida and Ensign Katsuyoshi Katsu.

If one is to accept Tsunoda's statement of the number of aircraft used there should perhaps be acceptance of his statement that two planes only were lost. It is difficult to do so. We have precise knowledge of four that could not have returned to the carriers, and the probability is that there were several others. Fuchida told me that seven aircraft were lost and I think that could be correct. Yet Fuchida himself, in some respects, has proved to be unreliable. He told me, for instance, that the task force was escorted by two battleships, *Kirishima* and *Haruna*.

This was denied by Tsunoda, who detailed the fleet elements, and by Commander Minoru Genda, who planned the Darwin and Pearl Harbour operations and was on board the carrier *Akagi*.

I am completely puzzled by the identity of the fighter pilot who crashed on Melville Island. Both Tsunoda and Fuchida identified him as Hajime Toyoshima. However, no such name appears in Australian records of Japanese prisoners. The first prisoner-of-war sent south from Darwin is listed in the Australian War Memorial records in Canberra as Sergeant-major Tadao Minami, an air-gunner in a high-level bomber from Ambon whose plane caught fire on the way. He told interrogators that he had bailed out and swam one mile to Bathurst Island, wandering around for two or three days until found by aborigines. Minami's name is not included in the Japanese records of the action, nor was a prisoner captured on Bathurst Island (adjoining Melville Island) at that time. These facts suggest that Toyoshima, for reasons known only to himself, may have changed his name, rank and unit.

Fuchida told me that on his return flight to the carriers after the raid he broke radio silence to tell Admiral Nagumo of the success they had achieved and also of Toyoshima's crash landing on Melville Island. A float plane was sent from one of the escorting cruisers to search for him. The crew landed on the beach but Toyoshima could not be located. As far as I know this was the only Japanese landing on Australian soil during the war. It has not been previously revealed.

To further confuse the issue, Hajime Toyoshima did not return to Japan at the end of the war. His name is not in the list of prisoners who died in captivity, nor is Minami's.

He has simply disappeared.

APPENDIX V

Japanese Activity near Darwin before February 19, 1942

Sea

January 1 : Submarine crossed the detection loop at the entrance to the harbour.

January 3, 11 and 16: Submarines sighted near Darwin.

January 20 : Australian corvette *H.M.A.S. Deloraine* (Lieut.-Commander D. A. Menlove) sank a submarine 50 miles west-north-west of Darwin. The American destroyers *U.S.S. Edsall* and *U.S.S. Alden*, escorting the tanker *Trinity* also took part in the action.

February 8 : *H.M.A.S. Deloraine* and the tanker *British Sailor* bombed 70 miles west of Bathurst Island.

February 15: *Houston* convoy attacked in Timor Sea.

February 18: The freighter *Don Isidro* was attacked by an aircraft 60 miles north of Wessell Island. Next day she was bombed and set on fire off Bathurst Island.

Air

January 28 : Unidentified aircraft came within 2½ miles of Darwin and was picked up by searchlights.

January 30 : Qantas flying boat *Corio* shot down near Koepang. Ten passengers and three crew lost. Captain Aubrey Koch and other survivors reached the coast of Timor after swimming five miles.

February 8 : Air raid alert at Darwin lasting 90 minutes following intense activity of enemy air force over Timor.

February 9 : U.S. Liberator attacked 200 miles north-west of Darwin by three fighters.

February 10: Single-engined monoplane was high over Darwin for approximately 35 minutes.

February 16 and 18: Further air reconnaissance over Darwin by single aircraft.

APPENDIX VI

Japanese Air Raids on Darwin after February 19, 1942

As well as the two raids on February 19 Darwin was bombed on 58 occasions between March 4, 1942, and November 12, 1943. These included raids against military installations at Noonamah, Batchelor, Coomalie Creek, Adelaide River, Brocks Creek, Fenton airfield, Katherine (where a lone aboriginal was killed) and Point Charles lighthouse. Some of these could be described as nuisance raids by small groups of planes but the majority were full-scale attacks by 27 or more bombers.

The first night raid occurred at 10.30 p.m. on March 31, 1942. Four days later the Japanese were caught unprepared by U.S.A.F. reinforcements and lost heavily in an air battle over the harbour. Subsequently some of the R.A.A.F.'s most renowned fighter aces were sent to Darwin as new aircraft became available, and Japanese losses mounted steadily.

One of the heaviest raids took place on June 16, 1942. On that day a large Japanese force bombed the oil fuel tanks around the harbour and caused severe damage in the town to the vacant banks and stores, and also to the railway yards. Oil tanks at Stokes Hill were then still being defended by the detachment of 14th Heavy Anti-Aircraft Battery which had performed so well on February 19. The tanks were hit and exploded. Gunner Ray Fogarty died of wounds. Bombardier Jack Ryder, Gunner Wilbur Hudson and Gunner Ronald Craig were severely burnt. Lieutenant David Brown also suffered burns which required treatment for a year. As a result of the action Brown was awarded the M.B.E. Sergeant Tom Fraser and Bombardier Fred Wombey won the Military Medal. Gunner Hudson had already been awarded the Military Medal for his actions during the raids on February 19. He was the first man to be decorated for bravery on Australian soil. Brown was the first officer to win such an award.

Index

A

Abbott, C. L. A., 13, 14, 15, 16, 18, 47, 54, 66, 67, 106, 107, 108, 109, 112, 118, 162, 163, 167, 184, 203, 204, 206
Abbott, Hilda, 106, 107, 108, 109, 152, 153
Acland, B., 40, 41, 43, 160
Adams, G., 120
Adams, Mrs. P., 189
Adelaide River, 146, 149, 154, 158, 159, 160, 162, 173, 174, 180, 200, 202
Admiral Halstead, m.v., 45, 48, 60
Adrian, Mother, 123, 124
Air Board, The, 194, 195
Akagi, 2, 6, 7, 9, 10, 206, 207, 208
Alderman, H. G., 192
Alfonso, Sister, 124
Alice Springs, 103, 107, 163, 167, 168, 169, 180, 190, 191
Anderson, J., 156, 159
Andrews, B., 75, 76
Annunciata, Sister, 124
Antoninius, Sister, 124
Aoki, Capt. T., 10
Army News, The, 164
Atkinson, C., 144

B

Bagot Hospital, 132
Bailey, Capt. W. C., 154
Bald, Alice, Mrs., 17, 94, 95, 99, 104
Bald, H. C., 17, 94, 95, 99, 100, 101, 104, 111
Bald, Iris, 17, 94, 95, 96, 97, 98, 99
Bald, Peter, 94, 103
Bank of New South Wales, 165, 166
Banya, 127
Barnard, Lieut. G., 87
Barnes, Brig.-Gen. J. F., 30, 35, 68
Barossa, m.v., 45, 48, 50, 52, 55, 70, 72, 74, 81
Barry, k.c., Mr. J. V., 192, 204
Bartlett, J., 55
Barton, L. A., 140
Batchelor, 30, 146, 194, 200
Bates, Capt. E. C., 45, 56
Baz, Lieut. A., 164
Bell, I., 76
Bergin, D., 78, 79
Bermingham, Comm. J. M., 45, 49, 50
Berrimah Hospital, 125, 126, 127, 128, 129, 130, 131, 132, 142, 144
Betts, E. G., 40, 41, 42, 43
Bevir, Cpl. P., 58
Bismarck, 177
Blake, Major-General D. V. J., 148, 149, 150, 152, 153, 154, 162, 163, 167
Bleeser, Mrs. A. M., 121
Bleeser, Florenz, 109, 121

225

Bliss, R., 156, 159
Blow, Sister L., 58
Bostock, Air Vice-Marshal W. D., 196, 197, 199, 200
Bowden, Dr. K., 58
Bowen, W., 119
Brennan, Lance-Bombardier M., 88
Brett, General G., 30, 46
Bridges, H., 68
British Motorist, m.v., 45, 48, 56, 77, 79, 87
Brown, A., 122
Brown, Lieut. D., 88, 89
Brown, G., 71
Brown, Capt. H., 27
Brown, R., 100, 112
Bryant, E., 156, 159, 173
Bryson, Billy, 172
Buel, Lieut. R. J., 30
Burke, Lieut. W., 62
Burnett, Sir C., 146
Burns, C., 27
Buscall, J., 16, 123
Byers, Billy, 71, 110, 111, 162

C

Camilla (Flying Boat), 80, 81, 82, 83
Carrodus, J. A., 205
Casey, Mrs. R. G., 123
Catalano, Dr. R., 129
Catalina (Flying Boat), 26, 64
Catlett, Lieut. W. J., 49, 50
Chapman, Warrant Officer H. W., 40
Charlton, Sister R., 141
Chavez, F., 74
Cheong, E., 114
Chikuma, 4
Citizens' War Effort Committee, 19
Civil Aviation, Department of, 28, 71, 128

Clark, C., 178
Clark, N., 178
Coleman, J., 164
Coles, Major J. H., 132, 133
Collings, Senator J. S., 18, 203, 206
Commercial Bank, The, 165, 166
Commonwealth Bank, The, 165, 168
Conanan, R., 72
Connell, A., 58
Connelly, Capt. L., 32
Connors, D., 96, 119, 120, 166
Connors, Father, 124
Coongoola, m.v., 46
Corio (Flying Boat), 80, 127
Cosgrove, Father J., 134, 135
Cousin, Capt. A. D., 50, 51, 52, 53, 54, 56, 57
Cousin, Sister E., 75, 129, 130
Crocker, R., 77
Crooks, K., 166, 167, 168
Crowther, Capt. W. H., 77, 80, 81, 82, 83, 121
C.S.I.R., 146
Cubillo, J., 69, 70
Cudday, C. H., 128, 136
Curio Cottage, 16, 123, 124
Curnock, L., 23, 42, 120
Curtin, J. (Prime Minister), 15, 68, 148, 205
Cutchie, J., 90

D

Dalby, L., 157
Dalton, E., 113
Daly Waters, 140, 146, 149, 194, 200
Dalziel, K., 40, 41
D'Ambrosio, E. F. S., 13, 112
Dangerfield, G., 72
Darken, Const. R., 96, 97, 100
Darwin Court, 114, 115

INDEX

Defence Co-ordinating Committee, 19
Dejulia, A., 70
Delissaville, 177
Deloraine, H.M.A.S., 48, 54
Dempsey, M., 75, 76
Dennis, Brother, 124
Dili, 27, 28, 29
Doherty, Sister E., 141
Dominic, D., 69, 70
Don Isidro, m.v., 46, 63
Doolittle, Col. James, 211
Drakeford, The Hon. A. S., 164
Duke, W., 102, 103, 105

Florence, D., m.v., 46, 63, 64
Floyd, J., 74, 75
'Flying Wharfies', The, 66
Foll, Senator H. S., 15
Fong Yuen Kee, 73
Foo Hee, 74
Foskey, R., 111
Fowler, Commander A. E., 62, 63, 80
Fraser, Ldg. Signalman D., 54
Fraser, Sgt. T., 88
Fuchida, Commander Mitsuo, 2, 7, 9, 10, 60, 84, 151, 200, 207, 208, 209, 210, 211
Funk, Capt. J., 140
Fyson, A., 107

E

Edmonds, W. D., 31, 68
Edwards, R., 42, 121, 122, 123, 171, 179
Egusa, Lieut.-Commander T., 8
Elcock, Sister E., 126
Ellifson, B., 89, 90
Ellifson, Cpl. C., 89, 92
Emmerson, B., 90, 91, 167
Emms, Leading Cook F. B., 61
English, Scottish & Australian Bank Ltd., 165, 166, 168
Erickson, R., 68, 69
Ericsson, Leading Seaman E. M., 78
Eucharia, Sister, 124

F

Fannie Bay Civil Aerodrome, 87
Fannie Bay Gaol, 117, 118, 131, 180
Fenton, Flying Officer L. G., 140, 146
Ferguson, J., 156, 157
Fisher, J., 80

G

Gabriella, Sister, 124
Garth, J., 105
Gee Fong Ming, 156
Genda, Commander M., 3, 6, 9, 151
Gibson, Warrant Officer A., 55
Giles, L. H. A., 109
Gilruth, Dr. J. A., 156
Glassop, B., 147
Glover, Lieut. J. G., 31, 32, 35, 38, 133, 134, 135
Goodman, C., 110, 162
Goodman, L., 108, 109, 179
Gordon, P., 77
Gordon's Don Hotel, 120, 121
Gowrie, Lord, 85, 184
Goy, Rev. C. T. F., 13, 19, 20, 129, 135, 144, 163, 170
Grant, Lieut.-Comm. E., 78, 79
Grant, M., 91
Greddon, J., 124
Gregory, Capt. A. C., 119, 120, 160, 161
Gribble, J., 24, 26, 196
Griegger, L., 142

227

Griffith, Wing-Comm. S., 25, 142, 143, 144, 145, 196, 198, 199
Griffiths, Lieut. O., 50, 54, 139, 140
Gsell, Rev. F. X., 109, 188
Gunbar, H.M.A.S., 45, 60
Gurney, Capt. C. R., 80, 81
Gustofson, Lieut. A., 50

H

Halcyon, m.v., 82
Hall, Const. V. C., 100
Halliday, Bombardier 'Doc', 88
Halls, A. T. R., 95, 99, 102
Hannam, H., 147
Hansen, Mrs. V., 81
Harding, D., 166, 167
Hardy, Surgeon-Lieut. L. A., 129
Harmanis, L., 171, 172, 173, 174, 175
Harney, Bill, 178, 179, 180
Harris, Rev. G. R., 189, 190
Harrison, E. T., 13
Harvey, Flying-Officer C. G., 194
Hasluck, The Hon. P., 192
Hawke, H., 99, 101, 102, 103, 104, 105
Hayles, W. J., 103, 120
Hector, J., 163
Henley, Lieut. E. J., 88
Henschke, Father W., 123, 124
Herbert, Mrs. C. E., 109
Hickey, L., 172
Hickey, P., 171, 172
Hiryu, 2, 6, 10, 206, 209
Hocking, Capt. B., 58
Hodges, E., 74
Hoffman, L. J. F., 130
Holmes, J., 58
Hone, Major R. B., 26, 27
Horan, Flight-Lieut. J., 141
Hotel Darwin, 81, 85, 93, 170
Houston, U.S.S., 47, 48, 49, 60, 86, 88, 132

Howard, G., 186, 187
Howle, Squadron-Leader D., 141, 142
Huby, Sgt. L., 87, 88
Hughes, Lieut. C. W., 31, 32, 35, 36
Hull, F., 147
Humphries, H., 58
Hurley, Gen. P., 139, 140
Hussey, Capt. H. B., 77, 80, 81, 82, 83
Hyde, Dr. J., 53
Hynes, J. E., 68, 69, 70, 71

I

Iles, S., 166, 167
Irisa, Lieut.-Comm. T., 8
Itaya, Lieut.-Comm. S., 8, 10

J

Jaffer, Sister A., 126, 128, 129, 130, 131, 135
James, Surgeon-Lieut. A., 126
James, Surgeon-Comm. C., 126, 128, 130, 131, 135
Jan, A., 73
Jan, Y., 73, 75
Jarvis, K., 120, 172
Jenkins, Flight-Lieut. T., 141
Jensen, O., 73, 155, 156, 157, 158, 159, 173, 174, 175
Johnson, Const. A., 190
Johnson, Lieut. R. L., 50
Johnstone, J. E., 61
Jones, R., 91
Joyace, Ensign P., 50

K

Kaga, 2, 6, 10, 206, 208
Kampur, Mrs. K., 108, 109

INDEX

Kampur, N., 108
Kane, V., 58
Kangaroo, H.M.A.S., 46, 61
Kara Kara, H.M.A.S., 46, 61
Karangi, H.M.A.S., 61
Katherine, 40, 105, 174, 180, 182, 184
Katoomba, H.M.A.S., 48, 50, 51, 53, 54, 56, 57
Keith, Comm. H. H., 49
Kelat, 45
Kentish, Rev. L., 189, 190, 191
Keogh, Sister H., 141
Kerr, Capt. R., 56
Kiara, H.M.A.S., 61
Kilmartin, E., 108
Kirkland, Dr. B., 102, 129, 130, 132, 187
Knight, A., 89, 90, 91
Knox, Matron D., 129, 130
Koala, 61
Koch, Capt. A., 80, 83, 127
Koga, Commander M., 208
Koivisto, Lieut. M., 50
Kookaburra, H.M.A.S., 46, 61
Koolama, m.v., 16
Koolinda, m.v., 16

L

Larrakeyah Barracks, 14, 86, 150, 151, 166, 168, 172, 178
Larrpan, 188, 189
Latham, L.A.C. P. S., 140
Lerew, Wing-Commander J. M., 194
Lewis, Able-Seaman A., 62
Lewis, Gunner L., 86, 87
Liddy, Mrs. T., 124
Littlejohn, Sgt. W., 73, 203
Lopez, J., 120
Lowe, Mr. Justice, 23, 145, 192, 193, 195, 196, 197, 198, 199, 202, 205
Luke, M., 161, 169

Luz, P. da, 28, 29
Lyne, V., 80
Lyons, B., 162
Lyons, J., 103

M

MacArthur, Gen. D., 211
McCarthy, D., 148
McCarthy, G., 104
McElhone, Lieut.-Col. J. B., 130, 131, 151
McDonald, K., 110
McDonald, Sgt. W. J. F., 27
McDowell, Sister M., 141
McFarland, Const. L., 112, 159, 162
McGrath, Father J. J., 23, 25, 120
McIntosh, L., 40, 41
Mack, Major J. M., 133
McKay, W., 58
McKenzie, L. R., 121, 122
McKenzie, P. A., 129
McKinnon, Sgt. W., 100
Macleish, Dr. A., 123
McMahon, Lieut. R. F., 31, 32, 35, 36, 37
McManus, Lieut. Comm. J. C. B., 24, 109
McNab, Const. E., 100, 129, 130
McNamara, J., 52, 120
McPherson, Lieut. C. E., 32
McQuade White, Matron E., 132, 133, 134, 135, 136
McRae, Lieut. R., 89
McRobert, Lieut. I., 78, 79, 80
Mangurupurramila, P., 23
Mansfield, A. A., 100, 101
Manunda, m.v., 45, 46, 48, 50, 57, 58, 59, 60, 69, 71, 76, 100, 106, 135, 136
Manzano, Comm. C. L., 64
March, Mrs. J., 189
Martin, D., 108, 179, 204
Matsuzaki, Lieut. M., 7, 9, 10

Mauna Loa, m.v., 45, 47, 48, 56, 79
Mavie, m.v., 45, 55
Maya, 3
Meigs, U.S.S., 44, 47, 48, 56, 79
Meldrum, Lieut. A. C., 54
Menlove, Lieut.-Comm. D. A., 54
Mestre, Sister M. de, 57
Michie, Capt. W., 45, 52, 74
Miller, A. R., 13, 14, 15, 17, 19, 110, 111, 112, 113, 159, 161, 162
Millford, Capt. T., 154
Mills, S. de, 119
Minto, Capt. T., 57, 58, 59
Mizuki, Petty Officer T., 7, 9, 10
Mofflin, Const. D., 96, 97
Montoro, m.v., 16
Moore, Petty Officer F., 61, 80
Mooy, Major F. F., 85, 86
Morris, Sister J., 129
Moss, G., 72
Mulholland, J., 86, 87
Mullen, E., 17, 95, 96, 98
Mullen, J., 17, 95, 96, 98
Mungalo, G., 123, 179
Murphy, J., 166
Murray, P., 114, 115
Muzzell, Lieut. N. M., 45, 61
Mynott, Ted., 56

N

Nagara, 208
Nagumo, Admiral C., 2, 6, 89, 150, 206, 207, 208, 209, 210
National Security Regulations, 12, 14
Nealyon, Aircraftman F., 140
Neptuna, m.v., 45, 48, 50, 52, 53, 54, 55, 56, 61, 70, 71, 74, 75, 76, 79, 80, 81, 82, 86, 88, 158
Newell, A. B., 19, 73, 114, 115
Ng, P., 73
Ngapiatilawai, M., 183
Nichols, J. W., 114, 116, 117
Northern Standard, The, 163

Nowaki, 208
Nuttall, H., 100

O

O'Brien, D., 99, 100, 103
Oenpeli, 189, 190
Oestreicher, Lieut. R. G., 30, 31, 32, 33, 35, 198
O'Grady, F. P., 95, 103
On, Fan, 73, 74
Orton, A., 117
Owens, D., 166
Ozaki, Lieut.-Comm. T., 8

P

Page, H., 103
Palfrey, Nurse J., 126
Paltridge, Senator S., 193
Parker, C., 97
Paspalis, M., 121
Payne, Second Officer P., 56
Peake, Sister O., 189
Peary, U.S.S., 45, 48, 49, 50, 52, 56, 57, 164
Pecos, U.S.S., 50
Pell, Major F., 26, 31, 32, 35, 36, 198
Pender, R., 76, 173
Penhall, L., 97, 98
Peres, Lieut. J. R., 31, 33
Perry, Lieut. E. S., 31, 33
Peters, Lt.-Col. C., 151
Phaup, Bill, 24
Piampirieu, B., 183
Piddington, Dr. J. H., 146, 147
Pires, Lieut. M., 27
Pither, Wing Commander A. G., 146
Plant, Major G., 151, 152
Platypus, H.M.A.S., 45, 50, 51, 54, 55, 78, 139
Port Mar, U.S.S., 45, 47, 48, 60

INDEX

Pott, J., 97, 162
President Grant, m.v., 16, 17, 171

Q

Qantas Flying Boats, 41, 77, 105, 121, 188
Que Noy, Jimmy, 166

R

Randall, B., 190
Rattley, R., 98, 99, 100
Read, C., 165, 166, 167, 168
Reid, R., 117, 118, 120
Rice, Lieut. B. H., 31, 32, 35, 38
Riley, F., 40, 41
Robenson, Col. J., 68, 124
Robertson, Lieut. G., 85, 86, 170
Rogers, J., 71
Rorke, L., 162
Ross, Col. A., 27, 28, 29, 166
Ross, D., 153, 196
Rossignol, Bill, le, 116
Rothery, J., 52, 53
Rowling, W., 98, 99, 100, 103
Ryder, J., 88

S

St. Francis, 64, 123
Saukuru, Rev. K., 127, 188
Saxton, Flight-Lieut. A., 26
Scherger, Sir Frederick, 25, 28, 29, 38, 39, 138, 139, 143, 145, 199, 200
Schmidt, A., 90, 91
Schumack, Matron C., 59
Scott, Able Seaman C. D., 61
Sea Dog, 172
Secretary, Bob, 179
See Kee, C., 108
Sellen, Capt. B., 164
Shazer, J. de, 212
Shelley, D. E., 63
Shepherd, A., 110
Shepherd, Ordinary Seaman H. J., 60
Shepherd, R., 100, 108, 179
Shepherdson, Mrs. H., 185
Shores, E., 74
Shultz, L.A.C., A. V. L., 140
Simons, Cpl. R., 140
Skerry, Sister A., 126
Smith, Brother A., 64
Smith, Third Officer A. S., 58
Smith, C. W. R., 50
Smith, Senior Sister Ila, 141
Smith, R. (Chief Writer), 55
Smith, R. (Cook), 58
Smith, S. G., 140
Somerville, Miss M., 189, 190, 191
Soryu, 2, 6, 8, 10, 206, 208
Southern Cross, H.M.A.S., 50, 188
Spain, C., 69, 70, 71
Spinney, W., 58
Stasinowsky, F., 17, 95, 96, 98
Stobo, R., 70
Stockman, Jimmy, 117, 118
Stoddart, E. W., 72, 73, 147, 157
Stretton, A. V., 109, 118
Sutherland, J., 76, 85
Sutherland, Major N., 85
Swan, Squadron Leader A. D., 40, 143, 199
Swan, H.M.A.S., 45, 47, 48, 52
Sweeney, G., 180, 181, 187
Sydney Morning Herald, The,
Symonds, Lieut.-Comm. C. F., 50

T

Takao, 4
Tarlton, A., 40, 41, 42, 43
Taylor, A., 101
Taylor, Dr. J., 129

231

INDEX

Taylor, Mrs. J., 113
Thom, Asst. Purser R., 58
Thomas, Capt. E. P., 25
Thompson, A., 103
Thompson, D., 114, 116, 117
Thomson, Capt. J., 61
Tindal, Wing-Comm. A., 40, 142
Tiver, R. K., 94, 103
Tolga, H.M.A.S., 61, 79
Tone, 3
Tonkin, Comm. J. P., 55
Toyoshima, H., 183
Tozer, Capt. L. E., 169
Tsunoda, H., 6
Tulagi, m.v., 45, 47, 48, 61, 76
Tye, G., 70, 71, 72, 78

V

Vaught, Lieut. R. H., 31, 32, 35
Victoria Hotel, 69, 81, 95
Vincent, C. W., 77
Vose, Major D. H., 85

W

Wade, Cpl. A., 90, 91
Wake, W., 40, 43, 77
Waldie, J., 43, 71, 76, 77, 78, 81, 83
Wale, K., 189
Walker, Squadron Leader B., 195
Walker, J., 68, 69
Walker, Lieut. W. R., 31
Ward, C. K., 114
Ward, E. J., 66
Ward, R. C., 114, 115, 116
Warrego, H.M.A.S., 47, 48
Warrnambool, H.M.A.S., 63, 64
Warton, T., 162
Wato, 55
Watt, Sister C., 141
Wavell, General A., 25, 148
Webster, J., 56

Weidner, Cpl. A., 91
Wellington, A., 95, 99
Wells, Mr. Justice, 112, 116, 117, 159, 162, 166, 168
Westbrook, Lieut. B. L., 80
Wheless, Capt., 35
White, Dr. F. W. G., 146
White, V. J., 171, 178, 180, 185, 201
White, W. J. E., 13
Wiecks, Lieut. M. R., 31, 33, 34, 35, 198
Wilkshire, J., 71, 78, 79, 80
William B. Preston, U.S.S., 45, 48, 57, 78
Williams, Air Marshal R., 39, 138, 139
Willmot, E., 13
Wilson, Air Comm. D. E. L., 25, 39, 146, 147
Wing Cheong Sing, 122
Wingham, J., 115
Winn, L. B., 13
Wombey, Lance Bombardier F., 88
Wood, Capt. H. K., 56
Woolmer, Sgt. W., 89, 90, 91
Wright, Miss F., 114

Y

Yamaguchi, Rear-Admiral T., 2, 6, 8, 208, 209
Yamamoto, Admiral I., 4, 6, 209, 210
Yampi Lass, H.M.A.S., 61
Yan, Y., 171
Young, Mrs. E., 17, 95, 98
Young, J., 97
Yuen, J., 72, 73, 74, 75, 76

Z

Zeelandia, m.v., 15, 45, 48, 58, 120, 163